THE FUTURE
IS OURS,
COMRADE

MOTTO

. . . I don't know a good Russian from a bad Russian. I can tell
a good Frenchman from a bad Frenchman. I can tell a good
Italian from a bad Italian. I know a good Greek when I see one.
But I don't understand the Russians. I just don't know what
makes them tick. I wish I could study them.

F. D. Roosevelt

(FRANCES PERKINS. *The Roosevelt I Knew. New York:
The Viking Press, 1946, p. 86.*)

. . . the Americans have created their own image of the Soviet
man and think that he is as you want him to be. But he is not as
you think.

Khrushchev to Nixon, Moscow, July 24, 1959

(New York *Times*, July 25, 1959)

JOSEPH NOVAK

THE FUTURE
IS OURS,
COMRADE

Conversations with

the Russians

INTRODUCTION BY
IRVING R. LEVINE

DOUBLEDAY & COMPANY, INC.
GARDEN CITY, NEW YORK

DESIGN: CHARLES KAPLAN

CONTENTS

INTRODUCTION

7

FOREWORD

11

•1•

THIS IS MY HOME

15

•2•

THE STREET AND THE CITIZEN

36

•3•

IN A CAGE

53

•4•

ON THE FRONT OF SOCIALIST WORK

68

•5•

THE SOVIET SOCIALIST ARMY—SCHOOL OF HEROISM

AND PATRIOTISM

100

•6•

IN THE HOSPITAL

113

•7•

HORSES, TAPE RECORDERS, AND THE RUSSIAN SOUL

122

•8•

REPUBLIC OF SCHOLARS

153

•9•

A TRIP ABROAD

173

•10•

PRODUCER'S MARKET AND GOOD WILL

187

•11•

THE HERO OF OUR TIMES

205

•12•

THE CHOSEN PEOPLE

224

•13•

WAR AND PEACE

243

WORDS INSTEAD OF AN EPILOGUE

285

INTRODUCTION

ALTHOUGH WE WERE IN RUSSIA DURING THE SAME PERIOD, I NEVER met Joseph Novak. I wish I had. He enjoyed access to Russian people and places that a journalist can only envy. In fact, a traveler to Russia of any category—diplomat, delegation member, tourist—cannot fail to admire the author of this book.

He did what every visitor to the Soviet Union wants to do—he shared and remembered candid, unguarded, uncensored conversations with hundreds of Russians in many walks of life.

Even visitors to Russia who stay only a few days almost inevitably seek something more than sight-seeing. Of course, a tour of the Kremlin's palaces and museum-churches is standard. And everyone goes on a pilgrimage of curiosity to the mausoleum where Lenin and Stalin lie embalmed, surely the most macabre monument since mummies were sealed in pyramids.

But the sight-seer in the Soviet Union wants more than merely to see the sights. He wants to talk with Russians. Often he goes to great lengths to do so. The crowning achievement of a trip to Russia is to be invited into a Russian home. Few visitors to Russia, whether they be tourists on a ten-day guided tour or diplomats stationed in a Moscow Embassy for a two-year tour, ever manage to do so.

This is especially difficult for diplomats. Contact with Russians, who themselves are friendly enough, is discouraged. There was the case of a promising, Russian-speaking third-secretary at the American Embassy who had a novel idea for meeting Russians. He signed up for a course in history at Moscow University. He met many students, as eager for contacts with foreigners as he was. They talked with him, invited him to their rooms, accepted his invitations. After only a few rewarding months in Russia the young diplomat was notified by the Soviet Foreign Ministry that he was *persona non grata*, and that he would have to leave. The Soviet official who handed down the decision said that the American had overstepped the proper limits of diplomatic activity. There was no appeal. Ten years invested by the young man in special schooling and preparation for his Moscow post had, ironically enough, been spent in vain, simply because he had made too good use of his background. If he is indeed permitted to work in Moscow ever again, it will not be for many years.

It is difficult also for foreign correspondents to have meaningful associations with Russians. It was a disillusioning experience for me, several days before I left Moscow, to have a Russian friend tell me that our association over the past four years had been not only with the approval of his superiors but, in fact, on their orders. Contrary to popular belief, correspondents ordinarily are not followed by secret police agents unless they have been making regular contacts with Russians. The "tailing" is usually obvious and awkward. This may be deliberate. It is intended to frighten or at least to discourage the correspondent and especially his Russian friends. Sometimes this sort of nerve warfare can be carried pretty far. There was a British newspaper correspondent, fluent in Russian, who managed quickly to build up a sizable circle of Soviet friends. He found himself being followed. He noticed mysterious men lurking in the corridors of his apartment house. The telephone rang regularly in the middle of the night and when he answered there was no one at the other end. He went to the British Embassy to report these antics. An overly cautious Embassy attaché felt compelled to cable a coded report to the Foreign Office in London, where a report was dutifully passed on to the man's editors. Isolated from the atmosphere of Moscow, the editors felt concern for their correspondent's welfare. They transferred him from Moscow immediately, thus prematurely nipping a budding Soviet expert.

Tourists are usually limited to conversations with interpreter-guides furnished along with meal coupons by the Soviet Government's *Intourist* organization. The tourist inevitably raises the question of why there is only one candidate for each office in Soviet elections. The guide gives the standard *Pravda* explanation, and retorts with a question about segregation in the South. The ideological exchange may provide anecdotes for cocktail party conversation for the returning tourist for many months.

Some tourists are not so easily satisfied. One man actually knocked at doors at random until a bewildered Russian housewife showed him through her family's two-room flat. The same American probably would have summoned the F.B.I. if a Russian had appeared at his door in this manner.

Another American, accosted by a trio of Russian teen-age black marketeers seeking to buy suits and shirts, offered to leave them all but the clothes on his back if they would show him the *real* Moscow. They agreed. They met him that evening, walked him up and down alleys to a taxi, drove a zigzag course, furtively changed taxis, and ended up at Moscow's most expensive restaurant. There they filled his ears with the most lurid anti-Soviet remarks, thinking this was what the American wanted to hear, while filling themselves with the most expensive caviar and steaks. About the time that he was presented with the bill, the American grasped that he had been "taken."

Joseph Novak's experiences were of quite a different sort. For him conversations with Russians were natural and uncompli-cated. He had opportunities to live in Russian homes, to eat meals with Russians, to travel with Russians. The reader is relieved to know of Mr. Novak's efforts to conceal the identity of his Russian friends who spoke to him with such self-incrimi-nating frankness.

Those who come to Russia expecting the worst are often pleasantly surprised. They are not followed. People are not in chains. They smile. No one looks hungry. Russians do not wear rags. Industry has made enormous progress. Massive housing construction is under way. But the visitor who comes expecting to find the *best* is often disillusioned, disheartened. If Mr. Novak's book sees little to recommend the Soviet society, if the author does not dwell on the merits of a system of free education and free medicine, it certainly is not because he is unaware of them, but rather because his experiences make other aspects more important to recount.

Oftentimes the first impression of Russia is the best. There is a façade on the buildings along Gorky Street behind which there are slums, but also the people present a façade to the casual visitor. Russians are proud, patriotic. They do not often complain to a newcomer. It is only after a foreigner has dwelt among the Russians for a period of time that he detects the pervading and dismal tragedy of their way of life.

Joseph Novak has made a significant contribution to an understanding of the Soviet society not only because his is much more than a first impression but also because of the timing of this book. We are in an era when Americans ardently desire peaceful relations with Russia. When I first went to Russia in

1955 Americans often asked me why my reports were not more critical of the Soviet Union. When I left Russia in 1959 listeners to my broadcasts more often asked why I had criticized a phase of Soviet life. Part of this is certainly due to the phenomenon that I mentioned a moment ago—that first impressions of Russia are often the best. But part of this may be interpreted too as reflecting a desire to get along with Russia even if it means sweeping repugnant realities under the rug. Joseph Novak's book makes it less comfortable to lose sight of the many unpleasant facts about Russia.

It's been said that reports on Russia resemble accounts by blindfolded men describing an elephant. Each touches a different part of the animal. The man who feels the trunk describes quite a different creature from the man whose hand explores the elephant's side. Joseph Novak has great advantages over most who try to describe the elephantine U.S.S.R. He did not wear the blindfolds worn by many; he spoke Russian, he wore the cloak of respectability denied to anyone who comes from a non-Communist country, and most important he carried letters of introduction and endorsement from high Soviet officials. He was able to feel and *see* large parts of the elephant missed by others.

The Soviet Union is an immense country. It is impossible to speak with or for 210,000,000 people. There is no single representative Russian any more than there can be more than a synthetically selected "typical" American or Albanian or Afghan. For example, many of the Russians I talked with expressed a deeper skepticism about the contents of *Pravda* than did those with whom Joseph Novak spoke. Many Russians conveyed to me a longing for peace and a confidence that peace could be maintained because war is too catastrophic to contemplate. Joseph Novak relates with obvious authenticity and accuracy what certain Russians told him. What they told him will leave the reader with one overwhelming emotion: the fervent hope that the title of this informative, unusual, and fascinating book will never come true.

IRVING R. LEVINE
former Moscow correspondent
National Broadcasting Company
Rome, Italy, August 8, 1959

FOREWORD

"YOU ARE VERY LUCKY, YOUNG MAN, VERY LUCKY." THE DIPLOMAT, on his way home from the Soviet Embassy in a satellite country, turned his suntanned face towards me.

We were sitting in the dining car of a train bound for Moscow. "Not every young man of your age, even from your country, has a chance to spend some time in the U.S.S.R.

"Don't ever forget, you are visiting a country that is altering contemporary history in a way which cannot be fully understood now. Use your eyes. Our today is tomorrow for your country, and the day after tomorrow for the whole world."

Our train clicked rhythmically over the tracks. Outside the windows, a never-ending landscape of fields, trees, and spots of green moved slowly by. Small houses or cabins leaped into view suddenly, then disappeared. Occasionally we saw the silhouettes of grazing cattle, as if asleep on their feet, outlined against the gray background of the monotonous landscape. Occasionally we flashed by people staring vacantly at the passing train.

"You must bear in mind," the diplomat continued, "that the U.S.S.R. is a huge country with magnificent scenery. Heterogeneous, it boasts of an old culture, powerful modern architecture, gigantic industry. If you try to see everything, you'll end up by seeing nothing. I'd advise you to concentrate on some specific field which is connected with the over-all picture. It's the only way you'll be able to get a real picture of the U.S.S.R.

"You know, of course, the greatest pride of Russia, the main Soviet contribution to the march of mankind——"

The sudden screech of brakes prevented the diplomat from finishing his sentence. From the lonely expanse of field and forest the buildings of a small station appeared. The first things we saw were two large bronze busts of Lenin and Stalin perched on high socles. Then we noticed gray, colorless people. A small boy, carried by a woman wrapped in a shawl, flattened his freckled nose against the window which separated him from us. His keen eyes discovered the oranges and bananas on the table in front of us.

"Well, this contribution," the diplomat continued, "our most precious possession, is the Soviet man, the citizen of the first socialist country of the world.

"Remember, young man, fascinating scenery, heterogeneous cultures, and monumental architecture may be found all over the world. But the generations of *new people*, raised by us, can be found only in the U.S.S.R., nowhere else.

"While in Soviet Russia, try to understand why these generations of Soviet people are our pride. Try to understand the deeply humane socialist system of education that molded these generations. Try to find, in the daily life of the Soviet people, the mechanism shaping the New Man, the Man to whom the Soviet present belongs, and to whom will belong the future of the world. . . ."

The train started to move over switches and cross tracks until it was again on the line running into the deserted fields. It picked up speed. The embassy official carefully peeled the golden skin of a banana. On the finger of his right hand shone a large, heavy signet ring with a red star engraved on a gold background. On his right wrist, seen under the cuff of a slightly soiled shirt, was the massive cover of a golden "Kama" wrist watch.

"While in the U.S.S.R., try to forget the world from which you came, and to which you'll return. Forget your present criteria, standards, opinions, evaluations, and comparisons conceived under entirely different conditions, in another country, and, even more important, in another society. They'll be of no use to you here. If you want to understand the U.S.S.R., if you want to know our Soviet way of life and live as one of us, you must adopt our standards, our values, and our opinions as your own.

"Unless you can do it, you'll get a fundamentally false and distorted picture of the country and its society. Like those trite reports about the U.S.S.R. published en masse in Western Europe and the U.S.A. based on impressions formed during a stay in Intourist hotels or from casual talks with the maids, hotel porters, or taxi drivers—provided that the authors know enough Russian to talk to them at all."

The train braked sharply coming into a station. The lights of a big city were reflected in the bottles of Caucasian wine on the table in front of us. Outside the window the white cap of a militiaman greeting the train passed by. Hurriedly the diplomat drank the remains of his compote out of the saucer.

"Here we are, it's Moscow. I have to run. Do you want me to give you a lift? I have a car waiting.

"No? Well, then, good luck, young man. I'm sure you'll come to understand why we so often say, 'The word "Man" has a proud sound.' Again, all the best to you—*wsyevo kharoshevo!*"

THIS IS MY HOME

"MOSCOW, LENINGRAD . . . THE THINGS THEY ALREADY HAD YES-terday, we, who live in other parts of the U.S.S.R. won't have until tomorrow. You'll see. Moscow and Leningrad are two of the most beautiful cities in the Soviet Union. The people in them are different. So are the houses, streets, and stores. If I could only live there for one day . . ." A dreamy smile had settled on the dusty face of the conductor on the Moscow-bound train.

And here I was, one of the lucky people allowed by fate to live for a while in these great cities—to enjoy what was the dream of tens of millions of people in the U.S.S.R. who live outside Moscow or Leningrad.

My stay in these cities, especially in the Moscow district, which interested me most, was actually quite unusual. As a minor bureaucrat from one of the satellite countries, enjoying the confidence of a number of highly situated U.S.S.R. officials who were responsible for my visit, I was invited to Russia for a protracted stay and allowed to arrange my Soviet life according to my own wishes, without being hampered or limited by anyone.

To a large extent I followed the advice of the Soviet diplomat. I decided to concentrate on the problems which interested me most, the questions which had led me to go to the U.S.S.R. in the first place. To satisfy my own curiosity, I wanted to know what the daily life of the average Soviet man was like, what his pleasures and troubles were, what he thought of the world around him, and how he saw himself in relation to the world surrounding him.

In getting to know the truth about "today" in the metropolitan centers, I was also finding out the subject of the dreams of all those millions of people outside of the metropolitan centers for whom this today was tomorrow.

I never formed ties with any one special social group during my stay in the U.S.S.R.; I sought out many people in various social groups. My practice was to hold on to old acquaintances. I preferred one close friend to ten casual ones.

In my contacts with people and the circles in which they moved, I endeavored to draw as much information from them as I could about them and their lives. Above all, I built a picture of their lives based on their own observations.

I formed the habit of asking questions and listening in my off-duty hours. Then, at a free moment, I would make short notes of the conversations or even write them down faithfully in their entirety. Whenever possible, I tried to do this immediately after my conversations.

I began my study where life itself begins, with the home and family. To learn more about them and at the same time to come into closer contact with more people, I didn't ask to be assigned permanent quarters. Instead, I made it a habit to ask people I met, and I met many, to let me stay with them for a night or two.

I lived in and visited homes of every description, inhabited by all sorts of people. I lived in apartments located in the solid buildings of the Czarist era. I lived in small wooden huts from the same era. I saw apartments in houses built in "Soviet times," after 1917, in the 1930–39 period, and in entirely new homes and housing projects of the 1945–57 period.

To find a common denominator for all these kinds of homes would be very difficult indeed, if possible at all. Soviet rules governing the number of people who are supposed to occupy a certain living area are elastic. According to my observations, the basis for assigning the "population" to an apartment is not the number of rooms or the family bonds of the people in the apartment, but solely the size of the living area.

If, for instance, the rule is that one person can live in an area of six or seven square meters, then an apartment of forty square meters should accommodate from four to six persons. This applies even if the apartment has only one room and if these persons are of different sexes and ages, and total strangers to each other.

There are cases where exceptions are made to this rule, for various reasons, and the number of persons in an apartment is increased or decreased. The Residential Buildings Administration and the Housing Office make the decisions. The average citizen may file appeals, but in most cases his appeal will be ignored.

"Ours is the most difficult housing situation in Europe," a newspaperman once told me, "and there won't be any change for many years to come."

In recent years the state has been building more residential quarters, but as yet this hasn't changed the existing situation. The newspaperman was something of an expert, since for his paper, he was in charge of matters which had to do with housing and he answered letters from readers about the problem.

"To our housing authorities," he told me, "the most important fact is that a man must live under a roof. Living in the streets, for example, would injure *the honor of socialism*. But when twenty people live in a small three-room apartment, this honor is saved.

"There's a saying, 'A man is a wolf to another man.' This is only true of capitalism, not here. It couldn't be. The trouble is that we inherited cities from Czarist Russia that are not adapted to an era of socialist industrialization. Industrialization of post-Revolutionary Russia brought in its wake the migration of hundreds of thousands of people from rural districts into the city. Furthermore, immediately after the Revolution, actually up to 1935, no mass renovation of housing was undertaken. Maintenance of apartments was left to the initiative of the tenants. The results were alarming. About 88 per cent of all the inherited buildings in the city required major repairs from top to bottom.

"But neither time nor people nor money could be spared for such things. Socialism had more important tasks in its first stage than the ending of holes in roofs. Then came the war of

1941–45. It ruined entire cities and towns. After the war the same problem raised its head, but to an even greater degree. Now it was the U.S.S.R. that needed mending, not the old houses, which continued to fall to pieces and are doing so to this very day.

"We still are not ready for new construction. We still have more important goals. The building industry is an embarrassing problem. It requires people, machinery, and raw materials. It would involve light industry, which has enough trouble producing clothing and articles for everyday living. Although heavy industry can produce certain consumer articles as a side line, it cannot build homes. That's obvious, isn't it?

"That's why, when we do build now, the buildings are constructed in a haphazard way. The more of them, and the quicker, the better. Naturally they can't be any good. Have you seen by any chance these large panel houses with bearing wall panels made in holder molds in a vertical position? We call it Giproiindustria Type. This is our best, but still rather primitive constructions. . . .

"Big government or institutional buildings in large cities, now that's something else. But our entire building energy is consumed by them.

"Still, there's no need to get hysterical over the problem. People go on living and being happy. Don't you believe me? Just look around and you'll see. . . ."

My first experiences and observations indicated that the housing conditions, which compel several unrelated families and individuals to live together in a limited space, had created a new co-operative pattern of life, in which each person had to accommodate himself to his fellow tenants and at the same time preserve a life of his own.

In each apartment the group of tenants is closely bound together by the limited area and by the common use of certain facilities—corridor, kitchen, and bathroom. As far as floor space goes, each tenant has a strictly defined area of his own. It does not always meet the requirements of the Housing Office, but it comes close to them.

Each tenant's share in the common facilities is religiously respected. I never ceased to be surprised at the way each person knew exactly where to find his place on various shelves, closets, and cabinets, and the precision with which he kept to his own zone.

Families and individuals try as far as possible to separate themselves from the other tenants. I have seen all kinds of screens, partitions, barriers, and curtains made of linen, cardboard, or paper used for this purpose. Sometimes a piece of furniture such as a wardrobe is used as a divider.

But it is obvious that no one can have much privacy. Whether they want to or not, people get to know a good deal about each other. They are more than ordinarily aware of the habits, inclinations, and rights of the people they live with, and they must conform to them.

Such conditions undoubtedly create new kinds of relationships between a man and his fellow tenants, the place he lives, his private life, and the private lives of others. What is the life of a family and of an individual among strangers? What are the bases of their relationships? What degree of intimacy exists, and what forms does it take?

I found that the main features of this communal life are mutual tolerance, a sense of reciprocity, a tendency to conformity, and general resignation.

My friend Vasia, with whom I was spending the afternoon, was deeply troubled. "I was going to invite you," he said, "to watch a TV program which begins now. But our neighbor K. is still sleeping behind this partition. He works on the night shift. Sorry we can't watch it. Shall we go for a walk?"

When I asked my various friends if I could stay with them overnight, they would first consult the other tenants of the apartment or room.

"Don't be annoyed," they would explain. "You can see that if we invite you without asking the others, then they would be able to invite anyone without asking us, and what sort of an existence would that be?"

When I turned up at some new "residence" with my temporary hosts, I was usually introduced to the other tenants, or at least some of them.

"This is Comrade N.," my hosts would say. "He just came

from K. He has a pass to visit the U.S.S.R., and he knows highly situated people here in Moscow. . . ."

I had brought a few articles of everyday use and some fancy goods into the U.S.S.R. with me, with the intention of giving them to my Russian friends. They were mostly objects imported from abroad and very rare in the U.S.S.R.

Among other things, I had a large, multicolored plastic table-cloth. One day, to show my gratitude to my hosts of the moment for their exceptional hospitality, I handed it to them. I was certain they'd be thrilled with it. To my surprise, their reaction was utter embarrassment.

The wife held the gift and lovingly ran her hand over its smooth surface. "The most beautiful tablecloth I have ever seen," she said after a moment's hesitation. "These colors, just like hand painting. But, now please don't be angry, we can't very well put it on our table. You see, there's the other couple living in this room with us, Zenotchka and Volodia. It's as if you were their guest too. They let us invite you and even lent us a bed. Perhaps you have another tablecloth for them?"

In another house I tried to give my hosts a large plastic shopping bag. They would not take it under any circumstances.

"If it were some little insignificant thing," they said, ". . . but a bag like this! The whole house would know about it immediately. You can't buy anything like it in a store. They'll all wonder why you gave us the bag and what we did to get it. Don't be angry with us. Please understand. We appreciate your offer very much . . . but . . . perhaps you can give it to someone else."

A good friend of mine, a civil engineer, lived in a four-room apartment with three families. The rooms were large and high-ceilinged, the kitchen spacious (it had been built before the Revolution). There were fourteen people in the apartment, five of them children, when he came, making the fifteenth. He made a portion of the kitchen into a tiny "room" for himself without complaining.

However, the engineer had a girl friend, a student in the Technological Institute. She was a stunning blonde with rather free ways. Unfortunately she was not allowed to enter the apartment.

"What can I do? These three families unanimously decided

that they didn't want her to come to the apartment. They told me this very plainly. So instead of perpetually arguing with them I see Vala outside."

My colleague Boris was twenty-four years old, a worker in a big industrial establishment. He was full of fun, had a great sense of humor, and liked to tell risqué stories. His interests were work, football, and girls. His parents didn't live in Moscow, so he lived in a room in the center of the city in a large, old house. He shared his room with a young married couple. The room was divided by a thin plywood partition.

Boris knew them, of course, but as far as I could see he disliked the young husband, possibly because the latter was about his own age, yet worked in an office where he occupied a comparatively high position. However, when I asked Boris to tell me some intimate details about the young couple he always refused.

"It would be a fine business if all of us listened to what the others did at night and told it to every Tom, Dick, and Harry."

"But," I insisted, "you must hear *something,* don't you?"

Boris grinned, "Sure, sometimes I hear plenty." But seeing my aroused interest he added quickly, "But don't ever think I listen on purpose. Of course sometimes when I come home late, or can't fall asleep, or wake up at night, I can't help hearing things whether I want to or not."

After a brief silence, Boris said with obvious satisfaction, "But in the morning, when I meet the young wife in the hall, she turns as red as a lobster. Even her neck and ears turn crimson. The poor little thing is ashamed for herself and for her husband."

Soon I had a chance to test Boris' veracity. A young married couple invited me to the theater, then we went dancing. It was rather late when we started for home. My friends suggested that instead of trying to go to the other end of the city where I was staying at the time I should spend the night in their apartment.

At first I refused, but not too strongly. At last I accepted their invitation. We entered the apartment in our stocking feet so as not to awaken the people who slept in the two rooms we had to pass through. My friends lived in the third room together with the husband's sister, who was already asleep. Quietly they opened a small folding bed, and a few minutes later I was in it, covered with a clean blanket, staring into the darkness. I couldn't fall asleep, and not because I wasn't sleepy. A mixture of noises came from the next room. My hosts had left the door open to let in fresh air. The noises excited my imagination. I tried to isolate them, ascribe them to individuals whom I had met the previous afternoon before leaving for the theater.

I felt ashamed of myself. I blamed my innate "bourgeois curiosity," but sleep still would not come. After a while I had proof that the young couple thought I was fast asleep. It was unfortunately too late to warn them. The night was almost finished, and here I was, still wide awake, fascinated by its voices.

When one becomes so familiar with the private lives of others, one realizes that they have an equal familiarity with one's own. There are no secrets in the group. I was impressed by a rather interesting detail in the apartments in which I lived or visited. Even when they go out, the tenants do not lock the drawers or closets. They leave their desks, cabinets, and drawers with personal documents and correspondence unlocked.

When I asked why, my hosts told me, as if they were describing the most natural thing in the world, "Lock the drawers? Whatever for? Don't we all know each other like brothers anyway? Besides, we have nothing to hide. . . ."

Somewhere else, in a quite different environment, I received this answer, "If someone is interested in the contents of my desk or cabinet, he'll find his way to them anyway. I'm out all day. But if a drawer is left open, everybody knows that there's nothing interesting in it. . . ."

Sometimes I would ask my friends about their co-tenants. What kind of people were they? What was their occupation?

The answers were invariably favorable. "Comrade W. and his wife? Nice as can be. Quiet, decent. Too bad they aren't here so that you can meet them."

If the answer was more restrained, it was a sign that the co-tenants were not on the best of terms. "The P. family? Yes, they live in the next room. He works in a canned-fruit factory. They are all right, I suppose."

Many years of living with strangers in a limited area have

produced a rigid pattern of behavior and custom. One of the signs of it that I noticed was the use of standard items of decoration. The most common were portraits of the ideological and political leaders of communism. Although not all the portraits were identical, some were displayed in every home I visited. Lenin was the most frequently seen; second in popularity was Stalin; third place was occupied by the least picturesque and least photogenic, Khrushchev. After him came Djerjinsky, Marx, Engels, and semipolitical figures like Gorki or Mayakovsky, or members of the Central Committee painted by the artist Gerasimov.

Frequently, instead of portraits or even in addition to them, you would see miniature statues or small busts of the leaders of the U.S.S.R. Once I even had to face the martial eyes of Marx staring at me in the bathroom; his stare intimidated me for a second.

I was probably the only guest in these politically decorated homes who found anything funny about seeing family portraits interspersed with the portraits of Lenin, Stalin, or Gorki. A picture of Lenin addressing a meeting had as its neighbor a dignified old lady, my host's mother, holding a large icon in both hands. The picture of my host as a baby in diapers was next to a photograph of Stalin shaking his fist from a platform.

Another permanent feature of the average Soviet home was mass editions of the Selected Works of the Classics of Marxism-Leninism, plus a number of other political and ideological works that had already become standard. They included very well-printed volumes of Marx and Engels, Lenin, Stalin, Kalinin, and Zhdanov in good-looking bindings. They are sold at amazingly low prices. A recent publication, also nicely bound, was the collected speeches of Khrushchev, omitting his address to the Twentieth Congress of the Party. The bindings, size, and number of volumes in the home library might vary, but the same titles were always at the center of it.

I had the impression that my hosts would never have thought of hanging oil paintings or landscapes instead of political portraits. I wondered if they were aware of their reasons for having these decorations and books in their homes, and I asked several of them about it.

These are some of the answers I received in workers' and white-collar circles:

"It's always been our custom. We've always hung—on the walls of course—the leaders and writers of the U.S.S.R. Before the Revolution, the Czar and his family hung everywhere. We're used to it . . . and besides, all the other people have them. . . ."

"Oh, the portraits. Aren't they pretty? We like Stalin's best, the one where you see him reading letters from plain people. What do you mean? . . . Something must hang on the wall. People come to our home. They look around. We aren't trying to avoid politics. Why shouldn't we have the portraits or these books?"

"This is the pride of our library, the works of Lenin and Stalin. See the lovely bindings. They are cheap, too. Sometimes we need them for reference. Once in a while we read them. Besides, everybody has them. This is the custom, don't you see?"

"You know, all the tenants in the building know each other, either through the house committee or through other contacts. It's much better if your home looks as it should, especially as far as politics are concerned. After all, a man is judged by his home. . . ."

Many people emphasized their personal tastes in the selection of portraits of leaders and politicians. Once when I was teasing a friend of mine, a drama student, about his conformity in furnishing the portion of the room he occupied with the works of Marx, Engels, Lenin, and Stalin, he pointed to a large bust of Kalinin as proof of his individuality.

I also remember a conversation with a history professor in a university. He noticed my surprise when I saw a large portrait of Lenin hanging on the wall and a tiny statuette of Stalin standing on the desk between the inkwell and the blotter.

"You're surprised by this large portrait of Lenin, aren't you? It's even larger than the portrait of my deceased wife. Well, you have to understand us. I'm far from being an adherent to the cult of the individual. I've never been one. *But this is only a way of speaking.* After all, I do have social contacts with people. Sometimes my students come to visit me. They look at the walls . . . well, I don't belong to the Party. You know, my origin, unfortunately, is a handicap. Perhaps now it's no longer of much importance . . . but for the past twenty years . . . Besides, you can't deny that these two [he points at Lenin and Stalin] are all the history we have up to date. . . ."

Just as characteristic was my conversation with a middle-aged mathematician who was an assistant at one of the research institutes. He impressed me as a man completely detached from everyday life. Absorbed in the problems of his science, he had no time, it seemed, for theaters, movies, or even a new book.

When he heard, however, that I was going to visit the Volga-Don Canal he became immensely interested. He said, "You'll find it most exciting. Be sure to see the statue of Stalin. It's monumental and beautiful . . . a colossus, you'll see." Then after a while he added, as an afterthought, "You should have been with me at the Congress of Mathematicians in Czechoslovakia. I'm telling you, I was flabbergasted. You ought to see the monument the Czechs built to Stalin! It's a real colossus! Much bigger than ours!

"But then we'll have a statue of Lenin seventy-five meters high in a few years. It will be erected either in front of the Soviet Palace now being built or on top of it. Putting it in front of the palace may make the statue seem smaller. Putting it on top of the palace may cause the clouds to veil it. This is a serious problem for our building authorities."

An administrative official once told me that there are icons and pictures of the saints on the walls of many homes. However, every such religious item is carefully labeled, "A Relic of the Eighteenth Century" or "A Family Heirloom," so that nobody could suspect that it served any other purpose than a decorative one.

The necessity of getting along with co-tenants at close quarters has a marked effect on family life. This is especially apparent in the case of old people or people with incurable diseases. They are a constant problem to most Soviet families who live in crowded apartments.

It is obvious that under such conditions an old or incurably ill person interferes by his very presence with the established order of co-operative living. He either requires special care, remains at home all the time, or uses the common facilities, especially the bathroom, disproportionately. It is absolutely out of the question for him to stay for very long in a multifamily apartment.

In one apartment I studied, nine people occupied two rooms and a small kitchen. Two married couples lived there, one of them with two children and the husband's father. The father was seventy-two years old and bedridden. The other couple had no children, but the husband's two brothers lived there, occupying the tiny kitchen in order not to disturb the couple.

The sick man used to moan all through his sleepless nights. He had to be given a bedpan, and naturally disturbed the other tenants. One day after the old man had had a specially bad night, the two couples had a terrific quarrel. The three brothers and the wife categorically demanded that the sick man be removed from the apartment. A few days later he was taken to the old people's home in the suburbs, and all was again quiet in the apartment.

After I heard this story, I decided to visit the Home for Old and Incurable. I must admit the visit affected me very much. It is true that the inmates had comparatively good living conditions, medical care, good food, organized recreation, radio, television, and other comforts, but this was not what interested me most, and this was not what was most important for these people. The real tragedy for these old and often incapacitated people was the knowledge that in the majority of cases they were sent to these places *by their own children* for the sake of peace and quiet at home.

Like children, old people have their own way of thinking. They see this world which they are about to leave in a different manner. Their weak, pale eyes stared at me as I listened to their tragic complaints, whispered through toothless mouths. They did not complain of the fact that life was soon to end. They did not complain about their ailing bodies, stomachs, or hearts. Nor did they complain of lack of care.

They complained about their children. They could not reconcile themselves to the idea that their children had discarded them like cumbersome pieces of furniture, had banned them from the circle of family life, had sent them away from their growing grandchildren. They were not allowed to live on life borrowed from the young or to die as their own parents had died, in the midst of their own people, near a daughter or son or grandchild.

Many had been moved from their homes by a ruse. The family, fearing resistance on the part of the old man or perhaps not wanting to expose him to much excitement, would tell him that he was going to see a doctor; then they took him to the Home instead.

Often persons removed in this way harbored a bitter resentment till the end of their days, not towards their children, for whom they tried to find excuses, but against the co-tenants whom they accused of hatching the plot and against whose heads they directed their curses.

After my visit to the old people's home I understood why the intoxicated janitor of one of the houses in which I had lived once said to me cynically, "You won't see any dogs or any old men in our streets. They aren't allowed. Socialism is for young people!"

The co-existence of a group of people and families who are unrelated to each other determines the attitude of parents towards their children and of the children towards their parents.

The parents are inclined to make their children independent as early as possible by sending them to the nursery day school or to the youth organization. This frees the parents from direct care of the children and at the same time makes more room in the apartment. The parents applaud any pretext which keeps their children away from home, be it camps for youth, harvesting groups, or potato-digging groups.

"Mishka is almost ten," a worker told me about his only son. "I'll have to get him accepted for some camp for the whole summer. The boy is old enough to understand many things. Sometimes my wife and I are embarrassed at night, that he may be lying there and listening."

Living among strange families and individuals has an effect on the attitudes of parents towards their children, and of children towards parents.

"Anna Vasiliyevna is still a young woman," said an acquaintance about a mutual friend of ours, a widow. "She'll surely marry again. I was told she managed to place her two boys in a boarding school. She'll have more freedom now. Before, she could never invite anybody in or go out late at night. The boys were in the way. . . ."

"Too bad you can't meet our children," said a married couple, "but there are so many old, nervous people in this apartment that we decided to send the boy to a cadet's school and the girl to a boarding school, about three hours by train from here. Want to see their pictures? The boy is a little pale, isn't he? But the school will do him good. They give them good food and good medical care."

But it isn't only that the children are in the parents' way. Sometimes the tables are turned. Young people can't live their own life at home because they are always in somebody's way. They must consider the co-tenants as well as their own families. The real, interesting life for them takes place outside the home, among large groups of children of the same age, in the youth organization, in a scientific circle, in a sports camp, at a dynamic meeting. A young man really does not know a family atmosphere. At most, he may know the lack of it.

But from his earliest childhood he knows the atmosphere of the group of which he is a member. The group provides him with emotions and passions. It gives him the feeling that he is not alone, that someone is always looking at him, appraising his actions. Even if this permanent control is sometimes a nuisance, he believes that it is for his own good and for his future. His family, father or mother, are removed by these circumstances to second place, sometimes even further, because they are not in any way related to this group and do not provide any creative emotions or stimulate any effort.

"I would like to remain in some camp for good and never return home," said a thirteen-year-old boy who lived under exceptionally good conditions because his father held a high post. "And if my parents wanted, they could always come to see me. I'm bored at home. I'd rather sit in school after hours. At least there's always something to do there."

"Everybody looks at me askance," remarked a fifteen-year-old boy who lived in an apartment with a number of other people. "I want to play the radio, and somebody wants to sleep. I start to fix my bike in the hall, and someone tells me that an apartment is not a garage. I start to read, someone else turns on the TV. It's always like this. I just don't count."

After such remarks, I was surprised to see that young people past adolescence were not anxious to own their own apartments, or at least bachelor quarters. Young people considered having an apartment to oneself as something strange, overstepping natural needs and accepted custom.

A girl I knew, a television actress, who had a small room in a comparatively new house in midtown Moscow felt that living alone was too bohemian, and usually lived there with a girl friend.

In the television studio where this girl worked I met another girl who was in the technical department. She was twenty-five and her name was Faina. I asked her whether she would like to have a small room with a separate entrance, a bathroom and a small kitchen, for herself. It would be nicely furnished, have a low comfortable couch, a telephone, radio, television, record player, and refrigerator.

Faina thought a long while, then answered, "Sure I'd like to have it. Who wouldn't? But I wouldn't like to live there alone. With a husband, all right . . . if I had a husband. But a single woman alone in a room like that? No! What would people think if you or some other colleague came to see me? Perhaps it's true that an apartment like that could turn a girl's head and spoil her."

Boris and his friends reacted differently. "Sure it would be fun to have a little place like that handy . . . for the five of us. Each one of us would have a key and we would agree to rotate. My turn today, his tomorrow, and another's the day after.

"You could use it to sit in the dark with your girl, to have a drink with your friends. If you want to play cards you grab a taxi and all of you go there.

"But for myself alone? A room and a kitchen? Maybe if I had an important position and had to give parties and receptions for important guests it would be all right. But I certainly wouldn't want to live there all by myself. People would start to talk. They'd say that I lead a bad life, or want to get away from people to drink, or to do who knows what with girls. You can never tell where this gossip might end. . . ."

Many of my young friends, men and women, said they'd love to live in such a place if they were married. But the idea of one person owning a whole apartment raised many objections, moral and political. They were afraid of "being suspected of leading an immoral life" or of "a desire to isolate themselves from society." Some thought that living alone in an apartment might encourage one's evil inclinations.

Others, the most serious, considered the idea of a private apartment fictional, and therefore any discussion of it futile and childish.

In recent years Soviet industry has begun the mass production of articles for use in the home. Refrigerators, television sets, radio sets, record players, electric washing machines have appeared on the market at prices city dwellers can afford. I was curious to see how these new appliances would affect the life of the people. I thought that they might not fit into the crowded apartments, that a conflict might arise between a tenant's desire to own an appliance and the lack of space and fear of disturbing other tenants. But an electrician who was installing a refrigerator in the apartment where I was staying at the moment dispelled my doubts when he laughed and said to me, "Do you think that a man who can *sleep* with his wife in the presence of five other people won't be able to listen to the radio or watch TV in their presence?"

Later I had an opportunity to verify his remarks. The use of the radio or television or record player has become integrated into the pattern of the privileges meted out within certain time limits to each tenant. The many years of experience in co-operative living have provided the solution to finding space for a refrigerator or a television set as efficiently as they have solved the problem of discarding old, worn-out furniture . . . and old, expendable people.

An example of this came to my attention when I went to visit a family and was greeted by a boy about twelve years old. Enthusiastically, he started to tell me about his new toys, concluding, "And we have a new TV set. Come and see how big it is. It stands where Grandpa used to sleep. Oh, and Grandpa is gone. . . ."

Olga, a twenty-five-year-old nurse in a Moscow Hospital, also must have given some thought to this problem. She told me, "You must understand that a human being can get used to anything, if he has to, and if he wants to. You can get accustomed to ignoring others just as they become accustomed to ignoring you. You'll learn the great art of becoming indifferent to the problems of the people around you. You won't be disturbed when trying to sleep by the light left on by a man studying in the same room, just as you won't be disturbed by the knowledge that he is trying to sleep while you are playing the radio. But you'll also learn tact and tolerance of others, just as they learn to be tactful in their dealings with you. You will learn to turn around so as not to disturb their private actions. You will pretend you are asleep in order not to frighten away a moment of love experienced by the people behind the partition. Isn't that the great socialist culture reflected in the cooperative existence of people?"

K., a white-collar worker and father of a family, saw it differently. "Under our conditions," he said, "housing is the least important problem. Today's man is outside of his home all day. First, he must go to work. After work there's always a meeting, or some entertainment, then a short stroll in the streets and it's late, time for bed. After a full day, you're exhausted. You throw yourself into bed and nothing can disturb you. In the morning you get up, and it all begins all over again."

"We Russians," said an intelligent and highly educated young man, "were always accustomed to collective life. For centuries, not only the peasants but also the aristocracy lived in big family collectives. Take the literature of the eighteenth and nineteenth centuries. At the same time that Western European aristocracy, and with it the bourgeoisie, sought a maximum of privacy even to the point of separating a husband's room from that of his wife, our aristocracy occupied their palaces together with their closest and most remote, relatives, plus a horde of other residents, entertainers, jesters, and hangers-on.

"Don't forget that our country by-passed the period of genuinely bourgeois culture, one of the main features of which was the separation of a man's private life from his public life. Our Soviet thinking did not inherit the cult of the boudoir reserved for 'the lady wife' or the 'love nest' for Sir Husband and his mistress! In a way, we moved directly from Russian feudalism into Russian socialism . . . and from the feudal to the socialist commune." And my friend laughed broadly.

Transferring the center of interest of a man's life to his work, to a life outside the family has basically altered his attitude towards marriage, his motives for having children, his relationships with his family. At the same time, and more important, this process occurs in reverse. Collectivity has entered family life. It has created the habit of interference with a man's privacy and subordination of his private life to the interest of the group of people with whom he lives. One of the institutions which has been promoting this process in the U.S.S.R. is the house committee, which is strongly affiliated with the City Housing Administration.

An employee of the City Housing Administration defines the work of house committees in this way: house committees were originally set up by an independent action of revolutionary councils (especially right after the Revolution). Now, a house committee is organized for large buildings, or for a few small buildings, which house thirty to fifty families. It works under and with the Housing Administration.

A house committee performs two fundamental functions. The first is actual management of the living area, along with the maintenance of the buildings and apartments. The second function is concerned with the management of the group of tenants. This includes keeping vital statistics, records of their movements, changes of addresses or employment. The house committee is comprised of tenants. Candidates are usually nominated in advance by the Housing Administration, and then voted upon by the tenants. The chairman, however, is usually appointed by the Housing Administration. The committee usually consists of three or four people, depending upon the number of people it represents and the type of building. The rules for the house committee are strictly defined only in connection with their administrative duties, which include keeping the records of all the tenants. Each city district has its registra-

THIS IS MY HOME

tion office which is independent of the house committee. It maintains its own files on every citizen in the district. The house committee may be called a local branch of the registration office, collecting data on the spot. However, it co-operates with other agencies besides the registration office and the City Housing Administration.

For instance, two tenants have exchanged apartments without asking the registration office or the housing administrator. A tenant may break down a wall in his apartment to install a window, while someone else walls up a door. It sometimes happens that a non-registered person will move into a tenant's apartment. All these incidents are investigated and checked upon by the house committee, which is on the spot and can act quickly. The committee can also supply information. It may receive a request for information on a tenant from the personnel section of his place of employment. They would like to know what his reputation is among his co-tenants, if he gets along with them, if he is disorderly, if he gets drunk, or even if he beats his wife. On the other hand, should a tenant's behavior be undesirable, the committee can report him, without informing him, to the proper authorities or to his employer.

In recent years the role of the house committee has been reduced to actual administrative and management tasks. However, up to 1954, they were vital agencies in the control of the tenants' socialistic attitude towards their private lives and the state. It is only natural that the committees often abused their power and involved innocent tenants for various personal reasons. In the past few years confidence in the opinions of the house committees has decreased greatly. At one time they were considered the ultimate and most objective source of information about a tenant and all that concerned him. Now these opinions are verified through other sources.

The committee's strong position does not stem from its official authority, for it doesn't possess any. Its position and the fear it arouses in the average tenant is caused by its unofficial activity. The members of the committee base their knowledge of a tenant on the knowledge shared by all the tenants about each other. I have seen actual cases in which the committee was able to obtain information without any difficulty because of this fear. One argument it uses to get information is that it represents the tenants themselves.

A talkative fellow who happened to sit next to me at the table at a private reception turned out to be a member of the house committee. He told me with a sanctimonious smile, "Mr. N., you can't even begin to imagine what people know about their neighbors. I'd be ashamed to tell you. . . . You know, we just can't help hearing these things. Wherever we go, someone comes up and tells us. . . . though we, I mean the committee, of course, aren't interested in intimate details. It's none of our business. Our business consists of the formalities, but they just won't leave us alone."

In years gone by, especially at the height of secret-police operations, the role of the house committee was simply to denounce tenants, to spy on them, to provoke them, to play off one against the other. At present, when reporting and spying are officially limited to certain persons rather than being a general game, and when the secret police take care of the job, these spying functions have been taken away from the house committees, so that their character has changed.

In one apartment, where I lived longer than in most, I was told about an incident which had taken place two months before my arrival. It wasn't considered exceptional by my hosts.

"It concerned the B. family, who had lived two flights below us," my hosts said. "You couldn't imagine a quieter, more average and normal man than B., who worked in an office." His wife was a saleswoman in a store. Their eighteen-year-old son, a member of the Lenin Young Communist League—Komsomol—worked in a garage as a mechanic and went to night school. The family occupied a tiny room in a five-room apartment. All the other tenants had to pass through it to reach their rooms.

One day B. had a violent quarrel with a colleague in his office. It was an absolutely private matter. One of them pushed the other or insulted him, nothing serious. However B.'s opponent brought the matter to the attention of the trade union, charging that B. had insulted him, "a socialist citizen and union activist."

The case was referred to the personnel department, where B.'s standing was not of the best. His record noted that he was "passive" and "avoided social work" plus the fact that he was "not interested in the affairs of his place of employment."

Since the chief of personnel had no valid complaint against B., he wrote to the house committee asking for data on the "moral and political life of B. and his family."

The chairman of the house committee investigated. However, B. had the reputation of a quiet man. The committee wasn't able to dig up anything against him immediately. Then a few days later, B., who had noticed the sudden interest in him and who was under a strain, exploded. He told a co-tenant to stop hanging around so much under various pretexts while all he really was doing was listening to B.'s conversations with his wife.

The co-tenant, offended, must have reacted violently. Anyway, a brawl ensued.

A few days later a meeting of the union passed a resolution, based on the opinion of the house committee, asking the personnel department to discharge B. He was charged with "violation of the moral unity of Soviet Society; an antagonistic attitude towards co-citizens, unworthy of a socialist citizen."

After some days B. received orders from the factory management transferring him to duty in a remote corner of the U.S.S.R. His wife was transferred too, to "avoid separating a socialist family." But their son remained in Moscow. B. and his wife left a week later.

Faithful to the old tradition that analysis of a man begins with his relationships to his home and family, I began my studies there, only to find out later that a Soviet man spends very little time at home or with his family.

Lack of privacy encourages active participation in group activities, which become the primary field of activity in the U.S.S.R. The efficient machine which never leaves a man alone, while at the same time pushing him into society from all sides, also feeds his mental, spiritual, and emotional life.

2

THE STREET AND
THE CITIZEN

"RUSSIANS ARE A FUNNY PEOPLE! WHO WOULD HAVE THOUGHT
that after forty years of socialism they'd grow to be such chau-
vinists! It's fantastic!" André, a Belgian journalist, weighted
down with his photographic equipment, turned to me with a
melodramatic expression. "Do you know what continually
happens to me here? When I try to photograph the exterior of
an old building, or the façade of any run-down house that
contrasts with the new architecture, I am forbidden to do so!
By ordinary people, by passers-by! Each time a crowd gathers,
and the people simply forbid me to photograph anything old
or run-down. Can you beat that! And do you know, this common
crowd, badly dressed, poverty-ridden, is actually hostile to me
and flabbergasted at what I am doing. I am automatically
their enemy because only an enemy would want to take pictures
of their old houses on their streets, when, on the same street,
as they say, 'there are so many magnificent buildings and so
much modern architecture!' The Russians are amazingly funny,
aren't they?"

It took me some time to answer that one. Only after I had
understood what the street means to the "amazingly funny
Russians," did I realize its importance and the special role it
plays in their lives. The street in a Soviet city or town fulfills
different needs from those it does in other countries. It was
only after I had become well acquainted with the rhythm of
everyday existence that I grasped the relationship of a typical
Russian to his street.

I have before me a few compositions written by students of two Moscow schools and ranging in age from nine to fourteen. A Russian language teacher, and a very good friend, a girl of twenty-eight who had recently graduated from a university, gave her pupils the assignment: "What I Like Best in My Life."

I looked over the neatly kept notebooks. The handwritings differed but the pattern of exposition was similar.

"My life, like the lives of everyone in the Soviet Union, is very pleasant," wrote a nine-year-old boy. "What I like best in my life is to ride a bus all over my city, the most beautiful of all cities in the world—Moscow."

Fourteen-year-old Olenka composed her essay more philo-sophically:

"Each man has his own likes. One likes to eat, another to amuse himself, still another prefers to study best of all. But there are certain things that are liked equally by everyone as well as by me. Those certain things are the things that must be liked, because we are always surrounded by them and they are inseparable from us: houses, streets, monuments and parks of our most beautiful city, the socialist Moscow."

The houses, parks, monuments, and especially the streets came up for praise in 80 per cent of the compositions. The teacher, seeing my interest and surprise, smiled at me, showing a row of healthy, white teeth.

"You are such a dreadful foreigner! What don't you under-stand, what is it that surprises you? Don't you think that I, an old maid of twenty-eight, if I were to write a composition like this, would write about the same things, the buildings, the parks, and the streets? Why, my life after work is the street. On the street I have everything, stores, theaters, the crowd. . . . Don't you yourself like to walk, look at things that are con-tinually changing, watch the people, their faces, their gestures, the way they laugh? Tell me, don't you like those things? Or are you really such a recluse?"

As I was taking leave of a high-school professor, he detained me and wagged his finger in my face:

"Do remember, young man, that Russia had *always* been a country completely different from the rest of Europe. Our country differs from West Europe not only because of a different

climate, the lack of good roads, or the alphabet. Our way of
life, our type of collective culture, always has been, and now is
even more so, responsible for our separateness."

Taking me to the door of the school, a young and sym-
pathetic teacher added: "When you stay with us a little longer
you'll understand the truth. Our life is not something dissimilar
from the life of the West, as they believe there. Our life is
heterogeneous, original, and typically Russian. It has always
been so. Our times only tend to underline this."

The face of a Soviet city: the wide avenues and sidewalks,
the hurrying crowds, the busses, the subway stations, stores,
theaters and movie houses. The same as everywhere else whether
it's Paris or London or Rome or New York. But are they the
same?

"Do you see this wide, white-painted lane in the middle of
each wide street?" a young man called Garik asked me. "On
that lane only police cars, ambulances, fire engines, and cars of
high officials with special license plates are allowed. It's easier
to drive on that lane and it's faster, less traffic. Oh look—"
Garik became visibly excited, "—see how they drive, and women
too, right there!"

And I started noticing. In the middle lane cars passed aglow
with chrome and white-wall tires, all bearing official licenses.
From time to time a police car raced by; but usually the cars
contained men with brief cases, or on sunny days, well-dressed,
well-painted, and smiling women. At the crossings, when the
cars slowed down or came to a stop, the passersby looked in
through the windows with respect and wonder at the smiling
"chosen of the gods."

"Did you see her? Pretty, wasn't she?" Garik looked dreamily
after the departing car. "And young too! It's probably her
father's car, either official or maybe even their private one. . . .
Oh well, when I get up into the higher circles, I will also drive
on the white line. . . ."

The owners of private cars are met universally with wonder,
respect, good wishes, and approval. The private car becomes
a symbol of co-operation with the system.

"You see, it's all very simple," a young engineer by the name
of Volodia explained to me. "This crowd you see on the streets,

walking, does not envy the owners of cars, as the poor envies the rich in the West. Each one of these people know that, should he be able to serve the Party and the country exceptionally well, if he should achieve a high position, he too, after a certain length of time, can take his place on the white line in an official or private car. . . . And that's why each one of us, the young ones, try to achieve these distinctions, try to climb higher and higher. . . ."

The day was unbearably hot. The streets of Moscow were crowded with people leaving their jobs. Luba, a friend I was with, was visibly tired. We went into a large store to get a drink. It was full of people waiting in line to be served. We stood and waited patiently. At one point a large car stopped in front of the store. An elegantly dressed woman got out and without seeming to notice the long line of waiting people went directly to the counter and was waited on by the clerk. She put her purchases in a bag, paid and, smiling beatifically, left the store. There was the click of the car door closing and an aroma of strong Russian perfume.

I was slightly upset because the incident seemed to have left an impression only on me. "Tell me, Luba," I asked my friend, "why is it that no one told that woman to stand in line with the rest of us?"

Luba looked at me shocked. "My God, how queer of you to ask that! Didn't you see that *she* came in a car? She's probably the wife of some director, or maybe she is in a high position herself. It's obvious that we shouldn't expect *her* to waste her time in line!" Luba rubbed the sweat off her face and suddenly looked animated. "But you must admit that she was extremely elegant, wasn't she? What a hat, suit, and shoes . . . and her perfume! Did you like her, tell me? Do you like such elegant women? But who wouldn't! You just wait, when I finish my studies and get ahead, I shall drive around in a car, I shall be beautifully dressed, and I shall smell wonderful, and . . ."

The street is the center of competition, it demands comparisons, it gives incentive to thoughts of bettering oneself financially in order to gain the respect and admiration of others. And at the same time a street in the Soviet Union, especially a street of a large city, satisfies the many needs of everyday life for recreation and rest.

Mura is twenty-four years old and undeniably pretty. She has two more years to complete her studies in physics. In spite of her scientific interests, she is romantically inclined, likes to dance and dress in fineries, and go out on the street. She lives with her father, brother, and sister-in-law. We liked each other very much, but we invariably met on the street. One day, a little irritated by her constantly insisting on going for a walk, I couldn't restrain myself any longer and asked her: "Tell me, Mura, why is it that we always meet on the street? The street isn't exactly the best place for two young people who like each other . . ."

Mura didn't understand my irritation. "First of all," she said, "I thought that you simply liked my company, that you wanted us to be alone, where no one would disturb us . . ."

"But that's just it!" I interrupted her. "That's just exactly what I want, to be only with you, alone. We don't need people . . . and that's why I don't understand why we spend all our time on the street."

Mura still didn't understand me. "You're childish! If we were to see each other in my house, we would never be alone. We'd either disturb somebody or somebody would disturb us. If we go to a restaurant, there would be all kinds of people milling around and staring at us. If we go to the theater or the movies, then we can't even talk to each other. But on the street we are alone, completely alone, don't you see? We are lost in the crowd, they don't bother us, and we don't bother with them. . . . Look around you right now. . . . There are all kinds of people passing us, old and young, men and women, children and soldiers, and here we are talking intimately with no one disturbing us and we are in nobody's way . . . Now do you understand? And if you want to, later on we can walk to the park and sit down, very close to each other. Isn't everything as perfect as could be?"

Many of my friends, young and old, felt the same way about the street. It gave them a certain feeling of intimacy, of being lost and separated from the others.

At a social gathering, the hostess introduced me to Gavryla, a handsome, well-dressed middle-aged man. "You will like each other," she said. "Gavryla knows a lot of the world. During the war he was in Germany, later in France. He is a great dancer and a greater talker . . . Besides, you'll see for yourself." She smiled at me meaningfully.

He was actually a very interesting man. He worked as a clerk in an export-import house and he knew a lot about the business. He had lost his wife and child during the war and now lived in an apartment shared by two other families, separated from them by a sheet stretched across the corner of the room.

He did not have many interests. "I am out of my element," he said, "this life is not for me." He was fascinated only by women and alcohol. He associated with people with the same interests. They were lonely men, middle-aged, with rather shady pasts. They all worked at unimportant jobs, having been passed over when they could have been advanced. They admitted to being "out of the running," and having no political or professional ambitions.

Alcohol and women . . . That seemed to me a bit fantastic under the circumstances. When I questioned Gavryla about opportunities for exercising his two hobbies, he smiled gently. "It's not so bad and it's possible, only you have to get used to the roundabout way of achieving your ends."

He and his friends had worked out an ingenious way for heavy drinking. Usually they met in a restaurant or café. From then on they followed a pattern. When the atmosphere became a "little heated" by high-proof vodka, they changed to another bar.

"You see," he explained, "you should never try to get drunk in only one bar. You run more of a chance that way of being picked up by the police. If they do pick you up, you'd have to sober up in jail, and worse than that, you'd go on record —and that might be the end. In two days' time your boss would call a meeting to discuss 'alcoholism among us,' and you might get kicked out, and who knows how far north that might lead. And that's why you must change bars. While walking you sober up, and if your intention is to drink really seriously, you and your friends should take a bus or a subway and go to a park. There you can 'wind up' your drinking in comparative peace, though not discarding all caution. Later, you should walk home as straight as you humanly can, and God forbid that you should bother someone on the street by getting into a conversation. In your own house you can drain the rest of the bottle, as long as you do it quietly without waking up anyone. . . . It's simple, isn't it?"

Gavryla had his own "recreational theory," as he called it. He did not drink without the company of a woman. "Vodka by itself—it's only half the pleasure. But the pleasure is complete when drinking is coupled with getting to know or building up the acquaintance of a woman. This drinking together makes for a fuller relationship, 'more complete conforming to existing circumstances.' "

Seeing my surprise, especially at his last sentence, he added, "Oh, you poor sons-of-bourgeoisie! You come from your bourgeoisized Europe and you understand absolutely nothing. . . . You can't catch on to the simplest things. . . . But just give it a little thought. Each of us has to find an outlet for his own impulses. We don't go against our nature just because the conditions of life are all against it. I am not like my comrades in the office. I don't want to be a high Party official or even a director of my firm. Why? I don't quite know why. I simply don't want to advance anywhere. Climbing up the ladder doesn't amuse me. Maybe it's because I am not so young any more. And maybe it's because I know that I can't perform miracles. I was away during the war, I am a little tired of everything around me. . . . What's left then? A good brand of vodka and a pretty woman. There is no lack of vodka here, but with women it's a little more difficult. . . . They are afraid of free love, they'd rather get married and have children, plan a family life. . . . If I were younger . . . The students have it easier, but I must work at it hard. . . . I know a few women, some of them you have met, but unfortunately they are not in the bloom of youth, as the saying goes. . . . And remember also our way of life. It's not France, where you can rent a room for five hours, you don't have your own apartment. . . . So what do you do, where do you go? What's left is the street, the park, the public square, the lot behind a building . . . and nothing else, dear boy. . . . But there is the other side of the problem. The women here respect themselves. After all they have the same chances at jobs and advancement as the men. There aren't many who'd want to neck behind the front doors or in the parks, or sit on cold marble on a cold night with the chance of being chased away by the night watchman. . . . And that's where vodka comes in. Get it? Vodka, which you drink in a civilized way in a café, lets you afterwards forget the doorway, the bare sky above, or the presence of the watchman. . . . Vodka draws you together, lets you forget the social rules of behavior, and by-passes all the lengthy flirtations and courting, with which Europeans with their own apartments have to preface lovemaking. . . .

"It's not easy to understand, I know that very well. But life is life and we must make the best of it. . . . Each society has its own ways of seeking recreation, the best ways suited to its environment. The French take their women into their beds with them. We Russians have social halls, meetings, parades, and factories building a better future. And I . . . I and the few friends I have are untypical, do you understand? We die out, go away, grow old . . . and in the meanwhile? Meanwhile we drink up the vodka and from time to time, next to a woman's warm body, we forget the world and all its problems. . . . But you don't follow me at all . . . why do I bother to tell you all this?"

One of Gavryla's friends said to me, "You see, the new generation, the one growing up now and the one already grown, hasn't the same problems. Their youth schools them differently. They have other desires, they live collectively, passionately so, they don't know—and never will know—what private, individual life is.

"They spend themselves in social work, dream of political or professional careers, they think of themselves, illogically, as the statesmen, leaders, pedagogues of the future. They believe in the destiny of their country. The majority of them are convinced that they will live to see the socialist conquest of the entire world, and that conviction alone feeds them fabulous dreams, fantastic new vistas. . . . That's the young. And what do *we* have? We are growing old, with not a chance of a change for the better career-wise, thrown off balance by the war or by the many upheavals that rock this country from time to time. What can *we* do? The answer is simple: as long as we last, we must think of ourselves. Little adventures, the pleasant dizziness after a few glasses, a woman's beautiful body near us. . . . Don't let Gavryla surprise you. There are many like him here. . . . But don't delude yourself that there is a great number of us. People like us fade out more rapidly. Sooner or later each one of us will be expelled from the Party, from our professions. . . . Sooner or later you make a row on the street or in the house. . . . And then you're sent away. . . . But there are others, you'll see. . . ."

"Each man must work, and after work he must have a chance for recreation," a well-known Party functionary said. "You see, we who were brought up in a socialist society have a distinct mode of living. From childhood we learn to exist within a group, collectively——we are never alone. What does that lead to? It leads to other needs. It means that we should not be compared, that we cannot be compared with other people who have been used to their own outlook on work, rest, and play. Our life is fundamentally a collective life. In this kind of life there is no place for privacy as it is known in a bourgeois country, a separateness from society. Here people are taught from infancy to play together, to work together. Does all this surprise you?"

The directress of one of the largest social halls, a well-known educator, smiled indulgently.

"I assure you that none of our members come up with such problems as you seem to have. When you live here a little longer, you'll understand many things. You'll understand, for instance, that if you subtract from the twenty-four hours the time you spend at work, Party meetings, social club meetings, special meetings, luncheons and dinners at your place of work, then you'll have no more than two hours for a walk. After having worked hard all day, one wants to rest outdoors. Indoors there is no possibility for such a rest, there is no fresh air. Indoors is for sleeping at night. One rests outside of one's home."

A journalist friend patted me on the back: "You're a capitalist son-of-a-gun! You must tell yourself, once and for all that Russia is another world, another people. Russia is not bears and Dostoevsky, not even communist conformity. Russia! It's a *collective way of being.* Don't you see, that's why you see groups of people on the street, in the parks, in the cafés, sitting until midnight talking, laughing, eating and drinking together. Don't you see, that's why they are so attached to their street? Don't you see that the street takes the place of a home, creates social excitement, and provides the moments of intimacy? If you don't understand that, then you don't understand anything."

Gregorij, a young student of philosophy, liked to analyze:

"The Soviet street takes up the greater part of a man's life. And therefore the street creates a *personal* relationship between itself and the man. The street fulfills the need for social contacts and makes it possible for those contacts to continue in a satisfactory fashion, in a chosen place and at a chosen time. The street allows the marriage of rest, play, and intimacy, the feeling of being 'lost in the crowd,' a strongly romantic concept we must all have to be happy."

A famous publicist told me, giving me the impression of being enlightened. "We mustn't forget the propagandistic, political, and educational meaning of the street in the life of our citizens. Look around——how many really magnificent, monumental buildings, subway stations, bridges, and sculptures do you see? Very many, and you must admit that they are not enough, that many others are under construction, that many others will systematically arise each year. You could say, and I am sure they do in the West, that for the price of only the adornments of those edifices, we could build at least a thousand large apartment houses for the workmen. . . . It's true. We certainly could. But those who say that, and think they are discovering something practical, basically don't understand and don't know our needs. You, having been here long enough, must have noticed how little importance is attached to the home. It's only a small, private corner where we sleep and where we keep our two suits of clothes. Our home, it's no more than a bed and a closet. And the street? I think that you are beginning to see a little, but you still haven't got the whole of the picture. Remember that our citizen personalizes the street, in a way. For instance, the street gives him the impression that everything that is being built on it is *for him*. Universities, museums, public rest rooms, subway stations, pavilions, railway stations, monumental warehouses for sanitation purposes, all for him, a man who actually

had only a room with a bed. . . . Furthermore, the street gives
him the impression that his own life changes for the better, because the street on which he walks changes for the better. . . .
For example, a year ago the colossal building right over there
did not exist, but now it does. Five years ago the park was not
there, but now it is. In two years' time, here and over there will
stand a new building. We change the look of our streets, our
parks, and our squares. Yearly we accomplish an architectural
face lifting for our cities, towns, and villages. At the same time we
change the consciousness of the people, for whom those streets,
the face of their towns, are a big part of their daily lives. We
give them faith that their own lives are better, happier, and
richer, as rich as the expensive decorations on the walls of those
new edifices.

"You, the people of other countries, will not understand all
that. For to grasp the significance of what I have told you you
must live with us not for ten years or forty. You should have
been here a hundred, two, four hundred years ago. You should
have grown inside our culture. And then you could understand
why we build supercolossal subway stations, palaces of learning
and art with precious stones embedded in marble. These edifices
have no more than 40 per cent functional value, and are primarily
there for the effect they give, a crushing effect of power, greatness, and glory. Only then will you understand that in our
socialist society, it's more important to have a monumental
street than a private life. And that's why we are constructing
pyramids of socialism instead of apartments. Now, is it a bit
clearer?"

A few days after this talk, I met my Belgian photographer
friend in a restaurant. He was as burdened by his equipment
as before, but now he was more sober-minded and inclined to
reflection.

"Finally! I am going to leave," he began. "I've never seen
anything like this in my whole life! Will you believe me if I
tell you that everywhere I have been, in all the towns and villages, the Russians are all the same? Many times they were on
the point of using violence when I tried to photograph anything
that was not 'new and beautiful'! And not individuals but
crowds of people, crowds, I tell you! Women, children, men,

young and old! They gathered as if someone had called them, and instantly and spontaneously they noticed that I was pointing at something they didn't want me photographing. And what anger! Right away they screamed that I was a scoundrel, that I wanted to ridicule them by exhibiting their few old and dilapidated houses once I got back, that I would show them as typical, and this and that!

"I said to them—I know enough Russian for that— 'Folks, why don't you relax? I am a socialist myself, Belgian, it's true, but a socialist. I wish you all well. I take pictures of new buildings too, but I want the old ones also. The new ones I can buy at any postcard stand. I want to show the Belgians how you live, and for Christ's sake you don't only live in new houses!' But they only waved their fists at me and shouted: 'What kind of socialist are you? We know such socialists, you're an imperialistic dog, a spy, a jerk. . . .'

"And when I wanted to photograph my only Russian girl friend in front of a fence, the crowd gathered and said terribly mean things to this very lovely and very cultured young girl. They all thought her a whore to let herself be photographed with a fence for a background instead of some great modern building. A queer sort of people, and mind you, a dangerous one! I've been practically all over the world and never have I seen anything like this before. I really feel bad. Never in my life had I so many curses thrown at me and my balding head. And why? I thought I was their friend. . . ."

We paid our check and went out of the restaurant. André walked bent low with his camera lenses and filters shining in the sun.

"Do you know," he said suddenly, "for the first time in my life I am afraid to take pictures. And I, a photographer for over thirty-five years!"

I told my Russian friends of André's adventures. They were not impressed; they listened as if those adventures were something very natural, something completely expected.

"Why are you surprised?" A couple working as mechanics in one of the factories asked me seriously. "It must be like that all over the world. . . . What don't you understand? You can see very well that for us, the Russians, our street is like our house, something we care for, embellish, are proud of. One invites guests to look at one's house and praise it, isn't that true?"

"That's exactly right," said the wife, "but why doesn't your Belgian friend understand that? If he is invited by someone inside a home in his own country, will he behave himself as he did here? Will he *also* want to take pictures of the dark corridor, instead of the beautifully furnished living room? Or maybe he'll photograph the spot on the rug instead of the handsome portrait of the hostess? Well? Are such things the customs in Europe? Are you taught to do those things?"

We were all silent for a moment. The Russian couple seemed upset. After a while, I timidly tried to explain that André had been a friend of the Soviet Union for many years, that he had very radical views, that his father was a longshoreman . . . that he was poor as a child and read Marx——

I was interrupted by the couple's sister, a woman in her forties:

"I wouldn't believe him if I were you. He's a journalist, isn't he? A journalist! He came from a capitalist country, he works for a capitalist paper, he belongs to the capitalist class, the class that exploits the workman! He can't be friendly to the Soviet Union. Never under any circumstances for any price. This man has obviously sold himself to the service of imperialism and he must serve its master! Even if he were personally honest, as a member of his profession he can only be dishonest. Anyway he's our enemy, no matter how you look at it."

The husband thoughtfully commented, "You must know that your friend's bosses are not interested in presenting Russia favorably. They are interested only in our deficiencies. If from time to time they do write something good about us, it's only to lull their working class, to make themselves appear impartial. Our nation knows very well what goes on, and that's why we treat all foreigners with suspicion, no matter what country they come from. And rightfully so."

Foreign tourists in the U.S,S.R. are invariably fascinated by the Lenin and Stalin Mausoleum in Red Square, Moscow, with throngs of several thousands waiting in a line miles long to enter it.

"It always was like that, as long as the mausoleum has existed," explained one of my acquaintances, a seventy-five-year-old man.

"Hundreds, no, thousands of people wait for hours to see the faces of Lenin and Stalin once again. Now think about it, young man." The old man raised his finger in a gesture. "Think well. It isn't curiosity that makes these people stand for hours in the hot summer sun or in the cold of winter. It isn't sheer curiosity. Think about it."

Foreign journalists have frequently described the mausoleum and the Russo-Asiatic throng waiting to get in. They write about the tension on the faces of the people, and of the martial bearing of the guards. But the question of the Lenin and Stalin Mausoleum cannot be understood in terms of the interests of tourists wanting to see a curious landmark.

Many of my friends have confessed to me that they periodically visit the mausoleum and that they always experience the same sensations and emotions. Some of them are highly educated men; two university professors, one surgeon, three high-school teachers, students, factory workers, clerks, journalists.

When I visited the mausoleum, entangled in the never-ending chain of waiting people, the silhouette of the St. Basil's Church with its unique and fantastic architecture loomed in front of me. At the right were the walls of the Kremlin. The comparatively low mausoleum was sheltered by them.

White-coated militiamen formed a symmetrical line running around the vast spaces of Red Square and kept the waiting people in order. The square was deserted otherwise. Traffic was forbidden.

The people moved very slowly. I looked at the faces around me. They represented all the races and nations which make up the U.S.S.R. Men, women, children, young people, old people waited patiently, staring around the big square.

First they looked at the people standing next to them; then, guided by the striking white coats and red armbands of the row of militiamen, they stared up at the dome and turrets of the church, and along the crenelated walls of the Kremlin.

Their tension grew as they approached the marble steps. They stood in a silent, orderly line, waiting for their turn in the silence of the vast square. Again I looked at the people. They moistened

their parched lips with their tongues. They nervously fiddled
with their hair. The tension spread. Even I found myself affected
by that tension.

The first guards at the entrance, in greenish-gray uniforms,
were like two figures of stone. But their eyes were alive in life-
less faces and searchingly followed each person who approached
the steps. A cold breeze blew from the broad mausoleum
entrance.

We descended the steps. Guards were on our left and on our
right. People stumbled on the steps and were reprimanded by
a sharp glance from each guard.

Somebody put a nervous hand on my arm to steady himself.
We proceeded, veering to the right, and found ourselves in an
interior flooded by blood-red light from a concealed source
somewhere in the vaulted ceiling.

A glass pane separated me from Lenin, who lay just beyond
it. He looked just as he does on thousands of posters, photographs, pictures, and monuments. An oval face with sharp
features, short beard, high forehead merging with a bald head.
But I couldn't see the eyes in his smooth, waxlike face. He was
sleeping, his arms folded on his chest.

The man before me suddenly lost the rhythm of the moving
line. He stopped for a moment. At his left was Stalin.

All the visitors stopped here, paralyzed by the nearness of
the man who lay only an arm's length away. Their eyes stayed
glued to the peaceful face. They searched for some trace of life,
for some movement of the eyelids or the lips, or of the hands
folded on the plain jacket. A few more steps to the left and we
could see Stalin's sharp profile. The red light made shadows on
the white face above the black collar buttoned up to the neck.

The people were unable to tear their eyes away from the yel-
lowish-red faces of the two sleeping men. While moving forward, they still looked sideways.

Only the sharp whisper of a guard, "Careful, citizen," brought
them back to reality.

And soon they were blinded by bright daylight. They were
back in Red Square. Lenin and Stalin remained underground
in eternal sleep, their glass cages filled with chill and ghostly

light, surrounded by the martial figures of guards with evil, searching eyes.

Once again I observed the faces around me. Tense features relaxed. People started to breathe normally again. Looking at the familiar surroundings, they started to talk. But not about the mausoleum or the two men in it. The experience was still too close, the impact too deep. They were not yet able to comprehend everything that had taken place in the last few minutes.

Analysis would come later, away from the spot, when daylight reflected from the white walls of the Kremlin would drive away all vestiges of the red light from the mausoleum. But what would this analysis show? What would be the results of a moment spent with Lenin and Stalin after the initial impact had given way to reason?

". . . This, sir, will *never* be fully understood or experienced by people from outside the U.S.S.R." The ordinary laborer with whom I was talking wiped the sweat from his forehead after we had left the mausoleum.

He fussed with his trousers, smoothed his hair, then sat down on a stone wall exhausted. "To understand it, you have to have lived *here* for these last thirty or forty years. Do you know what Lenin and Stalin mean to me? These are not just the names of two people. They are not even the two people themselves. To me, as you see me here, they are"—and here he stopped to think deeply for a moment—"my whole life, that's what. How should I put it? It is all that has surrounded me all of my life, and I'm forty-five. It has been my entire environment.

"First Lenin, then Stalin. Every problem, every day, every experience, every book that I ever read, every lesson in school, every meeting, and all the hardships in the army, they were always there.

"When some screaming commander yelled at me to jump out and attack, when I didn't know how many steps separated me from death, he, Stalin, was with me.

"I believed that if he knew about this attack of ours, about our life, our hunger and poverty, about the death raging amongst us, if he, Stalin, knew, then all this must be so that the future would be better.

"No, you can't understand it. To us it is the life we have led

all these years, all these hard years. To you, well, at most he is
a genius, statesman, creator of the U.S.S.R., and of the power
and greatness of our country, and that's all.

"But that's why inside the mausoleum I trembled all over.
I couldn't catch my breath because right there, half a meter
from me, lay Stalin. Do you realize it? Stalin himself! The same
Stalin who some time ago sat there like God, known to us only
by his portraits and films, and now he lies here as if in sleep."

A journalist friend spoke in a similar vein, "You see, no matter
whether you were a member of the Party and occupied a high
post, or were in a prison, Stalin, and Lenin also to a lesser
degree, was something that hit you from all sides.

"Cause and Effect, History and the Present, Communism and
the Future, the Power of the U.S.S.R., World Revolution. . . .
Everyone of these fundamental concepts was one man, Stalin.
Your work, your life, your dreams . . . all of them were tied to
him for thirty years!

"Just think, thirty years and always the same thing, the same
face, the same name around you and within you. Can you
imagine this? Can anyone outside of the U.S.S.R. understand
it?"

Evening was falling. The crowd increased and overflowed
into the street. Young people holding hands passed by me.
From somewhere came the sound of a harmonica; someone was
singing a song about Moscow and Russian heroism.

Night fell, a suffocatingly hot night. Suddenly among all these
people I felt very lonely and lost, not knowing what to do with
myself. I tried to telephone some of my friends but no one was
home. They too were probably out walking.

I had two more hours to kill because I had told my landlady
that I wouldn't be home until later. My earlier return might
disturb "the daily routine" of the other tenants.

I went to a movie. The poster pictured a young couple, arms
linked, looking towards the sky. The cashier, a pretty young girl,
smiled at me flirtatiously.

"A young man—and so alone?"

3

IN A CAGE

I MET MANY PEOPLE IN THE U.S.S.R. IT WAS, OF COURSE, INEVITABLE
that we talked about things such as love, marriage, and children.
I tried to understand their theoretical views on these questions
as well as their attitudes towards them in actual life.

Their attitude was characterized by realism. Marriage was
never the beginning of a new life for these young people but
just the continuation of things as they were, for two instead of
one.

I noticed what I came to call the "strategic" approach to
marriage, which meant considering marriage from what practical purposes it could serve. The main motivation was to
stabilize the kind of life which existed before marriage and
which was considered desirable.

For example, a young man would figure it out like this: "I'm
single, therefore my superiors might send me to some difficult
post far from here. They'll say, 'You're young, without depend-
ents. It's no special hardship for you to move.'"

Aliosha K. was twenty-two. He worked and attended vocational school at the same time. "If I marry before I graduate,"
he pointed out, "that means this year, and my wife becomes
pregnant, they can't transfer me. I would have to stay near my
wife since they wouldn't have adequate living quarters in the
more remote places for her and the baby."

An assistant instructor at Leningrad University told me why
his students marry. "Young people often marry while they're
still studying for fear of being assigned to work in a bad climate

. . . or even worse, far from any city. But marriage itself isn't enough to protect them from being sent into the provinces; they need children. Among students in their last year at the university, children are often born right after marriage. Fear of being sent to work in the provinces is stronger than any other consideration."

I was told that in the provinces the reverse was true. Young people in some miserable small town didn't want to have children which could interfere with a transfer to a larger city.

In the worker's environment, marriage is treated as a way of improving the material situation of both parties. I heard young workers with whom I was acquainted use the following arguments for marriage: "Two can always arrange their lives better. Two salaries are better than one." Or, "What's the use of waiting? It's better to marry when one is young. Here, it's almost impossible to induce a girl to have an affair."

"You can never tell, I might be sent somewhere to a new job and have to begin all over again. It's better to find a husband here, where I know everybody."

From talking to young people of various classes, I concluded that the two factors they considered as a basis for marriage are "love" on a sentimental plane, and intellectual compatibility.

Several teachers and educators with whom I had the chance to discuss this subject confirmed my observations. They pointed out to me that the attitude of Soviet youth towards love and their concept of the ideal union of two people, no matter what their social background, is vividly reminiscent of nineteenth-century poetry. The principle of physical attraction is eliminated.

I often was completely amazed by young men with their university studies behind them who confided their secret love for a woman to me or to each other. They sounded just like Pushkin's *Eugene Onegin* and Onegin's *Letter to Tatiana*. In their description of their loved ones they emphasized the emotional and intellectual factors exclusively. They talked for hours about the girl's moral qualities to the complete exclusion of her physical ones.

Similarly, when young men talked about women in general,

and their love affairs, they kept the conversation on a high, impersonal plane.

When I compared these discussions and confidences with similar conversations among their contemporaries in my own country, I found the difference so great that I couldn't understand it.

I met a young doctor, a neurologist, at some social gathering, and he explained the matter to me as he saw it from the viewpoint of his medical practice.

"I come into contact with young people either in the hospital or in my teaching, and I must tell you that in regard to love our youth is still deeply rooted in the nineteenth century.

"It is possible that they'll jump straight into the twenty-first century from the nineteenth. But talking objectively, our mass culture is a continuation of those patterns of the nineteenth century which best suit today's socialist morality.

"Our textbooks on literature, our latest films, our new novels, have changed the background of social relationships between people, but the essence of love has remained the same. Another factor that militates against any other treatment of love by our youth is the fact that the other attitude is peculiar to capitalism and widely cultivated in capitalistic countries. Incidentally, I believe with small benefit to the youth of those countries.

"Our old realistic literature of the nineteenth century is more socialist than our socialist literature of the present day is realistic. This isn't a paradox, either. Just think for a moment of the heroes of Leo Tolstoy, Gogol, Chekhov, Saltikov, Shchedrin and of their loves, let alone the poetic prototypes of love taken from Pushkin or Lermontov.

"Do you remember how the great realist, Tolstoy, describes the moment of physical contact between Anna and Vronsky? Even Dostoevsky, whom somebody called the sewer of the Russian soul through which everything runs, did not give us one single naturalistic description of a love scene.

"Just try and find anywhere in our literary heritage, to which our present culture is linked, the portrait of a great lover, a Don Juan, or the theme of an attempted rehabilitation of a loose woman who had changed her lovers because of her temperament.

"All literary attempts to introduce sex by Kuprin, for example, were emphatically rejected by socialist realism.

"Our socialist writers, Gorki, Alexy Tolstoy, Sholokhov, Fadieyev, and even Dudintsev, continue to follow this trend. They add to it by concentrating on everyday topics, the Party, ideology, the struggle against capitalist remnants, and the like.

"Did you know," the doctor said, returning to his own field, "that our medical specialists practically never have to deal with sexual degenerates? Our criminologists have even fewer cases of sex crimes.

"You'll also notice that our popular scientific literature almost never mentions sex, or at least treats it, as it treats any other question, very casually. It could be said that Russian pathology was buried with the genius who created it, Dostoevsky. But even this pathology was only of the soul and nothing else."

A few days later I had the opportunity to talk about the same subject with a girl working in a museum in Tula, an experienced teacher and art critic.

"It's true," she said. "Our nation has managed to steer clear of that phase of bourgeois culture. Those with this sort of culture fled abroad. Others died here under various circumstances, as counterrevolutionaries in Siberia, or in prison as enemies of the people, or they just found themselves without any means of making a living.

"On the other hand, don't forget that a genuine 'people's' culture is opposed to naturalism in the treatment of love and marriage by its very nature. The types of creativity and self-expression which conform to this culture are popular and patronized, other types which do not conform are banned.

"Here's a good example for you—the status of nudity in our socialist art. Not too long ago a female nude was exhibited in one of our art galleries. It must have been the first in twenty years. It was the work of a young painter, and the directors, after long debate and consultation, decided to exhibit it for a short time.

"Incidentally, it was a real work of art. Its young creator is undoubtedly a very talented painter. And yet the general reaction of the public was negative. Even we critics were confused and bewildered.

"You see, in our realistic creativity, in literature, art, and music, we deal exclusively with subjects that serve the cause of socialism and progress. But how can a nude serve socialism? I may sound vulgar, but I'm asking that question with a purpose. What I mean is that in real life, in a factory, school, or office, people appear as something definite, something with meaning socially or professionally. But nudity is anonymous! What I'm trying to point out is that nudity expresses nothing in the sense that we want a work of art to express an idea.

"In addition, a nude painting is a clear transfer of the center of interest from social man to physical man. Our critics condemned the picture very severely and expressed the hope that the young and highly promising artist would see his error.

"The answer to your question is very similar. In our life there is no purpose in playing up physical attraction between people. You won't find it in our films, theater, literature, or magazines. Our socialist morality has other goals and other missions than capitalist morality—a morality of degenerates, sadists, and rapists."

One day, talking with a large group of students in Kuibyshev, I mentioned a certain lack of feminine grace and coquetry that struck me about Soviet women. One of those present commented: "In our society the professional work of married women, including mothers, has become a set pattern of life. Please remember that in our country, women form 47 per cent of employed persons, excluding agriculture. And so coquetry, shrewd femininity, and cultivated sensuality are characteristics of an era that is gone and will never return. Only degenerated capitalist societies use sex as yet another 'opium for the masses,' stupefied by all kinds of advertising and propaganda. . . ."

I had an interview with Maxim, a sports instructor who was in charge of camps for young people which were open in winter as well as summer. He had been working in this field since 1936 and was well acquainted with the problems of youth. He had the reputation of being an excellent teacher and a great friend of youth.

We discussed the relationship between the adolescent girls and boys in his camps. "My young people have no secrets from

me, and I know their problems better than they know them
themselves. We spend so many days of the week together.

"There was a time when I thought young people were the
same all over the world. But . . . I was due for a rude shock!
Last year I was invited by a youth organization in Berlin to
attend a sports camp in the German Democratic Republic.
There I saw that our youth and the German youth, at least,
are completely different. What I mean, of course, is in the relationship between boys and girls.

"The young people in Germany literally treat sex as a sport.
A boy may meet a girl in the morning, and by evening they
are in bed together. All right, if they went about it normally,
as demanded by nature. . . . But no, they make a whole ritual
of the thing. It's a disgrace!

"Then among a group of apparently normal people you suddenly meet a lot of degenerates, boys with boys, for instance.
They are like animals, not human beings.

"They carry pornographic pictures in their pockets, hygienic
appliances, pills for stimulation, and who knows what else. Next
to them our young people are infants in swaddling clothes.

"If you overhear some of our young people talking with each
other, it's like a book. Your best friend may tell you he kissed
a girl, but that's all he'll tell you. Not only because he doesn't
want to. Even if he did want to tell more, our vocabulary for
these things is very limited and it would be very difficult for
him to express himself.

"Here, even adults can't talk to each other about certain
things in their married life because they are not familiar enough
with anatomy and we have no substitute words in our everyday
language.

"Of course our young people are healthily attracted to members of the opposite sex, but in a different way. Our youths find
an outlet in sports, social work, art, and in these activities their
sexual drives are rechanneled.

"And don't forget that our social organizations stand guard
over our morality. If, for instance, it is discovered that a girl and
boy have had sexual intercourse, they are faced with very serious
consequences both in the organization and in society. The affair will be discussed at a meeting at which both parties are

present. They could be expelled from Komsomol, even from school. Our young people are very much afraid of this, even university students, let alone high-school kids.

"Do you know what happened to the women or girls whose conduct was slightly loose during the last war, let alone those who had proven lovers? They were incorporated into special women's battalions and sent at once to the front line. In the army they were called TPZ 'tovarishch polevaya zona' which means 'comrade battlefield wife.' Now they are still sent to the front lines, but this time to the front line of socialist work, to remote Soviet republics where young, strong men are needed and there is a dearth of women for them to marry.

"Yes, my friend, we live in a group where the affairs of an individual cannot be concealed—the more so the affairs of two individuals."

The law permitting abortion by a government medical agency at government cost is surrounded by a number of legal and moral hurdles. A young woman who is pregnant and who wants an abortion, even for valid reasons, must go through end- less interviews, questions, answers, waiting, and humiliation which will poison her future life for a long time. And there is always the uncertainty as to whether or not the application will be granted.

To illustrate this hard road, I'll use the true story of Sonia E., a pleasant twenty-four-year-old worker in an industrial estab- lishment. Eighteen months before, on leave at a summer resort, Sonia met a good-looking young man, an employee of a com- mercial distributing center, who was also on his vacation.

Sonia told me her story because I was a close friend of her best girl friend, adding with resignation, "You'd hear all about it at the factory, anyway, and with silly remarks added.

"When I met him," said Sonia, "I liked him very much from the first moment. He could tell a good story, was intelligent, and very good-looking, really exceptionally handsome. All the girls were crazy about him. Well, I fell in love with him. It's human, isn't it? I was very happy in his company. I think he loved me a little too, at least he told me so. One evening we went to a dance. It was very gay. I drank too much wine, and,

well . . . it happened, you understand, and continued till the
end of my vacation.

"I left, and he remained for a few more days. But he promised
to write as soon as he got home, and we promised that we would
see each other again. He even spoke of marriage. Well, to cut it
short, I never heard from him. I wrote to him in Minsk, but
he never answered. They notified me from the housing committee that he had been sent away on duty for ten months.
Then I found out I was pregnant. . . ."

Sonia lived with her mother, father, and brother. She and her
mother worked, but her father was partially paralyzed, a nervous,
sick old man with heart disease. The thirteen-year-old brother
went to school. The financial situation of the family was far
from good. They lived in one small room in the attic of an old
house.

"I said to myself," continued Sonia, "that there was nothing
to do but get rid of it. I couldn't afford to raise this child. Besides, I realized what a hard blow it would be to my parents,
especially to Father. They always wanted me to marry a director
or engineer or inventor or scientist. You know how parents
are. So I didn't tell them.

"To receive permission for an abortion and to be sent to a
hospital you have to apply to the factory union. But first you
must talk to the secretary of the women's organization who must
give her written opinion on the matter.

"Well, I was lucky with the secretary. I told her what had
happened. The child's father had gone somewhere, I didn't have
time to look for him, and for all I knew he may have been
married. Finally, I told her that I wasn't financially able to raise
a child. She understood.

"But at the union it didn't go so well. I talked to the deputy
secretary for personnel. She was a woman. You'd think she'd
be able to understand. But all she had to say were the old,
worn-out platitudes, 'In our system every woman can support a
child,' and that I didn't have the right 'to deprive a future citizen
of the U.S.S.R. of life,' and so on.

"The next step was a hearing by a special medical-social commission in one of the City Centers for Mother and Child. The
commission consists of a doctor-specialist and delegates of the

women's organization, Party, union, youth organization, and someone from the department of health.

"I brought the opinions of the labor union and the Party with me in a sealed envelope (I'm a candidate member of the Party), plus testimony from the housing committee on the living space occupied by my family, my family's earnings, and my father's illness.

"The commission asked many questions. Wasn't I ashamed, as a Soviet woman and candidate member of the Party, to try to have an abortion? Didn't I know that our government provided children with the best conditions in the world? Did I really think that my father, a Soviet citizen and participant in the socialist revolution, would stand in the way of my bearing a child? They went on and on.

"But I continued to stubbornly insist that I saw no possibility of bearing and raising the child. That I wasn't prepared, either physically or morally, to have a child. Finally I did succeed in getting sent to a hospital and having the abortion.

"But"—Sonia stared at a fly crawling on the table—"don't think that this was the end of the story. At the next meeting of the union, to which I must belong with all the other workers, I was reprimanded for morality alien to socialist society. At the meeting of the Party, my membership card was taken away from me for two years for 'moral alienation from the ideals of the Party and Society.'

"Of course," Sonia smiled ironically, "it was a terrific subject of conversation for my colleagues of both sexes. They are still trying to guess who the father of my unborn child was, and who will be the father of the next."

Sonia's case was not an isolated one. I heard of many cases where young, unfortunate girls wandered from commission to commission, from secretary to secretary, from Party to Komsomol, from Komsomol to the department of health to get a permit for an abortion. Humiliated, insulted, forced to tell the most intimate details about their pregnancy and to call witnesses, branded at public meetings in school, university, or place of employment, serving as material for gossipers, often humilated in public, they were finally refused the permit. So they went somewhere North, "to the front lines of the struggle with nature." There, in a new environment, mostly surrounded by men, they usually managed to marry and legitimize the child. But return to their old environment was barred to them for many years.

Divorce is legally permitted in the U.S.S.R. But this too, like abortion, is complicated. A married couple who seek a divorce face an unknown factor as far as the court decree is concerned, while they realize perfectly well that the very attempt to get a divorce will jeopardize the careers of both husband and wife.

"Divorce is considered an element of social decay by the government, even if the law doesn't express it in these precise terms," explained a good friend, Judge P.

"In practice, we have worked out a way of treating divorce cases, based on our experience in the U.S.S.R. over the past thirty years. The basic attitude of the court always is that the divorce is not necessary since the married couple seeking divorce can achieve their purpose through a separation for an unlimited period. Now for a separation a court isn't needed. All the help a couple needs for a separation can be provided by the Party or the union. They can do it by simply transferring one of the parties to a new post in a different part of the country.

"In this procedure, which is the most common, the married couple are separated yet remain legally married. They have to arrange new lives for themselves, he here, she somewhere else.

"Then after a few years, when each has managed to get used to a new life with new friends, a new love interest, the court can grant them their divorce. The decree will state that from the angle of socialist morality granting the divorce will lead to a normalization of their new situation. Clear?

"Don't forget that a couple applying for divorce are perfectly aware that their case will be discussed by the Party, union, and youth organizations to which they belong at their place of business. They also understand that their socio-political standing and their vocational future depend on the reasons they advance to justify their application for divorce. That's why certain reasons, even if they are the true ones, must be avoided as 'anti-social' or 'rottenly bourgeois' or 'hostile to socialism.' They can't, for instance, use physical incompatibility, or sexual repulsion, or sexual negligence on the part of one party as a reason. Reasons like these, popular in capitalistic countries, would expose them to expulsion from the Party, or, if they're not members, would bar them from ever being accepted.

"In addition, their future lives would be affected because the record would remain forever in their personal file. Under our system, family is a fundamental unit of socialist society, based on marriage and kinship, characterized by mutual love, by equality of man and woman, identity of interests of individual and society, performing the functions of procreation, Communist upbringing, and mutual aid.

"Now where could you find room in a union like that for insignificant 'physical' problems? A Soviet man is not an animal, my friend." Judge P. smiled ironically at his own thoughts and at the clichés he had used. He carefully stirred the sugar in a cup of coffee brought in by his secretary.

"But our married couples anxious to part aren't so stupid. They try to give reasons for their desire to divorce which won't harm them, which may even improve their reputations in some place. They use political, ideological, social, and labor excuses, and lie like old veterans.

"For instance, a case will come up before me where the husband, a twenty-seven-year-old office employee promoted from worker, applies for a divorce. His reason? His wife, a twenty-five-year-old worker, refuses to 'improve her intellectual and political standards by attending an ideological course organized by the union.' The husband continues to give examples of the 'political backwardness' of his wife, quoting views allegedly uttered by her. Incidentally, ten years ago you could have been exiled for a long time and far away for such views.

"But we suspect he isn't telling the truth. The file on his case is forwarded to the union at his place of employment for review by them and the executive board of the Party. Together they attack the case with vigor. They summon the wife, verify, confront her with witnesses, and the case is clarified.

"The sleek husband has befriended a girl in his office, a divorcée, in whose house he spends all of his free time. He hardly ever comes home. When he does he beats his child and insults his wife.

"Well, there's a way to deal with such people. A week later he is assigned to the 'front line of socialist work' in the Ural Mountains for a year or two. He must take care of his wife and send her a given portion of his wages. If, after his return, it's found that he still hasn't come down to earth a divorce might be granted to him on the basis of the year or two of separation.

"Want another example? Let's take a wife this time, who sues for divorce. She is a thirty-seven-year-old clerk. Her husband is a respected scientist. The wife charges that her husband violates the norms of socialist morality, has a close relationship with a young actress, does not share his salary with his wife, and is a bad example for their two children. Again the case goes to his Party organization (he is a member) and to her union. Investigation proves that the wife is telling the truth. Pressure is applied by the Party, and it succeeds. Scared of being expelled from the Party, he promises to mend his way. If he doesn't, the case will be reopened at a future date.

"Here's another example. This time both parties sue for divorce. The reasons given are 'lack of mutual political understanding.' He accuses her of 'deficiency in ideology.' She charges him with 'political cynicism.' The factory and domestic committees find out that they haven't been living together for two years. The children are being cared for by a grandmother somewhere in the provinces. In this case the divorce is granted immediately. But right after the trial both were transferred to some new outpost of socialism. In Kazakhstan, I believe."

Judge P. finished his coffee and gave me a cordial handshake, "Well, young man, when will you invite me to your wedding? Better hurry up. You're at the best age, and the times are favorable. Our girls are pretty. You won't find any prettier anywhere else in the world."

The secretary entered the room with a batch of papers, and the judge threw his question at her, "Russian women are the most beautiful of all, aren't they?" The girl dropped her eyes and blushed.

At the time that I was studying the love and marriage customs of the U.S.S.R., I never dreamed that I would be affected by them personally. However, during my stay in a small town on the Moscow-Ivanovo railroad, I met a girl student of a technical school of whom I became quite fond. Let's call her Agniya.

Agniya was twenty-three, had a beautiful figure, somewhat oriental features, and exceptionally beautiful black hair with a chestnut gleam. We always had a lot to talk about, and we used to meet quite often. She was interested in my past. I was curious about her present. We were both interested in the turn our friendship would take in the near future.

Probably because of my influence, though it was far from my intention, Agniya tried to imitate the appearance of the western women she had seen in the movies. She wore her hair in a pony-tail, revealing her long, delicately shaped neck. She cut her tight-fitting blouse lower and definitely narrowed her skirt. In addition, she used a bit of lipstick. She was beautiful, and it gave me pleasure to look at her.

We had met only five or six times when a strange incident occurred. Late one night, someone knocked at the door of the room where I was staying with a friend. My friend wasn't home, so I opened the door. Two young girls, perhaps twenty years old, stood in the doorway. They wore sports blouses with Komsomol badges on the lapels.

"I beg your pardon, comrade," said one of them, "but may we come in?"

At my invitation they entered the room, looking around searchingly, then informed me that they were sent by the Komsomol organization to ask whether they could "help" me in any way, whether I wouldn't like "to meet a Komsomol discussion group" or something like that. I couldn't understand their interest in me, especially since I couldn't remember notifying any officials of my arrival in town.

So I thanked them and asked them to send me an announcement of their next meeting. My uninvited guests thoroughly scrutinized the whole room again. One of them seemed especially intrigued by the coat tree where Agniya's raincoat was hanging. She had lent it to me the day before when I was caught in the rain. The girls from Komsomol obviously recognized the coat; they glanced at each other significantly and left soon thereafter.

I had an appointment to meet Agniya the next morning. I

waited for a long time, but she never showed up. This had never happened before.

I went to her house in the afternoon, where her younger brother informed me that his sister had been summoned to appear before the Komsomol City Committee a few hours earlier. She hadn't come back yet.

Later that evening, the younger brother came to my room and with a mysterious air told me to follow him and he would lead me to where his sister was waiting for me. I was at a loss to understand this conspiratorial secrecy, but of course I went with him.

Agniya's hair was back to its original style, braided on top of her head. The blouse was closed high on her neck by a safety pin. Her skirt showed visible traces of widening. Her face was tear-stained and she obviously was under great strain.

She explained what had happened. This morning she had been summoned to the Komsomol Committee. At the meeting of the Committee, which was enlarged especially for the occasion, she was accused of "imitation of bourgeois attire, morality alien to the Soviet nation, improper behavior, and of being ashamed of the clothes and appearance of Soviet girls." She was told that pending consideration of her case at a meeting of her group, her rights as a member of Komsomol were suspended and her membership card withdrawn. In addition, she was advised that independent of the Komsomol inquiry, her case would be referred to her school authorities who would take disciplinary measures, including possible expulsion from school.

After that she was advised to apply to join a transport of "young Komsomol volunteers who have pledged themselves to the patriotic task of spending four months harvesting in a remote part of the U.S.S.R." The transport was leaving the next day.

Of course Agniya applied immediately, and was leaving tomorrow. She was broken-spirited and dejected. She expected the worst, even if she did succeed in becoming a shock worker during the harvest. She still would have to face these unbearable meetings and possible dismissal from school. The world, which yesterday was full of sunshine and happiness, had suddenly become a tiny cage with no exit.

I decided not to prolong my stay in that town and to take a train due to leave in an hour. We thought it best to say good-by right then and there.

I went to fetch my bag, and half an hour later was in my train compartment. A moment before the train left, Agniya appeared at the station. We both knew that we were seeing each other for the last time. It was hard to remain unemotional. The train started slowly. For a few moments Agniya walked alongside the window, then it pulled away from her. A minute later she was just a tiny spot pasted against the gray of the disappearing station. The train picked up speed. I drew the curtains closed across the compartment window and began to complete my notes.

4

ON THE FRONT OF SOCIALIST WORK

"WE ARE IN LIFE WHAT WE ARE IN WORK"—THAT'S HOW A YOUNG economist tersely formulated the role of work in the U.S.S.R. The area of everyday life affected by work in the U.S.S.R. is vast. Work actually decides the place of the individual in society, and at the same time defines the relationship of social institutions to the individual.

This is so not only because work has been made the individual's primary duty and a socio-political necessity ("if you don't work you don't eat" or "to each according to his work, from each according to his abilities") but also because, first of all, an individual who must work remains within the control of all those social institutions and groups which make up the concept of work. He must fulfill certain terms not only at the moment when he begins his work but for its entire duration. He must be an efficiently operating part of a complicated labor, social, and political mechanism which functions wherever a human being studies or is gainfully employed . . . in the factory, office, school, university, shop, hospital, army, everywhere.

"The man who turns up one day at work in our factory does not drop from heaven. He comes here for a reason—to get something from us—and he comes from some definite place," the chief of personnel in the K. factory explained to me. The personnel office occupied several rooms in the front building. A number of clerks, male and female, were at work on files of documents or bent over typewriters. The chief of the personnel office was a Comrade P., a man about forty.

"We may say," continued Comrade P., "that the tasks of the personnel section of each plant or office in the U.S.S.R. are: selection of personnel and control over the advancement of employees; keeping records on personal data such as salaries, vacations, and transfers; issuing required certificates for the employee's family or children and for the army; and implementing the policies of our Party and our government with respect to the training of needed workers.

"The personnel section of any organization is, we may say, its brains. Let me show you, comrade," and Comrade P. led me to the files and opened a drawer of folders. "Each worker has his folder, and in it is a picture of the whole man from every angle: family background; past places of residence; schools graduated; relatives abroad; police record, if any, where, and why; members of his family, where they work, were any ever in jail and why; condition of his health; military record, where served and when, ever court-martialled and if so why; his relationship to our Party, is he a member now or has he ever been one and then been expelled, or is he a candidate; his relationship to the Komsomol, is he a member, was he expelled, is he a candidate; where did he work before . . . and so on. All these questions are answered by the worker himself in a special questionnaire. Each answer is accompanied by the appropriate certificate.

"For example, when the worker says he graduated from a certain school he encloses his graduation certificate. When he writes about his family he encloses certificates issued to the members of his family by their employers and a certificate from the house committee stating that all these persons actually live in the same apartment.

"If the employee comes to us from some other organization, our section receives all the questionnaires and documents about him from his previous place of work, see? This, however, does not exempt him from completing another questionnaire and again submitting all the required certificates and enclosures relating to his experience *curriculum vitae*.

"But this is not all, comrade. The new employee doesn't only come to us from another place of work or school. He also comes from a certain labor union local to which he belonged in his previous place of work, and from a certain Party organization (if he is a Party member) or youth organization (Komsomol). These organizations send us complete information about him—their evaluation of his person, his work and its results, the vocational and socio-political courses he has taken, and the grades attained. Copies of this material are also received by our Party organization and by our union and youth organizations. Do you see? That's why I said that man does not go to heaven, nor does he drop into our factory from it." Comrade P. laughed jovially at his own joke.

"Such a folder is, you could say, comrade, the conscience of a socialist citizen and worker. From its contents you may be able to tell the changes in the characteristics of his handwriting by comparing questionnaires written at various stages of his life . . . and also the change in the character of the man himself by comparing the opinions issued about him at various periods. You also must remember that all of the essential information concerning the close family of the employee, for example his wife's or his son's employment, also reaches our folder. Conversely, our data on an employee reaches the folder of his wife in her place of employment, or of his son at the university. So we are thoroughly familiar with the external conditions under which our employee has been developing up to the moment when he comes to work for us.

"In turn, if one of our employees is transferred to some other place of business his folder follows him to his new job, enriched by our own comments and by his experience in our employ. But copies of the material remain in our personnel files, the big green closet you see over there in the corner. If we ever receive an inquiry about one of our past employees from another organization, we can recreate his professional, social, and political silhouette at a moment's notice. You might say, comrade as they learn in school, 'nothing disappears in nature.' Eh?

"Now this will interest you: the personnel section carries out the political and production goals of the factory. However, the personnel section does not formulate its own independent policy. It acts on the instructions of the Party and of the management. Obviously the chief of the personnel section is usually a Party member and a widely trusted man, perfectly oriented in the affairs of the business, the union, the Party organization, the Komsomol, and the various cultural and recreational organizations in the plant. His responsibilities are great.

"The business is actually managed by the office of the director, a board consisting of the director, the deputy director, the chief technician, plus several engineers . . . their number depending on the type of factory, its size, number of employees, production, and the like. Our highest authority is the ministry of the given industry, then the central board which supervises several similar plants.

"This is, then, the production-labor authority which collaborates closely in the factory with the political authority (the Party organization), with the union authority (labor union local) and with the youth authority (the Communist Youth Organization, Komsomol).

"All these authorities work closely together towards their common goal, the best interests of the business. But they preserve a certain independence by being responsible to their own separate superior authorities outside of the place of work. For instance, the Party organization in our factory comes under the district committee of the Party. The union local is subordinated to the district council of labor unions, and the Komsomol to the district committee of Komsomol.

"You'll understand this best if you try to visualize it from the view of every one of us manual and white-collar workers who come in contact with these organizations in our everyday life. Diagrams or figures won't help."

And so I began to change my views of the Soviet factory. I left the spacious offices of the personnel section, sped on by a cordial handshake with the chief and by Lenin's hand raised in brotherhood from the frame of a large portrait hanging above the green closet containing the personnel files.

On the way out I stopped at the director's office to say goodby and to thank him for the permanent pass which entitled me to visit his factory any time. His office was quiet and comfortable. His figure was engulfed in a massive leather-covered armchair which in turn was dwarfed by the huge portraits of Comrades Khrushchev and Lenin hanging on the wall. On top of the cabinet to his right were a few bronze statuettes and

busts of Stalin with shiny, engraved inscriptions, such as: "To
the factory of X, for its devoted work—from the Ministry," and
"For leadership in the fight at the front of socialist work—The
County Committee of the Communist Party of Soviet Russia."

Comrade Director was in the act of signing piles of papers
marked, in colored ink, "secret" or "confidential" or "top secret."
He automatically dipped his pen, shaped like an interplanetary
missile, into an inkwell made in the form of a MIG-16.

I left the administration buildings. The third shift of workers
was entering the production hall, passing by huge signs reading,
"Under the banners of Marxism Leninism—on to the struggle
on all the fronts of socialist work . . . on to communism."

As a rule, foreign journalists who visit Soviet industrial plants
are inclined to compare the working conditions of the Soviet
worker with those of his West European or American counterpart. However, the essential difference does not lie in the
appearance of the Soviet worker or of his plant, nor even in
the organization of the processes of production. The essential
differences are, above all, in the complicated relationships
between the worker as an individual and the collectivity of
workers as an aggregate of political and labor organizations.

"Let me see, how can I put it to make it perfectly clear?"
Anton, a worker in the Technical Control Department, tried
to initiate me into the area covered by these ties. "Well, look
around. You see workers like me, right? O.K., then. Now, from
the angle of work, laborwise, we all do the same work and we
make up one ladder, one hierarchy. A regular worker is
subordinate to the senior worker, the senior worker to the foreman, the foreman to the chief of a subsection, the latter to
the section chief, the section chief to the chief engineer, the
engineer to the director, and so on. See that worker over there
in gray overalls? There, to your right. In this hierarchy he is
my direct superior, the senior worker.

"Now forget everything I've just told you. Look around once
more. Still just a group of workers, aren't they? But stop
looking at them as workers and begin looking at them from the
angle of the place they occupy in the political organization
in our factory. First, you must divide them into members and
non-members of the Party. The members, in turn, must be

subdivided into many categories. Those who have been members for, let us say, thirty years, next twenty-five years, and so on down to candidate members. In addition, they must be divided according to their functions. One, for instance, is secretary of our Party organization; another just a regular member. One was once a member of the board of the Party's district committee, but isn't any longer. Another may have suffered a Party reprimand. So you see, these same workers around you, when studied from the angle of their Party standing, form an entirely different picture. I, for example, am a Party member, but the man I showed you is my superior in my work is Partyless. In the political hierarchy I'm above him, understand?

"See that tall, baldish man with eyeglasses? Employment-wise he's just a plain worker, but in the political hierarchy he is a very important person, being a member of the executive board of the factory Party organization. In the labor hierarchy we are equals, but in the political hierarchy he is way above me. He is on the board of the Party organization of which I am just a member. Or take another example. See that white-haired man behind the pillar? He is a regular worker like me, has been working here since 1929, but is not a Party member. So I, even though I've been here only five years, am above him in the political hierarchy because I am a member. Naturally, in the work hierarchy he is more important than I.

"But this isn't all. Don't forget that every factory, school, or office also has a labor-union organization with a hierarchy of its own. Look again at the men around you from that angle and you will get an entirely new picture. The senior worker I just mentioned is chairman of our factory union and as such is, of course, more important in the union hierarchy than I. In addition, he is more important in the political hierarchy as well, because I am a new member of the Party while he is an old member and is active in union affairs. As you know, the unions are considered 'the transmission belt from the party to the masses.' In certain situations he may even be more important than the secretary of the Party's factory organization, who has not had as much experience in social work as he.

"Now you probably wonder if we apply any other criteria besides political, union, and vocational ones to our daily lives.

Of course we do. There are other criteria, equally important, and sometimes, in concrete situations, much more vital. They are, I think"—here Anton stopped to think for a long while—"more difficult to change, more established. One very important criterion, applied in the U.S.S.R. at almost every step, could be called a moral criterion.

"By this I mean, first of all, the relationship of the citizen to the 1917 Revolution, to Soviet authorities, to the Party, to the war with the fascist invader in 1941 to 1945, to work, to study, to socialist ownership—briefly, to everything. For example, maybe you or some member of your family supported counterrevolution in 1917 or later, or served in a counterrevolutionary unit, or had a friend who was a counterrevolutionary. Or possibly a member of your family was a Trotskyite or had been expelled from the Party for some crime against the Party line. Or, to take other examples, a man may have been sentenced by a court for some crime against the Soviet authorities, for theft or bribery; he may have had an improper attitude during the last war, collaboration with the occupation army, unsatisfactory conduct in the Army or many other things. Of course the same moral yardstick is applied also to positive records and actions, such as heroism, some act of sacrifice, performing dangerous work under especially difficult conditions, or denouncing a spy to the people's authorities.

"From this angle, a man who neither belongs to the Party nor plays a prominent part in the union hierarchy has much more to say if he is, for instance, a Hero of the Soviet Union from the last war. He is supported by the blood he has shed endangering his life for his country. It talks for him. Similarly, a man who, if necessary, will sacrifice a member of his close family who is an enemy of the party or of the government and turn him over to the authorities will have great moral standing and will be cited to others as an example.

"So it is quite possible for a veteran Party member or union member to have less standing than a non-member whose moral stature is extremely high. The latter may have a decisive voice in certain situations.

"There is still another criterion. I would call it, historically, the oldest in the U.S.S.R. This is the criterion of social origin, in other words, a biographical one. There was a time when eligibility for membership in the Party was based on this. A man of bourgeois origin could not join the Party. In many cases the assignment to various posts has been and still is governed by this criterion. Many positions are still reserved for people of definitely peasant or working-class origin. To take another example, the son of a well-known Party leader has a higher status than a non-member, or the son of a non-member, or even a Party member of bourgeois origin, or a member with someone in his family living in a capitalist country. Similarly, a Party member whose father and grandfather have been members carries more weight than a Party member coming from a non-member family.

"As you see, all these intertwined evaluations play a very vital role in our everyday life. Each criterion, applied separately, has no meaning. Only in a dialectic relationship do they create a real and objective possibility of defining a man. In time you will learn to watch the people around you through several pairs of eyeglasses at the same time. Then you will see, on numerous occasions, how it applies to our work and our life. You will get used to it, I promise you."

"You must understand one thing, old boy," explained Leonid, who was a foreman. "A man doesn't have a certain value, in any area, established once and for all time. You can't say about anyone, 'He's a good Party member,' or 'Vasyli Ivanovich is a decent man.' The most you can say is 'Partywise, he's considered a good member,' or 'Nobody's proved anything wrong about Vasyli Ivanovich yet.' Each of us has a number of faces. With one he can smile and look contented, while with another he cries and is troubled. With still another he is fearful and afraid. That's why a man can never say about himself, 'I'm doing all right.' Because a man can never be all right from all angles at the same time!

"At the best, he may be all right in one respect and at one given moment. Remember, a man knows himself the least. Other people know the most about him. It can't be otherwise. A man can't live and at the same time calculate what other people think of him and how they see him from all angles. Brother, it's a mighty complicated philosophy."

And yet at the base of this complicated philosophy of Leonid there is a comparatively simple principle of organization in action. Vasyli, member of the factory's Party organization explained it to me to the accompaniment of clinking glasses of vodka.

"Did you ever study an anthill? I mean really study it, not just look at it while passing by? What do you see? I'll tell you. On one side you see order and organization, ants marching in a file in a definite direction to get specific things. If you look carefully you notice the principle of respect for authority and you see work performed seriously and thoroughly. But at the same time, on the other side, you see chaos. Ants rushing into each other, upsetting each other, running this way and that. And if you look longer what do you note? You see that the other side, the chaos and trampling and upsetting, *does not disturb* the order, that it is deliberate and purposeful, that it *helps* in the performance of work, that it introduces *individualism* into the ranks of the ants, that it brings out the personality of the individual ant who breaks away for a moment from the ranks of the ants, within a scope permissible by the collectivity, to subjugate another ant who had wanted to do the same thing. But after a while the victorious ant meets the same fate. Another partner from the marching file breaks away from it to subjugate our victor. And thus the seeming chaos and confusion in the ant society serves the cause of order, serves to advance the strained work of the ants."

In one gulp Vasyli emptied his glass.

"And now change your point of view and look at our plant from above, as you looked at the ants. What do you see? You'll see us all in ranks working. Everyone does his own work and everyone is watched by another. The principle of order and authority is preserved. But what happens next? Our human ants begin to exchange places. Instead of the job authority which has ruled up to now, another authority enters, let us say political. And lo, the former subordinate becomes a leader, the former chief a plain worker. One human ant drives another one into a file. But in this file, too, the exchange of places continues. Our human ants begin to jostle each other, to knock each other over. Each tries to discover the other's weaknesses which would make it possible to oust the competitor and make more room for himself. But soon satisfaction becomes illusion. The victor has weaknesses also—perhaps in his biography. If not in his own, then perhaps in that of his father or brother . . . and so he is doomed.

"Each of us could say to others, 'If you are without sin, you may cast stones at me.' But they cast stones because they know they are *not* without sin! Man protects himself by trying to find in others those sins which he commits himself. If he finds them, he is satisfied, happy, proud. His rival is eliminated for a while. But the pride and happiness last a short time. Soon the same method is applied to the victor . . . and who is without sin?

"So you see, here, too, the seeming chaos serves the cause of order. Disorganization serves organization. When a person magnifies individual faults in others, he enables the collectivity to define and combat his own faults. It's an ingenious mechanism, a true example of perpetual motion.

"You could say that this, too, was discovered by the U.S.S.R. It can't fail, because by applying pressure to the individual from all sides it exploits his energy, initiative, desire for progress, happiness, and contentment. There is always a goal before the man's eyes. But as soon as he reaches it, he realizes that he is still standing in the same place. So he starts after a new goal, and reaches the same impasse.

"But along the way his energy affects others throughout the group in which he lives and from which he can never free himself. The group continually puts new goals in front of him. It absorbs him completely. It watches him from all sides, especially from those where he does not see himself. It reprimands him continuously, and pushes him continuously. And thus around and around goes that wonderful spinning wheel, that dance of the human ants.

"But it's time to come back to earth. Someday come to our bi-weekly Party meeting. You'll understand much better what I've told you tonight in my somewhat tipsy condition. Be sure to come; you have my formal invitation. It will be an interesting evening. We always have many personal matters on the agenda, and these are always the most interesting."

The U.S.S.R.'s perpetual-motion machine, which Vasyli

described while staring into his glass, draws its motive power from the social organization to which it is constantly giving new impetus.

About fifteen people—engineers, technicians, and skilled workers—worked in the Technical Control Department of the factory I visited. The factory produced several types of cameras, so this section was especially important. It not only inspected the finished products, but also, indirectly, controlled production by checking the cameras for defects and for the quality of work performed. Thus the section of Technical Control, called OTK, was the very heart of the plant. It provided a good example for understanding the mechanism which Vasyli outlined in his analogy. Actually, Vasyli is a technician in the OTK and at the same time a member of the executive board of the factory's Party organization.

"Our OTK is an object of prime interest to all the authorities and organizations existing in our factory." A friend of Vasyli introduced me to the work of the section. "The technical control of the cameras produced in our plant includes inspecting the products for defects and for grade of work done. But first it checks the personal responsibility of a number of individual workers charged with the various phases of production in various sections. In this way, as you see, everyone can be examined, this time from the production angle, by means of the OTK."

A close analysis of the personnel of the OTK revealed a small representation of all the basic organizations existing in the factory. Thus there were a few Party members including two skilled workers, one technician, and one engineer. The center of this group was Vasyli, a member of the Party board. There also was a group of union members consisting of the balance of the skilled workers, three technicians, and one engineer. One of the workers was the assistant secretary of the union local. The last group consisted of the chief engineer of the OTK, his assistant, and a technician working on statistical analysis. The basis for this informal division into groups was the part played by the members of each group in the control of production of the workers. Each group represented the attitudes of a different organization. Vasyli's group represented the attitude of the Party organization; the union group, the attitude of the union organization; while the group from the OTK, led by the chief engineer, represented the attitude of management.

A few days later one of the technicians explained to me: "You see, the idea is to be able to find a way to each worker. The best way is through his production. You can hit him hardest if you find his work deficient, understand?"

When Vasyli and I discussed his work in the OTK, he was forced to think it out. He agreed with me that, actually, in the production sense, he didn't do much in the OTK.

"But my function is not work . . . you must understand this," he tried to convince me. "You see, production has several sides too. Production as such, from an objective viewpoint, is the job of the chief engineer and his assistants. But production also has a human side; let us call it a subjective side. That's where I and my Party comrades in the OTK come in. Our job is to watch the people—those in the production halls and those in the OTK as well. The comrades from the union also deal with people, with the workers. Their job is agitation, and investigation of the causes of decreased productivity.

"Their findings as well as the findings in the field of productivity are submitted to us. Of course, we also control *their* control function, understand? It's up to us to draw conclusions and to submit them, according to their importance, either to our Party organization or to the union organization or to the Komsomol, sometimes to the management itself.

"Others will decide the value of the findings. They may be discussed at a meeting of the union. Or they may find their way to the meeting of the Party organization, or even to the executive board of the Party. Or they may go to the desk of the director to be referred to the ministry . . . or to the district attorney.

"You see, comrade, we take our production seriously. Defective production is economic sabotage. Economic sabotage is the greatest enemy of socialism, of the U.S.S.R., of the cause of peace and progress. We, the Party, know how to deal with our enemies . . . is that clear? The comrade instructor from the district committee put it very well in our ideological training class when he said, 'This is a syllogism of socialism.'"

The cameras produced in the K. factory did not owe their existence solely to the "syllogism of socialism." Their manufacture was closely related to the department of the design engineering chief, engineer W. I had met engineer W. before, and we came to like and trust each other. He was middle-aged and all the education he had received was in the U.S.S.R.

He lived near the factory with his young and charming wife. They had two small children. In the morning he was brought to work by a factory car which also picked up the factory director and the secretary of the Party organization. The same car brought engineer W. home after work.

He was not a Party member. His father's brother was in command of a tank unit in the counterrevolution of 1917 and finally escaped to the West. W.'s father was executed by order of the Revolutionary court for "collaboration with the counterrevolution." W. admitted that it was by some "miracle" that he was able to finish high school and, sponsored by an influential friend, enter the Polytechnic Institute from which he graduated with top grades.

During World War II he worked in a factory making range-finding equipment for the artillery. After the war, he returned to camera construction, his original specialty. He married at that time. His wife worked in a nearby hospital as instructor of nursing. They occupied two tiny rooms and shared a kitchen with the factory janitor who lived next door.

We visited the department of design engineering. Proudly, engineer W. showed me a catalogue of all the magazines dealing with photographic technique that are published throughout the world. The catalogue was kept up-to-date by a special office of the ministry.

He told me about his work, which interested him even more when I spoke to him than it had in his student years. "In the U.S.S.R. a camera is no longer just a luxury. It is, above all, a product of mass consumption by hundreds of thousands of amateur photographers," he said with visible satisfaction.

Asked whether he ever was abroad or intended to go abroad, he answered with an astonished smile, "Abroad? What for? I have everything I need here. And if I need anything else, all I have to do is report it to the ministry and soon I have it. All the foreign countries I need are right here, next to me, in these books, magazines, technical reviews. The foreign countries come to me, why should I go to them?

"Our representatives in foreign countries can get us everything needed for our work. If, for instance, an interesting article appears in the West about problems that affect us, it is entirely possible to invite the author to come to the U.S.S.R. to lecture on the subject or to study conditions in our plant and help us solve our problem. Also, we can commission some foreign engineer or production man to work out a special project for us and submit a presentation showing what is required for its implementation.

"Incidentally, we receive masses of such material, often unsolicited. Ambitious foreign engineers, technicians, or production men simply send us their projects in the hope we will use them. They are, of course, well paid for them. You see, our industry has many contacts abroad, even in the U.S.A. These contacts are mainly intellectual, through various scientific institutions. And men of technical vision are the same all over the world, my friend. Lost in thoughts of some new equipment, improvement, or invention created in their brains, they see nothing around them. Their only dream is to see their idea carried out while they are still alive, to see it put to use. They gaze at the blueprints or the description of their project before them, and with the eyes of their technical imagination they see the machine operating at full speed, the transmission belts moving smoothly, workers swarming around.

"In the capitalist conditions under which they happen to live and work, very often nobody shows any interest in their ideas. Also, very often it is difficult to receive money for an idea, the money necessary for further development and for personal satisfaction.

"As you know, in Western Europe and in the U.S.A., the precision industries are monopolies. Anything that does not fit into their scheme of planned profits is not recognized as a useful invention. After all, what use are they? To whom? In addition, inventors are afraid to apply for patents for fear they may be stolen through the introduction of some slight change in the design. So they slip the product of their imagination, of

their knowledge, often of their genius into an envelope and
address it directly to us, or sometimes to our representatives
abroad, or to a friendly scientific institution in another Eastern
European country. They paste on an airmail stamp and in ten
days the envelope and its contents are here.

"When I recently attended a congress of Soviet design
engineers and inventors I heard a lot of talk about these sub-
missions. They said great numbers of such envelopes reach
us all the time containing the most valuable material. No doubt
the senders receive high fees through the same channels."

K. paused and mused for a moment. "Besides, this has always
gone on. Western scientists have always helped the U.S.S.R.
While our own scientists and technical men are completely employed in the service of socialism and the U.S.S.R., the bourgeois
scientists experience every crisis of capitalism as a crisis of their
own. These scientists, working for capitalist concerns that are
interested in the progress of technique only so far as it increases
their profits, are embittered. Many come into conflict with their
employers, who try to direct their work into strictly defined
channels. Many come into conflict with the equally anti-scien-
tific and narrow-minded army bureaucracy. This is especially
prevalent in imperialistic countries which are becoming increasingly militaristic and where many great scientists have been
put in mothballs and have sunk into oblivion.

"And, as you know, the scientists of the West still think in
terms of a great 'republic of scholars.' It is these mothballed,
forsaken, embittered men, with little say in production aimed
exclusively at profit, who turn their interests towards us. Naturally many of them sympathize with our ideology. But probably
many do it for material profit, to satisfy their ambition, or to
gain a chance to continue their scientific work. It is from these
people that the daily mail brings precious envelopes to the
U.S.S.R."

Engineer W. toyed with a German photographic magazine.
From the cover, two pretty girls on skis smiled up at him. "So,
as you see, there's no need to go abroad. Those of our scientists who do go, atomic physicists, geophysicists, do it for the
sake of propaganda rather than science. They give lectures promoting our peaceful policy and Soviet science. They perform

useful ideological work. But men like me stay home and produce. Anyway, we have enough recreation with the movies, television, and theater. We have a river to fish in during the summer. What more does a man need to be happy?"

We walked into another room. Models of all types of cameras and lenses produced in the U.S.S.R. were displayed in wooden cabinets. Those produced by the K. factory were prominently marked.

Lovingly, W. took one of the shiny cameras in his hand. "You see, this is a camera which will go on sale in 1960. Like almost all Soviet cameras it is not an original product. At least, in its fundamental features it isn't. It's a copy of a Swedish camera.

"Don't be surprised. Let me explain. You see our Soviet technology, from the moment of its birth, has run along two tracks.

"One track follows the principle that technical progress should be pushed in those fields which are revolutionary in technique. Fields such as nuclear energy, chemistry, applied mathematics (computers and calculators) and so forth. It is on this track that we concentrate our specially trained scientific and labor cadres. These are our best, most capable, most experienced people.

"On the other track are the fields of technical progress where we apply the principle of adaptation. For example, in the production of cameras, cars, refrigerators, radio sets, television sets, fountain pens, and other such items, we *adapt* those products which have already been tested and are considered the best and most modern in Western Europe or in the U.S.A.

"You understand? The adaptation of, for example, cameras, and even then only of certain types, relieves us of creative and technical effort plus the period of experimentation. The same principle applies to radio sets, car motors, agricultural machinery, and the like. After all, it's obvious in advance that the most startling invention in the field of fountain pens or refrigerators won't lead to a technological revolution. Whereas an invention in the field of new fuels or nuclear physics could have tremendous industrial, technical, and, especially in our time, political consequences.

"It's clear, isn't it? That's why in the field of 'small tech-

nique,' the technology of consumer goods, we now march, in
general, shoulder to shoulder with Western Europe and the
U.S.A. We might even be in the lead. Just think how much
human energy is wasted in countries like the U.S.A. where
hundreds and thousands of companies, competing factories,
construction firms, inventors, and scientists work for the sole
purpose of bringing out new models of refrigerators or washing
machines. The same applies to the automotive industry and
precision industry. We let them do it for us, do you see? Out
of their furious rat race of talent and creative brainpower, every
now and then they produce the perfect refrigerator or the
ideal fountain pen. Then we step in. We take over the design
of this most excellent refrigerator and this most efficient fountain
pen and mass produce it. Quite an economy for our state,
isn't it?

"As a result, hundreds of thousands of our young, able
technicians, mechanics, engineers, mathematicians, and chem-
ists find their way into our key industries, into the revolutionary
industries and technologies which will insure our domination
of the world, on earth and in the skies. The same methods are
being followed by our number one ally, the Chinese People's
Republic.

"By the way, have you seen the new fountain pen recently
produced in the Chinese People's Republic? No? Let me show
it to you. It's terrific!" W. reached into his coat pocket and
pulled out a streamlined blue-gray fountain pen. "I got it from
a friend of mine, an engineer who works in a fountain-pen
factory near by. He just returned from China where he was sent
as an expert to help organize new production lines. He said the
pen was just an adaptation of an American brand, I believe he
said Parker. Just see how it writes, like a doll." With a determined gesture he signed his name across the cover of the
German photography magazine, cutting across the smiling faces
of the cover girls.

"Good, eh? Well, I hope you now understand the rudiments
of our production system. My job, and the job of the entire
department of design engineering, is to pick out the models
best suited to our needs from the hundreds of types of cameras
appearing in the world, to pick out the easiest and compara-

tively cheapest to manufacture and put into production here.

"Of course, we sometimes make a slight change in the model if, for instance, our production set-up requires it. We know that the foreign countries don't like this whole system. They yell that we plagiarize and violate copyrights and patents and so on. But who can deny that modern technique is the contribution of all mankind and that each nation has contributed its proper share? Technical inventions, like literary works, are the common property of all civilized nations.

"There are several other factories manufacturing cameras in the U.S.S.R., but other types. Like our products, their cameras are also adapted from cameras produced in the West—mostly German or English—or in Japan. But remember, cameras aren't the chief product of these factories. In this respect our camera industry differs from its counterpart in capitalist countries. The camera industry, as well as all the other industries employing the so-called 'small technique,' are not independent industries. They are attached to heavy basic industries as a side line. As a rule, these, let's call them light industries, are practically a by-product of heavy industry and frequently use its waste materials. For instance the iron and steel industry manufactures agricultural tools and household articles from waste materials.

"Remember that our armament industry, which now is the most highly developed of all our industry, has a tremendous potential for this type of side production. For instance the plants which produce precision instruments for military planes or complicated range finders for the army also manufacture radio sets, television receivers, and refrigerators, using largely surplus material. Our camera industry works on the same principle. But that's another story. . . . How did you like our factory? And our workers and technicians? You can consider them a fair sampling of Soviet workers. Study them to your heart's content."

And I sat at the factory gate "to study" the crowd leaving work. Was this group any different from a group of workers leaving a factory in France or Italy? Did the difference lie in the way they acted?

No, I decided. Generally speaking, Soviet workers do not seem very different from Western European workers. Naturally they are not dressed as well. Their haircuts may be different.

Undoubtedly their homes are on a much lower standard than the homes of their counterparts in Western Europe. Undoubtedly they eat worse than similar families in France.

Yet these are not the real differences between the Soviet worker and the Western European worker. These differences lie mainly in the bonds which exist between the individual and the group in which he lives at all times; in the fact that this group, for the Soviet worker, is so organized as to bring about complete control of the individual by the group and by the other individuals in it.

But do the private opinions of the average Soviet worker differ from the opinions he expresses for the benefit of the outside world? How does he regard the world and himself? What does he really think of his environment? Does he consider himself happy, and if so, why? What does he want from life? On what does he base his positive or negative attitude towards the world which surrounds him?

There are no direct answers to these questions. In the U.S.S.R., the only questions a man answers directly are those in a questionnaire or those asked by some authority or other. As a rule, people don't discuss these matters in the U.S.S.R. The relationship of a man to his environment, to the world, to other people, and even to himself, have been established once and for all. Any ideological training, wherever it is, reminds him of this fact very plainly.

That's why, when talking with a Soviet worker, one must avoid abstract ideas. There must be no questions. Abstract ideas would immediately be associated with the phraseology of ideological training, while questions would make him suspect that they were being asked to see if he would give the proper, socially approved answers.

By culling from a great number of conversations on a variety of topics I was able to some extent, to get fragmentary answers.

First, how does the Soviet citizen view the relationship of the Soviet system to the rest of the world, and what is its future?

In all cases, my informants from the working class considered the present system as final and stable, though they reasoned it out differently.

The most common argument was: "The U.S.S.R. came into

being as the result of the operation of historical law, therefore nothing can overthrow it. Marx, Lenin, and Stalin predicted a long time in advance what would happen, and this always did happen. . . ."

One man said, "They (the Communist Party of the U.S.S.R.) know how to analyze the economics and politics of capitalist countries and how to use this knowledge for their purposes. That's why the U.S.S.R. has been progressing continuously since 1917 and will continue to progress and expand."

Another argument: "If at the very beginning (in 1917) the capitalist forces could not succeed in overthrowing us, how can they possibly succeed now?" Another point: "The U.S.S.R. is a unified force, while the capitalistic countries are divided by perpetual quarrels. Because of the very nature of capitalism they cannot agree."

Another worker: "The organization of the U.S.S.R. is superior to that of the capitalistic countries. There, every one works for himself. Not only every country, but even every industrialist. That's why they can't create scientific inventions as fast as we do here, almost as if on order, where all our scientists can concentrate on one single problem."

The acceptance of the system of society as an objective necessity was always accompanied by either a full or partial acceptance of the social arrangements.

It was expressed in various ways, "If there were no Party, no labor unions, and no rules, there would have to be something else to take their place. Such things have to exist in every society . . . only they don't take the same forms everywhere. . . ."

Or, "There has always been and always will be authority. A man must always have some authority over him, next to him. As a matter of fact, if one man does not have authority over another, he would like to have it. This is a law of nature."

". . . if there were no people, there wouldn't be any Party or organization. But people themselves create such organizations."

". . . there never has been a society in the world where justice is the same for everybody. It's easier to make injustice equal for all, but even this is difficult. . . ."

". . . You can still find among us those who never had any hope and those who eternally lose it. . . ."

". . . If you have a good memory, it is easier for you to forget many things."

". . . The sooner the government commits a crime, the sooner it becomes obsolete. . . ."

". . . In the perspective of Soviet history, even the most tragic actions of our Party look rather small. . . ."

". . . In the U.S.S.R. crime does not pay taxes. . . ."

A man's relationship to other people and to himself was also expressed in several different ways. Here are the opinions of several workers:

". . . with people it's like this. They always fall all over each other either to hug and kiss or to kick and fight. The best thing to do is to keep away. . . ."

"As long as a man sticks with the crowd nothing will happen to him. As soon as he tries something on his own he's bound to lose."

"A man must follow the majority. He can't go against it. But if, while going along with the majority, he manages to get a little ahead of it, he'll come out on top."

A worker about sixty years old said, "Sometimes, when I watch these young fellows at a meeting I get scared. They sit there just looking around to see whom they can use as a rung on the ladder of success. A man can take almost anything, but sometimes it's better not to live to see it. What kind of an existence is this? You always owe everything to others. About the only thing you can do by yourself is confess your crimes in front of a meeting. . . ."

". . . Why this silly talk? 'The Party appointed him, the Party expelled him!' What is the Party? It's people . . . people do it, not the Party."

"Here, a man can reach the highest positions in society if he is always positive. And he can easily be positive by active work in social and political organizations. . . ."

"A friend is a dangerous thing. He knows everything about you. A friend is a luxury that I, personally, can't afford. I'd rather buy a radio."

"If you know he is your enemy, the best course is to make

friends with him. The only trouble is that by the time you find out he is your enemy, it's too late. He has already done the damage."

"I'm a decent man. I always do what my superiors ask."

"Why should I plan? Smarter people are planning for me. The best course is to sit still and not be conspicuous. Those who climb too high always end up by falling into a quagmire so deep they can hardly be seen."

In evaluating life and happiness, Soviet workers have few standards of comparison. Again, to quote several opinions:

"It could always be worse . . . and it was. I don't complain."

". . . a man doesn't have time to think about these things. Work, meetings, classes, radio and television in the intervals . . . that's life."

". . . At first he wanted to be group secretary. O.K., he got it. Then he wanted to join the Party. So, he was admitted. Then he started to dream about being a director. A few years later he made it as a vice-director. He kept on being promoted. He got into the Ministry . . . and now he's in prison. So what good did it all do him?"

"What does a plain man want from life? To have enough to eat, drink, a bed to sleep in, to marry, have healthy good-looking children, a peaceful old age . . . and an easy death."

"If it weren't for imperialism, we wouldn't have to arm, and life would undoubtedly be better for people. But even as it is, it's better now than it was a few years ago. We can buy more things in the stores. In a few more years, I'm sure we'll be able to buy still more, and more cheaply. Anyway, it's always like this. A man is happiest in the future."

"Those who are now in their early twenties will live to see wonderful times. You can't tell where they'll live and work. The whole world will be one great U.S.S.R."

"When I stop to think how many people I know that were sent somewhere beyond the Lena River to Bulun or Zhigansk, I remember how well off I am. Of course I can never tell when, maybe even tomorrow, I'll be delegated to an important post in . . . Khabarovsk. But then as long as I don't know, I'm happy."

"You can never really tell when you're happy in this life.

Sometimes you may think you're unhappy. The best thing to do is to drink some vodka and go to sleep."

"It all depends on how you look at it. You may look and see faces, smiles. You think you see people. You look again, and all you see are hands raised in a vote."

". . . a man is happy when he feels secure, he and his family, when he knows that he's doing the best he can, that he lives decently and has all he needs when compared with his surroundings. I am . . . [a moment of indecision] almost happy. I'm healthy. My family is all right. We have a good radio and TV set. Next month we are planning to buy a refrigerator. The children have a record-player to play when they come home from kindergarten. In summer we'll have a vacation, sit on the sand in the sun and swim. In a few years we may even buy a car, when they become cheaper. If only they don't transfer me in the meantime. . . ."

The worker's relationship to his factory is also interesting. According to the conversations I had, and the notes I collected, it appears that the relationship of a man to his work really depends on his relationship to the social environment in which he works.

This was clearly expressed by a worker who, explaining the kind of work he did, concluded, "What you do isn't important. The important thing is your place among the workers, whether you are in the Party or whether you are an active member of the labor union. This is about all that counts."

And another one said, "No matter how well you work, it's of no value if you don't look well Partywise or unionwise. On the other hand, if they're satisfied with you from these angles, they close their eyes when they look at your work."

Given this attitude towards work, it was hard for me to understand the "shock workers," the Stakhanovites who are supposed to achieve high production norms and high efficiency. Though propaganda is usually exaggerated, the number of Stakhanovites and the size of their norms is a fact that you can establish in almost every Soviet factory. There are always a number of workers whose performance exceeds the norms and who periodically pledge themselves to an extremely high production

pared with the conditions under which he has been living and working till now.

"Thus you are facing the end of the world. Or at least the end of the world in which you have been living up to now with your wife and children, where you went to the movies and theater, watched television, in which you led the life of a human being. So what can you do to avoid this calamity? It's simple. You just say to yourself, 'Well, it's too bad, but I'm afraid I'll have to work like a dog for two or three months.'

"So you take a 'production pledge.' Let's say on the Anniversary of the Soviet Constitution you pledge to exceed your production norm by 40 per cent and you call on the other workers to compete with you. Suddenly you're a personality. Your name appears on a special bulletin board. You get a whole section of the board to yourself and to all the others who accepted your challenge and entered their names into the competition.

"Now you go through hell. You work like a dog and you succeed in delivering the 40 per cent over your norm. Deep inside you don't give a darn about production. What you do care about is the fact that your name has moved up in the scale of workers and in the union. And into your personal file goes the note 'shock worker in socialist work.'

"You can see that, can't you? When the Anniversary finally comes you are mentioned at the celebration, perhaps even decorated. And that's the end of it. After all, a man is only human. He can't work like that all the time. You are permitted to become an ordinary worker once more.

"However, your social standing is much higher than it used to be, though your health may be worse. Stakhanov wasn't the only one to pay with his lungs for work beyond his strength. All his imitators, the Soviet Stakhanovites, the heroes of socialist work, pay a price too. But after all, you don't risk so much when you take on this competition. Actually, even if you didn't exceed your norm by the promised 40 per cent it would have been all right. You would have become a shock worker just the same. It's clear, isn't it?"

My informant was seventy years old. He had keen insight. As an expert in his field, he had worked in the K. factory for thirty-five years, with a gap of a few years in the middle. He had never tried to join the Party. Nor did he ever run for any office in the socio-labor organizations, though he was nominated a few times. He seemed to me to be a straightforward man, kind but adamant, who would not accept compromises at any price if they conflicted with his standards of honesty. Many a time he suffered for this trait. Pressure was used to make this old worker and Revolutionary fighter join the Party. When he didn't give in, he was sent, for a few years, to a factory somewhere in the north, near Verkhoyansk.

"What could I do? I went." Ivan Vasilievitch smiled as his memory wandered backwards. "Thank God, I never was sick. But I came pretty close. The worst thing was that horrible cold! You couldn't even spit in anger, because your spit would freeze in mid-air. But a man can get used to everything. I worked hard, and after a few years was allowed to return here, to K., as a 'reward' for my work. Undoubtedly my job in the north was taken by somebody else.

"So I was working here again. I never did expect much from life. I was never afraid of work and I was never afraid to look human meanness straight in the eyes. But I never pushed for a better job or stepped on others.

"My father, though an ignorant peasant in the times of serfdom, used to say to me when he was alive, 'Don't pay any attention to others. You have a straight, paved road before you. Walk your way and make sure that you don't hurt anyone along the road.' And so that's what I do," the old man smiled. "The most difficult part is already behind me, and it isn't far to the end of the road. What a man learns in life is his, and what others teach him is his too. Only I have no one to leave it to. My wife died ten years ago. My son was killed in the war. And so a man waits alone for the end."

I tried to lead the talk back to problems that interested me. Ivan Vasilievitch had drawn his observations straight from the world that surrounded him. As a self-taught man, he had gathered an ample stock of information about various fields. That's why I believe his opinions are worthy of repeating as faithfully as possible.

He returned to his previous theme. "So that's how it is with our Stakhanovites. There also are other kinds of heroes of

socialist work. There are men among the workers who are willing
to get ahead at any price. They want to rise above manual work,
but their qualifications, or rather lack of them, stand in their
way. They aren't suited for political work because of lack of
education or ability. So they take another road towards pro-
motion, work competition. They make fantastically high pledges.
They form shock-workers' brigades. They make a physical effort
far beyond their strength. Accompanied, of course, by a lot of
noise and publicity. They are interviewed by the press and radio.
They receive valuable gifts from the factory management, the
Ministry, the Party, the unions, consisting of cash bonuses and
vacations in the Caucasus.

"You can watch them on television as, with broad grins, they
wipe the perspiration off their foreheads. Their example becomes infectious. Other new, strong, foolish workers, even
technicians and engineers, join the ranks of the competitors.

"This is very important, and not only because it increases
productivity. Basically, it is important from a propaganda and
morale viewpoint. It illustrates the model new citizen, who, in
addition to being completely positive, must also exhaust himself
working like a dog. It's an infallible treatment for the thousands
and hundreds of thousands of indifferent and discouraged workers who have already found out that great discoveries are not
in their line, who realize that they won't live to see the socialist
miracle and resurrection. These are the men to whom a poster
with the grinning face of a Stakhanovite is meant to appeal.
It says to them, 'If he *can* do it, you *must* do it too!' At the
same time, supported by the results of the 'mass movement of
competition,' as it is called, the Party raises production norms
to increase productivity.

"Of course it's another story entirely when, after a superhu-
man effort, the Stakhanovite goes to a sanitarium for a 'rest.'
The competition has left a rag of a man, incapable of any
physical labor in the future. Nevertheless, he is promoted. And
he is no longer 'threatened' with any physical work. As a favor
of the management, Party, or union, he is given some easy job
in an office or some light 'mental' work. However we mustn't
forget that our work hero is a nitwit who doesn't know much.
So the job must be fitted to his mental capacity. He fills out

passes at the gate, or adds short columns of figures in some office.

"Exceptionally strong men, perfect specimens, have been known to lose their health completely in this Stakhanovite race, as was the case with Stakhanov himself. However, work competition usually ruins those who are not really adapted for excessive physical effort, who were pushed into it by the desire to better their place in society or to upgrade their personal file, which in the last analysis means the same thing. They decided to become work heroes out of sheer panic, from fear of a transfer like the one I once had. So they undertake an effort too big for their strength in the hope that this will permit them to get rid of the sense of guilt and sin which is always and everywhere with them. Even the medieval Orthodox Church didn't go so far in creating this guilt complex in the faithful.

"Sometimes, something else happens that reminds you of the theater. When you watch an actor playing a role, you never really know how much of his performance is attributable to the director who dictated a specific interpretation to him. The case of our heroes is similar. Very often they are the victims of a stage director.

"Let's assume the following situation:

"An anniversary or celebration is approaching. But no challenges for a competition have been made in the factory. No one has spontaneously pledged to perform some heroic production feat in honor of the coming anniversary. The authorities, management as well as politico-labor organizations, are thoroughly frightened. They face the accusation that there is something wrong with the political-education work in the factory since no candidates for competition have appeared. These organizations may be suspected of having isolated themselves from the masses, or having lost contact with the masses, of having degenerated. These are extremely serious charges. If the superior Party or union authorities make them against the officers of the factory Party or union organizations, the latter face the consequences usual in such cases . . . transfer to some other post somewhere 'dalyeko, dalyeko, hdye kaczyut tumany' (far away, far away, where only clouds are roaming). Or possibly other Party punishment, such as discharge or reprimand.

"Well, our authorities find themselves in a real jam. But they've had experience with trouble and know what to do to avoid tragedy."

I saw that Ivan Vasilievitch, despite the confidence he had in me, was afraid to continue. Once more I proved that I had no interest in repeating to others whatever he told me, and that I would keep everything to myself, for my own understanding and knowledge, without exposing him to trouble.

After a moment of hesitation, he continued. "They start to work, but fast. The secretary of the Party organization, the secretary of the union organization, and the members of the factory council begin to interview various workers individually. They choose, of course, the workers who are easiest to convince. They may be men whose personal files are not of the best, or men who have some recent misdeeds on their conscience. In a man-to-man talk, the Party or union delegate tries to induce the victim to volunteer for competition or to pledge to perform an individual production feat. In exchange, he promises, in the name of the Party or the union or the management, either forgiveness for the misdeed or belittling of it, or simply a withdrawal of the damaging record from his personal file. Thus the worker is cornered. Soon a large bulletin board appears on the wall bearing the announcement of a work competition and his name is in first place!

"An active Party member, candidate, or union activist, may also be 'nominated' as a shock worker and hero of socialist work. In these cases, other arguments are used. He is told that the Party looks to him, as an activist, in the belief that he is the right person to issue a challenge for work competition. Unless he agrees, it would be embarrassing to let him continue as an activist.

"The victim realizes that the career he has been building so carefully may suddenly collapse. All the efforts he has made up to date to please the authorities may backfire. He sees no other solution but to volunteer.

"Now it may happen, and does quite often, that the initiator of the competition simply is not equal to the work he pledged to perform. Then the management or the Party run to his rescue. Sometimes, for the good of the cause, the weakling is helped by a decrease in his regular norm which makes it easier for him to exceed it. Sometimes his protectors in the Party, management, or union will tamper with the figures and skillfully increase the results reflecting his productivity.

"It isn't done to shield him, but to bolster the prestige of the factory and the success of the competition. Other competitors must really believe that the norm was exceeded by the weakling, say by 40 per cent. Sometimes, when a competition faces a complete fiasco, the challenger is removed from the stage at the critical moment and sent for a vacation or delegated to take some ideological or vocational course, thus saving the honor of the competition.

"When a large number of workers joins a competition, the affair proceeds more smoothly. New applications come in in a landslide. The remaining workers can't afford to remain passive while their colleagues are in the competition. They must join too. Nobody wants to be accused of boycotting a socialist competition, 'the noblest form of the struggle of man with nature.'

"The next stage is competition between two or more departments in the same factory. Here the stage setting includes groups of workers who are persuaded by various means to sign their names to the list for collective competition, independent of any individual competition in which they may already take part.

"The last stage is interfactory competition, organized under the auspices of the Ministry with the assistance of the Party and the unions. All this is accompanied by intensive propaganda and veritable American publicity. Boards, flags, banners attached to machines, celebrations, speeches, photographs, slogans, decorations, and medals. The winning shock workers receive prizes: cash bonuses or gifts, sometimes even a car or a motorcycle. The winning staff receives a cash prize to divide among themselves or excursions are organized for them or they get permission to spend their vacations in one of the best resort hotels in a spot like the Crimea.

"The winning factory usually receives funds for new equipment, for enlarging the library, for building a nursery for the children, for remodeling the factory cafeteria.

"Of course the work methods of the victorious shock workers, their staff and factory, are widely publicized. Propaganda pamphlets and articles are published about them. Educational films are made.

"This is one side of the coin. But there is another side. We mustn't forget that victory by one factory in the competition necessarily means a defeat for another. The losing factories become the target for searching analyses. Why did they lose? They are visited by all kinds of ministerial and Party-union commissions. They are subjected to various checks and investigations. Working councils, calls for self-criticism, and just plain criticism fall on them like rain. All this is followed by a grand reshuffling of personnel. New directors are appointed. Party and union organizations elect new secretaries. New people take over the posts in the factory councils.

"Frequently, some real or fictitious abuses are discovered to help unmask the guilty and justify all this fuss in the socialist cause. All this takes place, naturally, accompanied by loud publicity replete with shibboleths. Indictments often follow, when those guilty are found out at last and brought to court charged with exceeding their authority, conscious or unconscious sabotage, or any of a thousand other things like bribery, negligence, or desertion of the socialist front of labor.

"After a while everything quiets down again. New competitive slogans appear, 'My work is my witness,' 'Let's hit the face of imperialism with the fist of work.' The rotating stage of work competition is entered by new shock workers, the real prima donnas of socialism. And new directors take over. The scenery is changed according to the new situation at home and abroad. In our socialist puppet theater the audience changes too.

"The first rows are occupied by the last group of shock workers, while the new ones enter the stage. In the middle rows, the mass of future heroes of socialist work wait meekly for the signal, glancing at all sides to be sure that the signal hasn't been given yet. In the last rows and in the balcony squat the scared victims of defeat waiting for a new, more favorable moment. The performance goes on. The trained heroes leap, shout, swing their pickaxes, pose proudly on cardboard tractors. The performance goes on, except nobody is having a good time because the play is old and it's been ten years since its first performance."

Our talk ended. We were approaching the walls of the factory, visible behind the trees. Ivan Vasilievitch said good-by, and, as if afraid he would be seen with me by someone from the factory, left quickly. His bent figure receded slowly as he plodded in the direction of the workers' housing project, large blocks with flat roofs covered with television antennas.

I continued towards the factory. The colored bulletin boards devoted to work competition were densely covered by names with the percentages of norms performed. They made a pleasant contrast to the gray background of factory walls. I went closer and studied the faces of shock workers looking at me from large photographs. They were the normal faces of normal people. They stood very stiff in carefully pressed suits. Obviously, most of them tried to assume earnest and martial expressions for the camera. They looked somewhat ludicrous, but the high figures representing the percentage of norms performed that were printed under the photographs filled me with respect: 175 per cent, 160 per cent, 202 per cent, 138 per cent. . . . A few workers stopped and read the figures with great attention. They seemed to be deep in thought.

It started to rain. The rain quickly changed into a downpour. Sheltered under the bulletin board I watched the traffic in the courtyard. The drenched workers didn't interrupt their work. The loading of cases from platforms in the middle of the court-yard proceeded. Other workers came out of the factory halls. They came and went, stumbled into each other at the doorway. They gesticulated, shouted, and laughed. A secretary, hugging a batch of paper with one hand, and holding up her skirts with the other, jumped over the rapidly forming puddles.

The rain did not stop. Thick drops splattered the bulletin board with the competition lists. The water found its way under the glass pane protecting the photographs of the shock workers. A stream of purple ink ran down from the caption, "Through Socialist competition, on to victory at the front of socialist work, on to socialism." It ran down the inside of the glass distorting the faces of the shock workers and washing away the big-bellied figures representing norms exceeded.

I, too, performed a heroic deed. As fast as I could, I ran through the courtyard and burst like a bomb into the gate-keeper's office.

The gatekeeper turned to look at me and asked half seriously, half jokingly, "And what are you running away from, comrade? What from?"

5

THE SOVIET
SOCIALIST ARMY—
SCHOOL OF HEROISM
AND PATRIOTISM

SOVIET SOLDIERS, WHEN MET SOCIALLY, SEEM TO BE THE MOST cautious and suspicious people in the world. I remember an incident which is very much to the point. One day, at the house of a mutual acquaintance, I met a non-commissioned officer on furlough.

We talked about everything and nothing. Finally, my acquaintance got around to asking the soldier how much longer his furlough would last. The non-com became very stiff and answered earnestly, "I'm sorry, Grisha, but I can't tell you. It's a military secret."

This mania for military secrecy assumes fantastic proportions. It includes almost everything, including such "key" matters as what the soldiers eat or how often they change their underwear. The soldiers are terrified at the thought of answering the simplest questions because behind each question they smell a dangerous spy who is just waiting to draw a state secret from a softhearted Soviet soldier.

Civilians are very tolerant and understanding about the taciturnity of the defenders of their country. In general, the Army is the favorite organization of every citizen. Soviet people, regardless of their social level, are ready to expatiate at length and at any time on its power and technical equipment. These conversations, of course, bear only slight resemblance to facts. The citizens assume the facts, basing their views on press reports and general articles printed in military periodicals, which are full of the most glowing adjectives, plus occasional motion pictures on military subjects. The only concrete things the people have to go by in these discussions are the tanks, cannons, and arms which they actually see in military parades.

However, the suspicions of Soviet soldiers are limited to purely military matters, such as armaments, deployment of units, or information connected with military institutions. If you can steer the conversation to the operation of identical institutions which form a part of civilian life, such as youth or Party organizations, or if you talk about everyday "human" matters, you may occasionally glimpse a bit of the truth about the military.

During his Army service a soldier is given thorough ideological and political training under the supervision of Komsomol and the Party organization of his regiment. This training is set within the framework of military service and is one of its most important parts. It consists of classes and practical testing to determine whether the soldier has an understanding of what he has learned. Evidence of this is found in proper performance of military duties and blind obedience to disciplinary regulations. Under these circumstances, any violations of these regulations, any slackness in military efficiency, count not only as political and ideological deficiencies, but also as military ineptitude. Thus, Army service may seriously affect the citizen's future life.

Scrupulous reports issued by political organizations (Komsomol and the Party) on the soldier's performance in the Army will constitute later, in his civilian life, a guide to employment, type of work, wages, and so on.

Soviet Army discipline, therefore, has a difficult and complicated task. Fundamentally it operates in a vicious circle. It must maintain a strict separation between a soldier's political and military activity. It must accurately establish where the sphere of absolute obedience to officers begins, regardless of their political standing. The criteria here must be military rather than political. On the other hand, political training reminds the soldiers and the officers on every occasion that their military performance is also appraised from the political point of view.

Since 1957 it has been emphasized that the decisive factor in a unit is the commander who guides both military and political training of personnel. Practice, however, does not live up to this principle. In reality political and military authority parallel and sometimes complement each other.

It frequently happens that Party officers, though inferior in rank, function, and military experience, have a much more important voice in regimental affairs than their superiors, who are Partyless. And it is not uncommon that Party privates are often treated with more leniency by their superiors than the soldiers who do not belong to the Party. This is readily understood when we consider the political importance of the Party and of the Komsomol in the unit, for it is they who decide what will go into the records which follow the soldiers into civilian life.

This division between the political on the one hand and the military on the other can lead to what U.S.S.R. Army authorities call "the ossification of military units." This happens when the military and political organizations of the regiment cease to exert control over each other and both become equally interested in maintaining the status quo. All their efforts are now directed towards representing as perfect, to their superiors, the situation in the regiment, even if it isn't true. They submit false reports on the results of training, on the economic use of material, degree of deterioration of equipment and uniforms, and so on.

To fight this ossification there is a special counterintelligence section in the U.S.S.R. Army whose principle task is to check up constantly and discover the real state of affairs. They must break up and destroy the ossification of units by unearthing evidence which enables superior military authorities to make radical shifts in personnel on a large scale and fill most of the posts with new men.

Military service, being obligatory in the U.S.S.R., gives millions of young men a concentrated dose of moral and political training, and a schooling in life. Although this school is not listed in literature on Soviet education, we may accept it as one of the most effective and successful schools.

The lessons learned by a Soviet soldier may perhaps best be illustrated by a rather long story told to me by a friend named Aliosha about his days in service.

Aliosha's regiment was on its summer maneuvers. It was a

typical summer evening. Right after the evening company roll
call, it was discovered that a man was missing from Aliosha's
platoon. "It was reported to me," said Aliosha, "by my platoon
assistant, Private First Class Anton. It came out that the soldier,
by the name of Usbakhov, had been missing since recess in
drills. He had missed his dinner. Anton thought Usbakhov, who
was his friend, would show up any minute and therefore did
not report his absence to me until after the roll call. During
maneuvers Usbakhov was his usual cheerful self, making the
whole platoon laugh with his jokes. He was a nice boy and far
from stupid. He was a member-candidate of the Party and talked
to the point whenever he took part in any discussions. Anton,
of course, was certain that I'd punish him severely, perhaps even
arrest him. However, I didn't intend to do this at the time. I
asked him not to tell anyone and to send Usbakhov to me as
soon as he came back. Personally, I was certain that nothing
serious had happened to him and that he would soon reappear
inventing some alibi or other to explain his absence. Usbakhov
was an excellent soldier, one of the best snipers in the regiment.
He knew his regulations.

"I knew, of course, that I was violating the regulations by
not reporting his absence. The rule is to report any A.W.O.L.
cases at once to your superior officer. We were taught that the
division commander should know about the disappearance of
a soldier within one hour after it happened. We were also taught
that in times of war neglect to report such a disappearance
could cause immense losses to the Army.

"But at the moment, I didn't take it too seriously. After all,
we weren't at war. The regiment was on normal maneuvers.
It was summer, and the soldiers were young boys in their first
year of service.

"At the same time I was aware of what might happen to
Usbakhov if I reported him. The record which would later
follow him through his civilian life in factory or office would
always have an unfavorable mark on it. Besides that, Usbakhov
would be punished for leaving his unit without permission. He
could be expelled from the Party.

"But then I realized the consequences that could result for me
from my failure to report the disappearance of a soldier. These

were even more serious than the penalties facing Usbakhov. As a platoon leader, I was responsible for my platoon and for every individual soldier in it. That was the dilemma I faced. Should I wait for Usbakhov to return, and in a way save his future, or should I hand in a report of his disappearance at once and protect myself?

"I remember I worried about it for a long time. No solution satisfied me, but I had to do something. Especially since there was no trace of Usbakhov. The night passed. There was another roll call in the morning, and Usbakhov was still missing.

"I decided to draft a report in order to be ready for any emergency and to put yesterday's date on it. I resolved to turn it in after our return from drill. I don't know why, but I had the feeling that Usbakhov would be afraid to return through the main gate, walking by the sentries, but would try to slip back into the ranks during drill.

"I thought it quite probable that Usbakhov had lost himself in the one of the nearby *kolhozes* (collective farms). Perhaps he had a girl, or perhaps he simply took advantage of their hospitality and drank too much vodka, which was very potent in this area. For all I knew, he may have been lying in a ditch by the road dead drunk.

"During the drill I kept a sharp lookout, and so did Anton. But no sight of Usbakhov. I slowly realized that it was too late for me to hand in a report. The investigation would show that Usbakhov had been missing for over twelve hours and that I knew about it from the beginning. Or that I should have known about it, as platoon leader.

"In any case, Anton would be sure to confess under questioning that I knew about the disappearance and had procrastinated. I couldn't be sure that the rest of the platoon hadn't noticed Usbakhov's absence, though at my request Anton was supposed to have mentioned casually to the other boys that Usbakhov was on the sick list. However I didn't know whether he had or not, and I didn't want to ask.

"I was terribly nervous. The hours passed slowly, and still I didn't know what to do. Before the evening roll call, I visited the regimental doctor, whom I knew personally, and asked him to put Usbakhov on the sick list. Of course I did not tell him that Usbakhov had disappeared. I just explained that while he was not sick enough to go into the field hospital, my man was not up to par and should be put on the list just in case. I promised to send the official report in later.

"So, at the evening roll call Usbakhov was reported as being sick in the hospital. I saw disapproval written plainly in Anton's eyes, but he knew as well as I that I was helpless. It was too late. I had to try to muddle through.

"On the third day of Usbakhov's absence I was desperate. I made up my mind to go to the company leader whom, incidentally, I thoroughly despised, and tell him the whole truth. But the awareness that I might needlessly expose myself to all sorts of trouble when Usbakhov could reappear at any moment kept me from it. I reasoned the way any other person in a similar situation would have. If something had happened to Usbakhov, if he had had an accident, if a car or tank had hit him during maneuvers, someone would have notified me at once.

"After dinner the doctor came up to me and declared that he was taking Usbakhov's name off the sick list since he had not received an official report. He said, however, that our friendship prevented him from reporting this 'shady' affair to his superior in the hospital.

"The ground began to burn under my feet. In a moment of downright panic I began to draft a report, 'The Disappearance of Private Usbakhov,' trying hard to invent some arguments in my defense. My writing was interrupted by the ring of the telephone. It was the battalion headquarters calling to say that a control commission had just arrived from the division command. They were going to inspect a few selected units, of which my platoon was one. The platoon was to appear fully equipped in the square in front of regimental headquarters in an hour. I was to bring along all reports about the exercises my platoon had gone through, their state of preparedness, marksmanship rating, and the like.

"My legs buckled under me. I had never thought that fate, or chance, or so-called objective reality could be so cruel, so unbelievably malicious. Of all the platoons, it had to be mine selected for inspection. I decided to try to get out of it. I called up the battalion commander, thus violating the compulsory 'channels of command' by by-passing the company commander. However, the aide to the battalion commander informed me that the commander had left the office for the day and that my platoon had been selected by the control commission itself from a list submitted by the regimental headquarters.

"So there was nothing I could do in this channel. I began to rack my brain trying to invent something in forty-five minutes. Suddenly I hit upon a solution: find someone to replace Usbakhov! I clung to the idea, and thought that I might be able to see it through. My reasoning was that if I turned up for inspection with an incomplete platoon, the commission would undoubtedly want to know what happened to the missing man. It would come out that he wasn't away on either furlough or duty, and that he wasn't on the sick list. So where was this soldier of the Union of Soviet Socialist Republics? Where did he disappear, this defender of peace, citizen of the first socialist country of the world, while performing honorable military service?

"I couldn't possibly," Aliosha continued, "let the truth come out during the inspection. It would have been a disgrace, not only for me and my immediate superiors, but for the entire regiment. I also realized that if the truth came out during the inspection, my punishment would be much more severe. You must remember that just as I was responsible for my soldiers, all my superiors, up to and including the regimental commander, were responsible for the leaders of the units subordinate to them and for regimental discipline.

"Usbakhov's absence could become the affair of the entire regiment. And it all would be my fault! I moved very quickly now. Without telling the members of my platoon anything about it, and knowing that they wouldn't have time for questions, I rushed to a friend of mine, who was leader of another platoon which was not scheduled for inspection.

"I briefly told him the whole story and asked him to lend me a soldier for the inspection. I explained how I had to have a full platoon so that no one would notice Usbakhov's absence. My friend agreed. I'm not sure he quite knew what it was all about, but he assigned one of his soldiers to me. The boy was smart and understood the situation very quickly. I told him that if the commission should call on Usbakhov to answer some questions, he should reply for Usbakhov. I certainly did not expect that fate would be cruel enough to make the commission single out Usbakhov of all the soldiers, but I preferred to make sure.

"So, half an hour later I brought up my platoon, resplendent in carefully pressed uniforms, for inspection. The boys were not quite clear about why a new soldier had replaced Usbakhov, but they probably thought he was still ill.

"You can imagine how tense I was when I presented my platoon to the officer who was inspecting it on behalf of the commission. He was an elderly colonel, who seemed to me to be a veteran with many years' experience. The other members of the commission, two or three captains, two lieutenants, and a sergeant sat at a long table together with several senior officers from our regiment. The commander of our regiment stood near by, anxiously watching my boys who stood at attention in a single line.

"The inspection began. The commission examined the condition of the uniforms, called on three soldiers to show their weapons. Two other boys very efficiently took apart, then reassembled, their carbines. Another soldier demonstrated the ready position for attack. Still another dug a square foxhole, quickly and with great precision, on a given spot in accord with the dimensions specified in the regulations.

"After this, the commission questioned the soldiers at random about regulations and political training. As a rule the answers were satisfactory. I stood on trembling legs and kept counting the minutes until it would be over. My borrowed Usbakhov also answered some questions. However, he had not been called by name. Just when it looked as though my platoon was through with the inspection, and the other platoons were already waiting on the edge of the square to begin their inspection, the worst happened . . .

"A book containing the personal data of the platoon was lying on the table. It contained entries about the character of each soldier, and condition of their health, their education in civilian life and in the army, grades on tests they had taken, and so on. Now, one of the members of the commission opened it casually, glanced indifferently at one or two pages and then, just when it looked as if he were going to put it down, decided to call out a name. Usbakhov. I became numb; the blood seemed to drain from me. My heart was beating wildly. At that moment everything depended on how my borrowed "Usbakhov" would act. He looked at me imploringly, then after only a moment's hesitation, he stepped out erectly from the ranks.

"The remaining soldiers of my platoon looked at each other, then, without changing their at-attention position, turned their eyes to me questioningly. They were at a loss about what was going on. Some, I'm sure, suspected some hoax in connection with this new, mysterious Usbakhov. However, there was no time to think.

"'Usbakhov' stood at attention and waited for the next question. It was long in coming. The captain stared at him for a while, and then asked in a quiet, and almost fatherly tone, 'Well, Usbakhov, how does it go in the Army?' The erect Usbakhov became a little more erect, as is the custom in such cases, took a deep breath and uttered the accepted formula: 'I serve the Soviet Union, Comrade Captain.' The captain smiled discreetly, looked searchingly at the taut Usbakhov, looked at the book in his hands and with his eyes fixed on its pages asked: 'Yes, yes . . . very well. . . . And now, tell me, Usbakhov, where were you born?'

"Both 'Usbakhov' and I froze. In my wildest dreams I couldn't have foreseen such a situation. I had not, of course, drilled this man on the personal data of the real Usbakhov. The situation was becoming ludicrous in its tragedy. 'Usbakhov' remained silent for a minute. This silence attracted the attention of the entire commission. Then 'Usbakhov' whispered, 'I don't know, Comrade Captain . . . I . . . forgot!'

"Everyone present was stunned. Imagine, a Soviet soldier, after almost a year of training and ideological classes forgetting where he was born!

"In the meantime, the captain continued.

"'What do you mean, you don't remember where you were born? Hm . . . it's strange. Well, would you remember the name of your father perhaps?'

"The hapless soldier stood under the pillory of searching

glances which almost clung physically to his perspiring, livid face. And I? I just didn't care any more. I wished I could sit down and shoot myself.

"Another long silence followed, ending in a still weaker whisper, 'No, I cannot remember that either, Comrade Captain . . .'

"The officers roared with laughter and for a moment the tension was eased. But, after a while the deputy commander of the regiment for political affairs, stood up behind the table. He was a big fellow with a broad red face. Trying to conceal his rage, he asked:

" 'You . . . Usbakhov, do you want to make a fool of yourself —or what? Now tell us where your parents are living. How do you address the letters you write them? Eh?'

"Again a dead, crushing silence. I knew everything was finished. I looked at the swaying tree tops and at the birds flying among them. Finally I heard 'Usbakhov's' voice filled with despair.

" 'I beg your pardon, Comrade Commander . . . my name is not Usbakhov. My name is Bolyakchovskij. I am from the Second Platoon, Company Four. I am here on the order of the comrade leader of this platoon, to replace Usbakhov, who is not here. Please forgive me, I beg of you. It isn't my fault. I was ordered here.'

"All was quiet for a moment and then pandemonium broke out. In a sonorous voice the regiment commander ordered the poor soldier to be put under arrest. I was ordered to my quarters to await further orders. The commission made a report on the incident. The inspection went on, but even more minutely and severely, and it revealed—guess what—four or five similar cases! Four or five more platoon soldiers were missing and like me, the other platoon leaders were loath to ruin the future of the missing boys and procrastinated about filling their reports. Only one did. People are not machines yet!

"On the evening of the inspection Usbakhov returned. He was hale and hearty. The other missing men also returned with him. And where do you suppose they had been? What had they been doing? At first they wouldn't tell us but later they told their story. This is what Usbakhov told me.

"During recess in maneuvers he went for a walk along the road at the edge of the forest. He wanted to pick wild strawberries which grew there abundantly. A panel truck came up to him and stopped. A colonel got out from the front seat and asked him how to get to the division command. Usbakhov saluted, then pointed out the direction. The colonel, however, said he was in a hurry and couldn't wander around all day. He ordered Usbakhov to get into the truck and show him the way. He promised that the truck would bring him back to his regiment on its way back from the regimental command. Usbakhov got in and even surrendered his rifle to be put in the back of the truck so that it wouldn't be in the way. When the truck reached its destination, he was ordered to get out along with several other soldiers of our regiment who had been hidden in the back of the truck.

"They were all taken to a room where they were severely reprimanded for their mistakes. A soldier is not supposed to obey the orders of unknown officers who could easily be disguised American spies interested in finding out details about their regiment. Furthermore, a soldier is not supposed to surrender his rifle, nor is he supposed to walk away from his regiment.

"As punishment they were assigned to K.P. and had to clean the latrines for the few days they were there. In the meantime the officers of the counterintelligence (for that is who they were) probably drafted a report on the incident. I was told later that they had played similar tricks on other regiments too. In one case they inspected the whole regiment and nobody thought of asking them for their identification papers or orders. The conclusion they reached was that the regiment's training was faulty and that they were not alert enough. In another regiment their tests were even more amusing. They told the soldiers to disperse, then, taking advantage of not being watched, they took one rifle lock from each of several platoons. In another case no one stopped them from stealing a set of regulations marked 'for internal use only.' They also helped themselves to secret instructions from higher Army authorities. In still another case, during inspection, they spilled a chemical into the food kettles on the stove, making the food absolutely inedible. In all these instances the idea was to test the alertness of Army authorities, to see if regulations were being followed, and whether they kept proper records of every incident which took place in the regiment. They also wanted to see if the regiment command would investigate the matter of the missing locks and instructions, and of the contaminated food, and whether pertinent reports would be sent to the division command. But, it's easy to guess, nothing was done about these things in the regiments. No reports were sent in, and the soldiers whose locks were stolen promptly turned around and stole locks from other soldiers. Even the command hushed up the affair of the missing instructions, blaming it on chaos in the files. The command concluded that the instructions must be somewhere and would turn up in time.

"After some time a control commission appeared in these regiments just as it appeared in ours. An inspection of the condition of arms was made, especially in the platoons from which the rifle locks had been stolen. In other regiments methods of taking care of instruction sheets were investigated. The health division was grilled about the food, how it was distributed to the soldiers, and so forth. The results were terrific. The commission discovered the prevalent thefts of rifle locks among the soldiers. It was easy to find the guilty soldiers, for each lock bears a number which is registered in special files of the regiment together with the number of the rifle it belongs to. The name of the soldier who has that rifle is also in the same files. The consequences were crushing. In some cases almost half of the regiment was sent to hard labor. Many commanders were demoted. A number of career officers were expelled from the Army. Others were transferred to punitive military units, working under the most difficult conditions in the worst of climates.

"Returning to our regiment, after the Usbakhov incident serious changes were made here too. A few persons from the command were immediately transferred to inferior posts in other units. Meetings were held of the boards of Party organization and Komsomol. Former Party functionaries were excoriated. Some received reprimands. One was expelled from the Party. All this for lack of alertness and control over the performance of orders and failure to maintain the discipline stipulated in

the regulations. Several platoon leaders, including me, and the
'kidnapped' soldiers were sent to the Manchurian frontier to
very hard labor."

Aliosha stopped for a moment and then added emphatically,
"Really very hard, you may believe me. Once in the new place, I
energetically started to better my impaired record, which could
cause me a lot of harm in the future. In two months I was
one of the few shock workers. I also learned a lesson: a kind
heart does not pay. The most important thing in life is to perform
your duties according to the rules set by society. And I don't
mean only in the Army, but in general. Everywhere we are
surrounded by regulations, laws, and rules. I came to understand that since they are made for people, thought was given,
in making them, of the people they were to affect. They were
not made to have some miserable individual like me try to improve them on his own.

"Now I'll remember for the rest of my life that, if you try
to help someone, the most you can do is harm yourself, without helping him in any case. I don't expect eternal salvation
nor am I waiting for it, therefore I certainly will not martyr
myself for others. I have enough troubles of my own. . . ."

Aliosha said the last sentence in a hard, abrupt voice. He
was deeply convinced of the righteousness of these practical
principles which had been proven to him by life.

6

IN THE HOSPITAL

AFTER AN ATTACK OF FLU, I BECAME ONE OF A COMMUNITY OF sick people isolated from the world by the thick walls of a large hospital in a Moscow suburb.

My first acquaintance was a young lady doctor, always composed and slightly smiling. "You're lucky in your misfortune," she told me laughingly after a few days. "At least you'll have a chance to see a Soviet hospital from the inside. We seldom get tourists here."

She was thirty-five and had been working in this same hospital for several years. "I was fortunate," she said. "I was placed here right after finishing my studies and somehow have managed to stay here. There were attempts to transfer me to a 'more responsible post' somewhere 'far, far from Moscow' as it is called. But a more suitable person happened along who was sent there as punishment. Frankly, I love the theater, movies, the hustle and bustle. I prefer to work in Moscow as a second assistant rather than as a hospital director somewhere at the end of the world. I have many friends and acquaintances here. My parents don't live far from Moscow. Out there I would be all alone, and for a long time, too.

"Besides, I'm used to this hospital, to our Party organization —I've been a member for three years—and to everything as it is here."

Our conversation was interrupted when a tall, well-built man with slightly graying hair appeared at the door of the room. He was wearing a white, beautifully pressed linen uniform. My charming doctor leaped up from her chair and with an almost military step marched up to him. She made a report in an equally military manner. The man nodded his head indifferently and left the room.

She came back blushing. "That was the senior doctor," she explained. "He was looking for someone."

I asked about the senior doctor. When had he finished his studies? Was he married? Had he any children?

She was surprised at the questions. "I must tell you frankly, I don't know, even though we've been working together in one section for a few years. After all, he is a senior doctor, and it isn't customary for an inferior in service to be on even slightly friendly terms with his superiors. We only have a service relationship, and I wouldn't dare to be the first to try and change it. He finds his friends among his equals and so do I. Besides, he's some kind of an advisor to a Ministry committee. You know how it is. If you get too familiar with your superiors, and then you have a quarrel with someone in the hospital you can very easily be accused of nepotism, of trying to get out of doing your work through pull. This is a very serious charge and very difficult to repudiate even if untrue. Just look around for yourself and you'll see how it works in practice."

And so from my bed and my walks in the corridors I began to analyze the small world of the hospital, both the world of the staff and the world of the patient.

The staff impressed me first of all by its military attitude in mutual contacts. The younger nurses reported to the senior ones standing at attention. The senior nurses did the same with their superiors, who in turn acted similarly when faced by their superiors.

One day a supervisory nurse appeared in the ward. With one searching glance she checked the patients and the beds. Though everything seemed to be in perfect order, she called for the nurse's aid, an elderly white-haired woman with lined face and veined hands. The supervisor pointed to a bed, allegedly unmade, and scolded the nurse's aid. Meanwhile the patient swore that his bed had been made and called on all the other patients present as witnesses. The supervisor paid no attention to him. The old woman listened to the unjust reprimand standing at attention.

Later, after the end of the scene, I asked the aid why she hadn't availed herself of the favorable testimony of the witnesses.

She tried to explain. "It's not the subordinate's place to show the supervisor that she's wrong. The Party and the management knew what they were doing when they appointed her as supervisor. And if they ever decide to discharge her from her post, they will also know what they are doing. It's up to her to scold, and up to me to listen.

"Anyway, it's better to listen obediently, even to humiliate myself if necessary. As a supervisor she could find thousands of accusations to make against me if she wanted to. They would believe her because she is a supervisor, while I would be accused of trying to undermine her authority and by the same token the authority of those who had appointed her, the Party, the union, and the management.

"What's the use of looking for trouble? It wouldn't accomplish much anyway. A few more years of cleaning the wards and I'll change from a nurse's aid to a patient, a candidate for death. She is young, energetic. The world belongs to people like her. Let her climb, if she has the strength. Let her push ahead. It's none of my business. . . ."

Astonished by the military rigmarole of doctors, nurses, and aids that went on continuously before my eyes, I casually asked my lady doctor why this went on in a hospital when even in a factory relationships between subordinates and their superiors were not accompanied by such stringent discipline.

This is how she explained it. "You see, a hospital and a factory are quite different. In a factory a worker has no opportunity to become intimate with the director or the secretary of the Party organization. There exists a physical separation between subordinates and their superiors, a separation in space. But this is lacking in a hospital. Doctors work together with nurses, nurses with aids. In this situation, if it weren't for military discipline, which seems to amaze you, the differences which result from the positions occupied by these people in the management or Party hierarchies would be wiped out.

"Don't forget, either, that in a factory a plain worker may reach a position such as secretary of the Party organization. But in a hospital, higher positions in the Party organization go hand in hand with higher positions in the management hierarchy. It would be absolutely impossible for a nurse's aid to become secretary of a Party cell in which senior doctors are just plain members. This could lead to all sorts of complications.

"Preservation of military forms, as you call them, in the contacts between employees prevents us from taking our duties lightly and at the same time preserves work discipline and a sense of responsibility, qualities absolutely necessary for hospital service.

"Look at the patients. They are no more and no less than a cross section of the Soviet people torn away, perhaps for the first time in their lives, from the *social order* in which they have been living. In the hospital they are suddenly cut off from their neighborhood, work, union, and political groups. Their attention concentrates on their illness, on their persons, and on us who help them. Their eyes follow us constantly. Not a single movement, not a single facial expression escapes them. That's why, if we step out of line, our superiors may make the very serious accusation that we *demoralize* the patients by setting a bad example.

"And another thing, you can't just ignore the patients. There are bound to be some responsible functionaries, high officials, journalists, and Party members among them. They may file a complaint or write an article for the papers. You see, we must watch out for all these angles. A sick man is liable to do anything."

And, indeed, the pale patient in the bed at my right was a journalist. He had been in the hospital five months with prolonged bronchitis. While there, he observed the hospital life both as a patient and as a journalist. After the doctor left, he commented on her last words, "She is wrong. A sick man is not liable to do anything. He is not likely to forget the world from which he came. In a physical sense, patients consider themselves different from healthy people. However in the socio-political sense they are a continuation of healthy people except that they are in the hospital. Isn't this amusing?

"Just think how they are brought here in various conditions. Some are unconscious, some are moaning with pain, others are in a panic waiting for an operation or diagnosis. When I see them at such moments, they are human, natural. They are, you might say, individuals, and different from healthy people.

"But they change as soon as their health returns. When they feel better they cease being different from the healthy people outside the hospital. They begin to demand the same status among the sick that they had occupied outside the hospital among the healthy. A member of the executive board of the Party in a factory or office, whose health is returning, would like to play the part of a big cheese here too, among the people in blue pajamas. He'd like to call his fellow patients' attention to himself. And he'd especially like to be the center of the staff's attention. Anyway, most of the time he succeeds.

"That's why the work here is so difficult and why they resort to military discipline. The patients find that they are surrounded by a strong organization that they can't easily affect as a result of the posts they occupied in their healthy life.

"How envious they are of the doctors' attention, even in the case of the seriously ill who really do need special care. They cannot accept the fact that suddenly, as a result of being in a hospital ward, they cease to represent a 'post' or 'function' and have just become bed number so and so or a case of this or that illness. Their demands on the staff are not demands from sick people. They are, instead, demands that they be treated according to their standing, their decorations, the services they have rendered to the Party or the government; not according to the needs of the sickness they happen to be suffering from. Each boasts of things that make him better than the others. Some boast of their work records, others of family connections, still others of battles in which they were wounded. Here, in this hospital we exist outside the framework of any political or organizational unit. Each patient, therefore, tries to prove his social and political value.

"In their regular place of employment they are known from all the angles, while here they are just patients, and it's not possible to know them. But wait, that's not quite correct. I just happened to remember the case of a Party dignitary we had here. But ask the senior ward nurse about it. She knows the story better than I."

At first the senior ward nurse couldn't remember the case. "So many people pass through my ward, I can't possibly remember them all. Let me see, an unpleasant incident in my ward? . . . Oh, you're talking about the comrade from the Party city committee. But that happened long ago. He was an old member with many decorations, a man of great merit. He was here for heart trouble. Remained about two months, I would say.

"He looked like a very nice man. When he felt better he would hold lively discussions with the other patients. He talked so well that you could see he was a veteran speaker, a good agitator, and a good Party propagandist.

"And then some national holiday came along; I think it was the Anniversary of the Revolution. Our patients asked him to address the people in a celebration at the hospital auditorium which was attended by all patients well enough to walk. They asked him very nicely, but he just refused. He just said 'no' without giving any reason. He said he was too sick to speak, but we knew better. He had no temperature, his blood pressure was normal, there was no stomach trouble. He wasn't too sick to talk with the other patients all the time or to read. He was almost entirely recuperated and soon to be discharged.

"So the patients asked me to intervene for them. Well, we all went to him together and pleaded with him. But he was stubborn. The answer was 'no' and 'no', without any reason given. We finally got good and mad. 'So this is the way you play, comrade. It's all right to argue with the patients and disturb the others in their sleep, but talking for the common cause at the celebration is too much for you, eh? Well, brother, you've shown us your real face.'

"And that was the end of him. The celebration went off beautifully. There were addresses by other patriots. Loud-speakers in the wards carried them all.

"The next day we all wrote a joint report to the Party committee about that comrade and his anti-Party attitude. We enclosed a certificate signed by the ward doctor testifying that the patient was almost entirely well and that there were no physical reasons to prevent his delivering a speech at the celebration. I made out a similar certificate, and all the patients

signed the report as witnesses to his anti-social behavior and
hostility towards the celebration. The report was transmitted
through the secretariat of the hospital.

"A few days after our obstinate patient left the hospital we
received a written notice from the Party committee that his
case had been studied by the executive board of the Party.
After hearing his self-criticism, they punished him with a reprimand, entered the incident into his personal record, and
transferred him to a more difficult sector of Party work outside
of Moscow.

"Yes sir," said the ward nurse emphatically, "in our work we
don't just take care of the patients' physical health, we also try
to influence their moral attitude. Often, if a patient's behavior
is improper and not worthy of a Soviet citizen, we report
it to his place of employment."

A few days later I heard the following story about the improper behavior of another patient. This time it took place
in the operating room. The patient was a man, about forty
years old. I think the nurse who told me the story said he was
from Uzbekistan. He was suffering from some intestinal trouble
that needed surgery.

He had never been in an operating room before and was
extremely panicky. The preparations for the operation filled him
with terror. With fear-stricken eyes he watched the operating
table, the instruments being laid out, the anesthetic mask, the
gas tank, the doctors putting on their masks.

When the doctor approached him with the anesthetic mask,
the patient suddenly refused to go through with the operation,
declaring that he did not believe it would be useful and that he
doubted if he would survive.

Consternation reigned momentarily among the doctors and
nurses. It seemed that this sort of thing didn't happen very
often, especially after a patient had been brought all the way
to Moscow for an operation.

The staff pleaded with him to no avail. He wouldn't even
permit an injection for fear it would put him to sleep or weaken
his resistance.

Finally the surgeon, in the last stages of irritation, resorted
to the ultimate argument. He knew that the patient was a

member of the Party and held a high post in his local Party organization. So he called the secretary of the hospital Party organization to the operating room.

The secretary reminded the terrified patient that, according to Party rules, while in the hospital he was subject to the hospital's Party organization.

"Let's put it this way," he argued. "You were delegated by your Party organization to undergo an operation in Moscow. In the name of the Party organization of B. hospital I order you, as a Party member, to consent immediately to the operation."

The patient, now half dead with fright, still stubbornly refused to obey and let himself be anesthetized.

The secretary, furious because the whole incident was undermining his authority, tried a stronger attack. "So you refuse to obey a Party order, is that it?" he demanded of the trembling patient. Then, without waiting for an answer, he continued, "I want to remind you that since you refuse to undergo this operation, for which you were expressly brought here at government expense, you'll have to face the consequences not only as a Party member, but also as an employee who misled the management of his factory by using the alibi of an operation to get a trip to Moscow and evade work. I'm warning you once more that our Party. . . ."

At that moment the patient yelled, "Don't try and scare me with your Party! You know where you and your Party can kiss me . . . right here!"

Before the petrified eyes of the secretary, the doctors, and the nurses the patient slowly moved his trembling hand to the small of his back.

Less than five minutes later the patient was back in his bed, tucked in his blankets, still trembling from his recent experience. For the moment he was left in peace.

The next day he was slipped some tablets that dulled his powers of resistance. He was given an anesthetic and the operation was performed successfully.

After a few days of recovery he was summoned before a meeting of the hospital's Party organization. In a solemn, tense atmosphere the secretary read a review of his case. In a monotonous though impressive voice he described the patient's attitude as definitely hostile to everything that the Soviets stood for. Using all his demagogical ability he demanded of those assembled what must be the moral attitude of a man who, after being brought to Moscow for an operation, shows his ingratitude by hurling insults at the Party and at the Soviet Government; who turns his back on Party functionaries; and who to add insult to injury, does it in the presence of people who are not Party members.

The secretary ordered a vote. There were no abstentions. The accused was unanimously expelled from the Party. His Party card was taken away from him.

"Your case will also be reviewed by the union local in your factory," the secretary assured him as he left the room. "And the minutes of our session will be forwarded today to the party cell of which you *used to be* a member. They will be there before your arrival!"

When I told the story to my neighbor, the journalist, he listened with a comprehending smile and then replied, "The operation was a success, but the patient died . . . a civic death."

He thought for a moment and then added, "What did you expect? Any man must be careful of what he says, but a Party member must be twice as careful. There's a reason why we have the saying, 'your tongue is your enemy.' If a man is careless, well. . . ." The journalist didn't finish, but he drew his index finger across his throat.

Finally the day for my discharge from the hospital arrived. I had been quite sick and I couldn't recognize myself in the mirror. Dressed in street clothes, I took my final walk through the aisles and corridors, saying good-by, as was customary, to all my co-sufferers.

I went downstairs to wait for the hospital car which would take me to downtown Moscow. I left behind the characteristic odor of the hospital, the white figures of the doctors and nurses, the patients in their rows of beds, the whole hospital world with its inhabitants, sick and well.

7

HORSES, TAPE RECORDERS, AND THE RUSSIAN SOUL

TOURISTS FROM ABROAD VISITING THE U.S.S.R. ARE DEEPLY interested in the role of authority in Soviet life. They watch the ubiquitous militiamen with respect. It is true that the militia, with their white coats and red epaulets, form a striking contrast to the gray Soviet crowds and look most important. However, in reality, the militia's only duty is to keep order, and its role in the Soviet system of control is secondary, a fact of which the Soviet citizen is well aware. However, since the militia is one part of governmental control, it deserves mention.

One day, in a small town about 150 kilometers from Moscow, I was invited to attend a dress rehearsal in the local theater, which was the pride of the town. Because of the excessive heat or fatigue, my head began to ache. Towards the end of the rehearsal I left my seat in search of a headache powder.

Luckily I found a merciful soul who gave me one. After taking it, I went to the third floor of the theater where there were some extra dressing rooms and where costumes and props were stored. It was deserted at that time. I sat down in an old and inviting armchair that smelled of dust and old, forgotten scents. The whole floor was blissfully dark and silent. No sounds reached it from the stage. My headache slowly disappeared. But, without knowing when or how, I fell asleep.

When I woke up, for a moment I didn't know where I was. Then the pictures of venerable actors and actresses staring down from the corridor walls reminded me. I glanced at my watch; it was 3 A.M.!

I started down the stairs which were covered with soft, high-pile carpeting. Downstairs, I saw two militiamen on duty standing next to the night watchman who was seated in a chair. At the same moment, they noticed me.

They froze, then quickly regained speech before I could say anything. They ordered me to halt and raise my hands, screaming out shrilly, probably in order to bolster up their own courage by this unholy noise.

I tried to explain my presence, but they wouldn't listen. The representatives of justice telephoned in a panicky report, probably directly to the secret police. Anyway, a few minutes later a car pulled up in front of the theater and eight comrades in plain clothes piled out of it. Their coats had padded shoulders, and revolver butts bulged from under their armpits.

I was thoroughly questioned. All of my identification papers were carefully examined. My little address book, passport, and even a few old trolley tickets were fished out of my pockets. After an hour of questioning I was set free. I was even driven to my address by a taciturn agent who did, however, explain to me with a kindly smile, "The militiamen took you for a foreign spy."

The old night watchman had been so nervous and frightened that he didn't utter a word during the whole incident.

My second contact with the militia had a different character. It came after the end of a football game in the large Luzniki Stadium in Moscow. There must have been about fifty thousand people there. When crowds of them began to pour out of the stadium through the exits and stream towards the subway, a chain of several hundred militia on horseback and on foot surrounded the stadium. The mounted militia treated the quiet and orderly crowd in a way that touched me to the quick. The trained horses faced away from the people and, directed backwards by the riders, broke up the crowd by the movement of their shiny rumps. Children, young people, oldsters, mothers with babies in their arms . . . all of them were pushed in the direction of the subway entrances. Several people in my immediate vicinity were hurt by the horses when they had no room to move out of the way.

Outraged, I asked a militiaman to take me to the commander of this action. At first he refused, but when I said I would file

a complaint against him, he asked me to follow him. A few
yards away, in an open military car, a robust militia captain
sat attentively watching the doings of his heroes and their well-
fed horses. Very politely I asked him for the reason for this
cavalry action.

He smiled and said that he could tell I was a foreigner from
my question. "Our people are used to it," he said. "Where
there are crowds there must be mounted militia. Otherwise the
people would trample each other to death. It's happened. As
you would know if you had seen the doings on the day after
Comrade Stalin's death, when his bier was displayed in Red
Square!

"Oh, there's no use talking about it. We've always done it
this way. Ever since Czarist times the mounted militia have been
best able to deal with crowds. If a horse does happen to step
on somebody's foot in the process, or pushes him to the ground
with his rump . . . who's going to worry about it when the whole
problem of maintaining order is at stake? Look there, to your
right. See? That horse pushed two people down. Now they're
up and patting him on his rump. Our people are used to it.
Where are you from, anyway?"

A few weeks before, when I was sick in a hospital, I managed
to get the nurses to tell me about the scenes in Red Square on
the day when Stalin's body was displayed. It was a great day in
the history of Moscow and of the whole U.S.S.R. This was the
first time that the people could have a close look at Comrade
Stalin's face.

Thousands of delegations came from all over the U.S.S.R. to
stand close to his body for a moment and to stare at his closed
eyes. Just as at the coronations of the Czars, human beings
poured into Red Square. For the first few hours some order was
maintained. The route to the bier was marked by rows of heavy
trucks, and controlled by thousands of police and troops on
horse and on foot.

Then at one point the crowd, excited by its own hysteria
and by the wailing and sobbing throughout the Square, broke
through the disciplined ranks of militia and troops. Under the
pressure generated by hundreds of thousands of persons in all

the corners of the huge square and the streets leading into it the heavy trucks were overturned like children's toys.

The moans of trampled, crushed, and collapsing people were hidden by the general wailing and sobbing of the crowds. However, next to the bier order was preserved. The leader of two hundred million people lay there, proud and indifferent, his face turned away from the members of the central committee and the crowd of people standing guard over him. His sharp profile was outlined against the background of the Kremlin walls and gray Moscow skies.

After a few hours, the crowds were again under control and order was restored. But the last victims were still being carried to hospitals or to the morgue. About 250 people were brought to the hospital at which I was a patient. They had broken legs or arms or had crushed ribs. Many of them would remain cripples for the rest of their lives. But only a small share of the victims were brought to this hospital. Eye witnesses with whom I talked estimated that three thousand people were injured.

One day I watched a crowd of perhaps five hundred university students and teen-agers in front of a circus box office. All the seats had been sold out; the crowd was getting riotous, shouting its demand that standing room be sold to them.

A single militiaman came by and forced the crowd to calm down and disperse. He was unarmed and didn't even carry a club. I must admit that this demonstration impressed me.

I was with a friend who was a pharmaceutical chemist. When we had found seats in a restaurant and were cozily ensconced behind a table, I asked my friend about the incident.

"You see, those university students and teen-agers," he said, "who dispersed so readily without even hurling an insult at the militiaman were not afraid of him. They were afraid of the "government among the crowd," the agents who were in the crowd. The consequences of an insult hurled at the militiaman would be answered not by the militiaman, who probably wouldn't even hear it, but by an agent who would promptly lead the loudmouth to the nearest doorway, check all his identification papers, and make a record of the incident.

"That's why we never risk disobedience. Don't believe it when someone tells you that he saw university students demonstrate against authority. It's all nonsense. These students are well aware of the fact that authority is not only *above* man, but also *behind* him and next to him. As our comedians say, government is *closed to* the needs of the ordinary man. It must be close to him and his affairs and never far from him in his daily life. Authority in uniform is like God's image. It reminds us of its existence at every step, of expected obedience, and of punishment which we can suffer from its hands. But actual authority is always amidst us. It is non-uniformed and unrecognizable. It is the authority composed of secret-police agents and all their collaborators. Don't think, however, that our present agents are the same as those of the thirties. Oh no, then our secret service was only equipped ideologically. Now technical equipment has been added. The longer you stay with us, the more you'll see and understand."

I came to appreciate the truth of this brief analysis, and had a chance to learn about the work of the secret service indirectly through the case of my friend S. living in Leningrad. I had known him quite some time and admired his courage in openly saying what he thought. His views on the current problems of the U.S.S.R. and world politics were extremely accurate and excellently thought out. Often they didn't quite conform with the official theses of Soviet propaganda. S. was a mechanical engineer and interested in art. He claimed that he was a victim of the despotism of his parents. They had made him study science against his will. He knew French and admired everything that even hinted of French culture, literature, and art. He even admitted that after the victory of the proletarian revolution in France he would like to live in that country. He kept Sartre's plays in his house as something sacred and knew each word of them by heart. He also had some French philosophic publications and illustrated magazines hidden deeply in the linen closet. He was gay, an easy talker, and always ready for a discussion. This was S. during my first visit to his house.

When I returned to Leningrad after a long absence, I saw S. again. The change in his behavior stunned me. I could hardly draw him into a conversation. He was frightened out of his wits and full of prejudices. At one time we were walking down the street and talking about modern Soviet architecture. Sud-

denly a stranger came up to us and pleasantly introduced himself to us as an architect. He was of medium height and had
a nice face. He said that he had been walking behind us and
couldn't help overhearing fragments of our discussion. Would
we allow him to join us? I said "yes" without giving it a second
thought, but S. stood there as if rooted to the ground. He
became pale and started to perspire and would not budge. I was
at a loss. I couldn't understand what was wrong. The architect
felt awkward also, for S. began walking without saying a word
to him. We walked along in this manner for a few minutes,
then suddenly S. bade us good-by and disappeared in the slowly
moving crowd along the avenue. The architect proved interesting
and friendly. We continued to walk, with the architect supplying
many arguments in favor of Soviet monumentalism in architecture.

The following day I called on S. I was curious to know the
cause of his odd behavior of the previous day. He was sitting
in an armchair writing furiously in a large notebook. I sat opposite him, waiting for him to finish. When he was done I asked
him what the matter was. For a long while S. evaded my
question, but when he heard that I was leaving Russia soon
and that probably we'd never see each other again, he softened
and put a bottle of wine on the table. We drank in silence
for a while, then S. began to talk. He told me what had happened in the last few weeks which had so completely changed
his personality.

Some weeks ago S. had said farewell to some French news-
papermen at the Leningrad railway station. He had become very
friendly with them, had shown them the city during the few
days they had been there. With his admiration for French culture, he was delighted with the company of the French guests. A
few days later, still under the spell of the Frenchmen's visit, he
was summoned to a secret-police office. He arrived at the appointed time. However, he was asked to wait in the waiting room
and told not to leave since he would be called at any moment.
He sat down on a narrow, uncomfortable chair and waited,
nervously watching the hands of a wall clock and smoking cigarette after cigarette.

After two hours of waiting and smoking, he had run out of

cigarettes. There was no one in the room from whom he could borrow a smoke. The entrance pass, which the doorman had given him, did not entitle him to leave the building unless it was signed by the department which had summoned him. S. went to the men's room in the hope of finding some cigarettes there, but no luck. He became unbearably thirsty, but no water was available. The two-hour wait, with nothing accomplished and no cigarettes, irritated him.

He finally knocked on the door of the secretariat. It was opened by a small man with short-cropped hair. S. explained that he'd been waiting over two hours. . . . The small man interrupted, "And what's your hurry, Comrade S.? You're not going to work today, are you? And you aren't planning to go abroad just yet, or are you?" and he shut the door in his face. Nervously exhausted, S. fell into the hard chair and continued to wait. "I knew," he said to me, "that something was wrong, something that I had done or something that they wanted from me, but I had no idea what it could be."

Twilight came. A powerful lamp was turned on in the waiting room. S. could not look out of the window, for it had thick, opaque panes. So, he sat on and waited and for the nth time arranged his personal papers in his wallet.

Finally, after nine hours, a clerk opened the door and said, "Come in, please, Comrade S." S. entered, trying in vain to assume a pleasant and unworried smile. He was asked into the next room. Behind the desk sat a lean, fair-haired man with an "undescribable" (as S. said) look on his face. "Comrade S.?" he asked, "sit down, comrade, please sit down. You had to wait a little, didn't you? I'm sorry, but we're so busy."

S. said he sat there, staring at the open cigarette box on the table. The official was smoking and the aroma of his cigarette was driving him crazy. What he wouldn't give for just one smoke! In the meantime, the official was looking over some papers, rocking in his wide chair, and every now and then sending rings of white smoke into the air. Suddenly S. realized that he had a splitting headache. He hadn't eaten all day, having missed even breakfast because he'd been too nervous to eat. At the moment the official put away the folder with the papers and, looking searchingly at S., said, "Well, Comrade S., speak up!"

S. didn't understand. "Speak up? But, about what, comrade?" he asked.

The official smiled slightly and said almost amicably, "Speak up, Comrade S., *if you have something to tell us.* And if not, please go back to the waiting room and wait. *Perhaps you will think of something there.* How about it?"

"So there I was," said S., "back in the waiting room, sitting and staring at the clock again and trying to figure out what it was that I had to tell them. What had happened? By this time I was faint with hunger. The faint odor of tobacco, which was probably in my clothing, was torture. After two hours I was called into the office once again. The official looked at me with friendliness. Between puffs of his cigarette he asked, 'Well, Comrade S.? I'm listening; I'm all attention. Won't you sit down and tell me about it?' In an effort to gain a lead I asked him to ask me a question. The official looked at me calmly. 'Really, Comrade S. Don't you really know what you should talk about? Honestly? Is it true that you cannot recall and wish to go back to the waiting room and—'

"I wouldn't let him finish. I was deathly afraid of returning to the waiting room with my blinding headache and growing faintness. I began to talk about myself, my plans, my professional work, my friends, my books and magazines. I told him about all the conversations I could think of that I had had with people within the last two months. I mentioned you, too, and the Frenchmen, and almost anything else I could think of.

"He never interrupted or asked any questions. He sat still, looking at the ceiling, sometimes glancing at me carefully and then back to the ceiling. When I finished—and I must have talked for about thirty minutes—he smiled leniently and disconnecting an outlet under the desk, said, 'Eh, Comrade S., what a child you are. Did I ask for a confession? No. I simply asked you to tell me, *you know what,* the thing that might interest us. All these other matters don't interest us, Comrade S. —not now, at least. They are not of the slightest importance to us, understand? I'm asking you once more. Tell me all that is

on your conscience, where you think you are not in order towards authority, society, yourself. Will you do that, please?'
The official was silent for a moment and then added with a
teasing smile, 'and remember, Comrade S., that whatever you
say will go down in history . . .' Seeing that I didn't understand what he meant, he explained, 'I have connected the tape
recorder and what you have to say will be recorded on it. You
see? Well, Comrade S., go ahead.'

"Once again I started my story about everything and nothing.
This time, however, it was more chaotic. I had no idea on what
to concentrate. The awareness that every word I uttered was
being recorded by a cold, precise mechanism, that my life was
turning around with the tape recorder, frightened me. I realized
that now I was speaking of different things than I had before.
I was beginning to believe that I was guilty before I even knew
what I was guilty of.

"I found myself piling up accusations against myself, doing
it almost consciously. I accused myself all along the line in
accordance with the accepted principles of self-criticism. I
accused myself of indifference in my contacts with foreigners.
I quoted my cynical opinions of certain aspects of our 'reality.'
I confessed servility in relationship to Western culture and
decadent, bourgeois art. When I was finished, I was faint from
the exhaustion and tension which accompanied the hearing.

"The official must have noticed my condition, for he gave
me a small glass of water and a cigarette. I thought that this
was the end of the hearing. I thought that I had told him
everything that he wanted to hear from me, that I had nothing
more to say. I smoked my cigarette slowly, enjoying its taste
and aroma. At that moment, it absorbed all my attention. I felt
sure that in a couple of minutes I'd get up with a cheerful
smile and leave. In half an hour I'd be home in bed."

But S.'s hearing didn't end so soon. After S. finished his
smoke, the official went to the next room and returned with
another man, tall and almost entirely bald. He introduced S.
to the new man and left, probably for home.

Weak from fatigue, hunger, and tension, S. had to go over
everything once more from the beginning. He could not, of
course, remember exactly what he had said on the two previous

occasions. Underneath the top of the table, the tape was moving
slowly on the recorder, permanently setting down the third suc-
cessive version of S.'s story. The new official sat quietly staring
at the ceiling, as had his predecessor. He glanced occasionally
at S., sweating and pale from exhaustion.

At midnight, after about twelve hours in the secret-police
building, S. staggered home, after being told to return the next
day.

On his return home he fell into a heavy, exhausted sleep.
But the next day the procedure of the previous day was repeated.
Only this time he was asked questions by several officials one
after the other. The questions were based on his recorded
testimony. The questions dealt with almost anything, and it
seemed obvious that their purpose was to convince S. that by
his contacts with foreigners he acted against the best interests
of his country and the Soviet Government. The same questions
were repeated several times.

They were strange questions. Often they were constructed so
that they suggested the answer expected from the accused.
Frequently only a "yes" or "no" answer was allowed to a question
that couldn't be answered like that.

"But I didn't care any more, and I gave the answers they
wanted. After three days, I was told to come back to sign my
deposition. From the material I gave them during those monstrous hearings they compiled a really fascinating dossier. I
looked like some perverse, ambiguous, shifty character, an enemy
of the Soviet Government and the Party . . . a cosmopolite
. . . almost a degenerate. And this was a permanent record!

"The worst part of it to me was the fact that these were
things I had said about myself. With my own lips I had written
this self-accusation perpetuated by the brown tape of the recorder.

"And how many people I had involved! For I had to give
both examples and witnesses. Now it would be their turn, and
they would write the continuation of this tragic story, heroes
half dead of fright."

S. stopped suddenly and started to laugh, unnaturally loud.
It was a bitter laugh, directed against his own thoughts, associations, comparisons, and judgments. On seeing my curiosity, he

laughed even louder and said, "You are waiting for the end
of the story, aren't you? You're surprised that I'm still here?
Well then, listen carefully. After I signed my uneven signature
in a trembling hand and the ink had barely dried, the official
who had been the first to interview me walked me to the door.
He stopped at the threshold.

"Looking at me with a slightly amused expression, he said,
'A guilty conscience is a strange thing, isn't it, Comrade S.?
You know, you did a terrible thing to yourself. You were called
down here because two weeks ago your Ministry requested that
we compile data on your personal life, conduct, and private affairs. The request was labelled very urgent. Naturally we concluded that you had done something wrong, politically or
vocationally. As is usual in such cases, we proceeded to give
you the works. However a few minutes ago, while you were
signing the deposition, a call came from the Party committee
asking whether the material had been sent. They needed it ur-
gently, for the Ministry had made your appointment to some
high position in Moscow dependent on our report.

" 'But now it's obvious from your deposition that you're quite
a boy. Well, you may as well go home and wait. You may be
in trouble, serious trouble. If you are, it's entirely your fault,
Comrade S.'

"I felt as though lightning had hit me. Why, oh why had
I told them all those things? I did it all myself. I had dug my
grave with my own hands!"

We sat in silence. S. had stopped laughing and was covering
his face with his hands. I felt as cheated as he did; and I felt sad
that there was nothing I could do to help this wise and kind
man. I noticed his unshaven neck, covered with slightly curled
black hair, which reached almost down to the dirty collar of his
checkered shirt stained with grease and dandruff.

Only then did I see how badly S. had neglected his appearance, the disorder in his apartment, the two empty vodka bottles
on his night table. I tried to leave the room quietly, but S. arose
and for a moment was almost hostile.

"You too? You're leaving me just like the others did, running
away from somebody contaminated by plague. You think I'm

already in Siberia, even before those who can send me there do it. Well, to hell with it all!"

I don't know what became of S., but in my memory he will always remain as one of the most intelligent people I've ever known.

When later, on my way home, I again passed through Moscow, I told some of my friends S.'s story. They put me in contact with a Mr. Kr., a man whose brother had just been sentenced to four years in a labor camp for alleged crime committed under truly fantastic circumstances.

Kr.'s brother was a minor clerk in an unimportant job. He was in rather poor financial circumstances. About forty-five years old, he was married and the father of one son and two daughters. For a long time Kr. did not belong to the Party, but at the time our story begins he had become a member candidate and possessor of a Party card. The family lived in mid-Moscow in a multi-family apartment, occupying two small rooms.

Mrs. Kr. worked as a maid in a large Moscow hotel which catered primarily to foreigners. It was just at the time when more and more foreigners were beginning to visit Moscow. The son was in the Army. The daughters attended the University. Both of them were engaged and were soon to be married.

One afternoon Kr. came home from work earlier than usual. He was in an exceptionally cheerful mood. He hurried through his dinner, then decided to pick up his wife at the hotel. Since it was very hot, he left the jacket of his suit at home.

The hotel was full of foreign tourists. On entering the lobby, Kr. had to show his credentials. He explained that he was coming to get his wife, and the doorman let him in. The lobby seethed with women in colorful dresses and spiked heels and men in checked jackets with vivid scarves tied around their necks. News photographers milled among the crowd, carrying cameras over their shoulders. It was not the first time that Kr. had been in the hotel, but he had never before seen so many foreigners there at one time.

He stopped to watch them. The sound of the clock striking reminded him of his wife. Instead of asking for her in the hotel's personnel department, he went straight to the maid's dressing room to look for her. She wasn't there, so he took the crowded but elegant elevator to the floor where he knew she worked.

There he was reminded by another maid that his wife, as she did on that day every week, was working in another hotel near the Agricultural Exhibit. Kr. scratched his head and grew irritated when he realized that in his hurry he had forgotten to look at the calendar and so had made an unnecessary trip. Now he would have to cross the whole city by subway to meet his wife.

On his way out, he stopped in the modern, luxuriously furnished (in comparison with Soviet standards) men's room. And that's where tragedy struck. Not used to modern, efficient equipment, Kr. bent over while flushing the toilet bowl. Unfortunately, all his personal papers whose old covers were soft and pliable, fell into the toilet bowl. He could save nothing!

The rapid stream of whirling water seized his passport, Party card, both his union card and his wife's, and in a second the bowl was empty. Kr. hoped against hope that the trap in the pipe had stopped the documents. He found a piece of wire and tried to fish them out. But to his complete discomfiture he found the trap was empty. The worn papers were on their way to the city sewers.

His last hope gone, Kr. stood for a while in the hotel corridor not knowing what to do next. The floor maid testified later that Kr. stood by the window with a foreigner, and that they were smoking cigarettes. But we don't know if this was before or after the episode of the men's room. Anyway, Kr. decided to leave the hotel. But in the downstairs lobby he was approached by a man who identified himself as an agent of the secret police. He took Kr. to a room and asked to see his papers. Undoubtedly Kr. had caught the agent's attention because dressed as he was he stood out like a sore thumb in the hotel lobby. The agent simply wanted to know who he was.

Well, Kr. explained his mishap. Naturally enough, the agent didn't believe a word of it and proceeded to question him. During the interrogation, Kr. probably forgot that he had smoked with some stranger at the hotel window. When he did remember, he said that the man merely happened to be standing next to him. They did not exchange a word.

The maid, however, testified that Kr. had talked with the

foreigner. Kr.'s statement that he had forgotten that his wife did not work in the hotel on that day wasn't convincing. Other witnesses testified that Kr. always wore a jacket and never impressed anyone as being a forgetful man. An examination of the toilet in the hotel men's room proved that though it was possible for the papers to pass through the trap, any halfway adroit person would be able to salvage them in time. These findings confirmed the district attorney's theory that Kr. was trying to find an excuse for the missing papers and therefore invented a story about the toilet, about rushing out without his jacket, and about searching for his wife.

On the basis of this testimony, Kr. was accused of giving his personal papers to a foreigner who needed them for purposes of espionage. However, no one could describe the foreigner.

Kr.'s guilt was not entirely proven in court. No answer could be found to the question of what Kr. gained by giving his papers to a foreigner. No one saw him negotiate any business or receive any money.

Kr. did not plead guilty to the crime he was accused of. But he did concede the district attorney's point that a man who is able to lose his Party card and his other identification papers in a toilet bowl is just as liable to inadvertently betray his country. He also conceded that he hadn't taken proper care of his papers, especially his Party card, the most valuable thing that a Soviet man can own.

The judge retired to consider a verdict. The sentence was four years in a labor camp. Kr. accepted the verdict with composure, his eyes wandering over the rows of spectators to see once more the small, tear-stained face of his wife.

". . . Too bad you couldn't have met him," said Kr.'s brother, a worker in a metallurgical plant. "He was an exceptionally decent man, as anybody will tell you. He was honest, not pushing, never did anybody any harm. He loved his wife, his daughters and son, and enjoyed playing chess. Just a plain man, neither a saint nor a scoundrel. He decided to join the Party after the Twentieth Congress. He told me then that though he wasn't one of those who had destroyed socialism, he would be glad to try and repair it, working together with other people like himself. And of all people, it had to happen to him. If only he had been healthy, but he wasn't. He had serious stomach trouble and a diseased kidney. Both of these ailments needed constant and good care. Even if he comes out of it alive after four years, he won't be of much use."

Kr.'s brother thought for a while. Suddenly, as if recalling something, he asked me with anger in his eyes, "Tell me, abroad, where everyone has such toilets, do people lose their papers or money in them? Perhaps the construction is deficient and should be improved?"

I could not answer him then; nor can I answer today. It is possible that valuable papers get lost in toilets, but do people perish because of toilets?

In my talks with different people in various places I often discussed the problem of secret agents and secret police. I must say that this was the only field in which people had some doubts that the changes going on in the U.S.S.R. were for the better. The people I talked with, even if their attitude towards the social order around them was most enthusiastic, refused to commit themselves as soon as we started to talk about the secret police. They didn't want to discuss this touchy subject which often robbed them of their faith that a change for the better was taking place in their lives.

I spoke to people whose relatives or friends had been "taken away" from home a few months ago. No one knew, not even the closest relative, why, what became of them, what they were accused of, or when they would return—if they returned at all.

I talked with the wife of a man who had been taken away while at work half a year ago. She was still torturing herself trying to guess why her husband had been arrested. His colleagues at work were also baffled. "Don't fret, comrade," she was told by a secret-service official in her district to whom she was admitted after many difficulties. "Your husband is not lost. He is in the U.S.S.R. together with you. He was not taken abroad, nor will he be. Nothing can happen to him. All you have to do is wait and be calm."

Sometimes a man would just disappear and his family would come up with the most far-fetched guesses as to the cause of his disappearance. Had he been arrested . . . and why? Perhaps he got drunk and did something wrong? Perhaps he was seen

with a suspected man? Perhaps it was just an accident? Perhaps
. . . perhaps . . . perhaps. . . .

The thing that amazed me most, however, was the composure
with which all the affected people reconciled themselves to their
fate. In the most flagrant cases of lawlessness committed by
authority the people were always ready to look for the guilt of
the accused rather than to accuse authorities of absolute dis-
regard of the elementary principles of law. They would wonder
about what crime had been committed but would not wonder
about those who imprisoned him.

At one time when I expressed my doubts and astonishment,
a man older than I looked at me for a long while and then said:

"You must understand, young man . . . a man is only a man.
He must have faith in the justice of the authority under which
he belongs. If we doubt this, what is left? How will we live
without this faith? Do you really believe that faith in injustice
helps you in life better than faith in justice, even if you don't
think everything is right and proper?"

Another man, a plain worker, expressed the same thought in
other words:

"Authority rules millions, so it is entitled to make mistakes
where individuals are concerned."

During my stay in Moscow, I once had a talk with a doctor,
a retired psychiatrist who was then almost seventy. When I
brought up the problem of the apparently small number of mentally ill in the U.S.S.R., the doctor, once one of the distinguished
experts in the field, said to me:

"This matter is not at all as simple as some of my younger
colleagues, the so-called representatives of the new Soviet medicine and psychiatry, may have pictured it. In their conception it
appears as if certain psychiatric ailments disappeared in our
country after the revolution. They will also tell you that the new
Soviet psychiatry has contributed to the almost complete elimination of a whole series of mental illnesses and deviations from
our clinics. However, the reality is somewhat different. First of
all, you must remember that for a good number of years of the
post-revolutionary period the mentally ill were left to fend for
themselves. In borderline cases they were often executed by
revolutionary or counterrevolutionary forces as being an uncer-

tain, harmful, or dangerous element. In other cases, the mentally ill were forced to physical labor, and when they rebelled against commands or did not carry them out accordingly, they became the victims of the guards, who preyed upon them especially in order to give an example to the others. Thus it is possible to say that our revolution somehow raised those who were not normal to the level of normal people, although many malicious persons claim the contrary. Naturally it was these unfortunates who suffered by it. Sick, beaten, tormented, abused, they were executed for their actions, which were evaluated in terms of normal behavior.

"Those, however, are the old times. Today we must deal with an opposite situation. If you take a good look at our psychiatric clinics, you will be impressed by the absence of certain classes of mentally ill which in other countries—the United States, Britain, or Sweden—form a large proportion of the inmates of clinics. I have in mind certain types of neurasthenia, schizophrenia, and a whole series of sexual deviations—in other words, those types of mental illnesses which can exist hidden in everyday life. To qualify these illnesses as such demands a proper approach by society in the first place and then by doctors. Meanwhile, in our circumstances, very many of such mental illnesses are considered forms of social maladjustment and combated with a very individual therapy. This therapy consists of exerting pressure upon the person, in the direction of, as we say here, submission to the interests of the group in which the individual finds himself. In this way a large number of people who abroad would be directed to hospitals for the mentally ill and would undergo appropriate treatment do not qualify as being mentally ill at all. I would say that it is even the reverse. Such individuals, often treated as "socially lazy," "inimical to the group," etc., must suffer the consequences of violating patterns accepted for normal people. Thus they are criticized at group meetings, forced to self-criticism, delegated to forced labor, and very often, perhaps most often, they are transferred somewhere, "far to the north," as we say here, to the forefront of hard socialist work, which will ostensibly turn them into valuable members of society.

"As you see, behind our statistics which proudly emphasize the minimal number of mentally ill in the U.S.S.R., there is hidden the tragedy of thousands of mentally ill people suffering for actions which they are not committing in bad faith. This is the price they must pay for being considered normal, for it seems that normality also has its price in our socialist market." The doctor paused for a moment and then added: "A friend of mine, a psychiatrist, was sent to a labor camp because he took it upon himself to certify as mentally ill a patient whom the Party organization regarded as being 'unstable, malicious, secretive, and irresponsible in the decisions he undertook.' In the opinion of my colleague, it was a classic example of a mental illness in an advanced stage. But what of it, when the authorities were of a different opinion? For his effort to 'whitewash an enemy of the Party,' my friend had to pay with a term in a labor camp. What I think is very important is that during his stay in the camp he determined that fully 25 per cent of the inmates, condemned for laziness, anti-social attitude, etc., were people who were mentally ill."

In one more effort to regain my faith in Soviet justice, I asked my friends to help me meet, if possible, someone set free from a labor camp or prison under the program of "Repairing Past Errors" initiated by the Soviet Government in 1954–55. After some time contact was established with such a man. Arrested and sentenced to lifelong imprisonment in 1936, he was freed in 1954 as innocent. However, his application for rehabilitation as a member of the Party was rejected by the Party court. When I met him, he was fifty-five but he looked at least seventy-five. The story of his life as told to me by a friend was simple.

He was a teacher and had been connected with the communist movement from early youth. He took part in the Revolution and since 1918 had been active in labor unions, a group in which Lenin had been especially interested. He was promoted from year to year and occupied increasingly responsible posts in the Party. By 1936 he was one of the highest functionaries in the directorship of labor unions and close to the Central Committee of the Party. The wave of trials, mass arrests, and executions of 1936–38 caught up with him. Together with the last group of the Lenin members of the Central Committee, a number of high Army officers, almost all the ambassadors, chiefs of the secret police, and a few vice-prime ministers, he was arrested and subjected to severe interrogation. Tortures, such as breaking the joints in his hand and drilling his teeth, forced a complete "confession" of the crimes he was accused of. Under interrogation, he gave the names of alleged collaborators and friends, who were then arrested and also convicted.

I finally met this man at a small table in a smart restaurant in Leningrad. From a distance we probably looked like any two typical Central Europeans. The dignified waiters busied themselves among the tables, nimbly maneuvering their trays. The soft sound of the orchestra dimmed the murmur of conversation. The restaurant filled gradually.

I was trying not to look at my companion's face. I was afraid of hurting him by staring at him and thus reminding him of his looks. Instead, I looked at the snow-white tablecloth, but there I saw the hands of this man. Their abnormality was repulsive. They reminded me of pictures I had seen in my childhood of monsters, half-men, half-animals. His hands were flattened and angular, and the fingers ran in all directions. The joints were swollen and jutted out and to the sides. On some fingers the nails were ingrown. They stuck out and their layers formed shapeless lumps. The flesh was blue and brown, dried and creased, full of wide open paths and grooves cut by the lines of the veins. It was difficult for me to realize that these were the hands of a living man, hands that had been so terribly violated by other human beings.

My companion seldom mentioned the eighteen years he had spent in the labor camp and I shrank from being the first to refer to them. Now that he had returned to normal life, to living people, and had regained his faith in being a human, it was not easy to talk about the times when he differed little from a wild animal, doubting his own humanness and that of the men around him.

We talked about his return to life, about the grace of a government which by giving him a sum of money for "further life" had made it possible for him to sit at an elegantly set table. But in our conversation the problems of life continually entwined themselves with the problems of death, problems of freedom with problems of prison. In the conversational snarls, I completely lost any sense of the world's stability.

My companion was quite obviously afraid to mention concrete facts, names of men or places. From his chaotic narration, during which his hands trembled frequently, I can remember only those fragments which touched directly on his survival and his return to life and freedom.

"When they arrested me," he said, "I did not realize what had happened for a long time. I was summoned to the director's office where two men were waiting. They handcuffed me and led me to a closed car which drove us to the jail where I was to be questioned. There I was put into a small, damp cell. At home my wife had been cooking supper, my son had been doing his homework . . . that was how I left them and how they remained in my memory. Both died later during the war. I survived *odietij kamniem* (stone-clad) in a distant quarry with several thousand men like me. Day in and day out, we wormed our way with pickaxes into a never-ending wall of stone.

"You know, at the beginning, when I was in jail in 1936, I was convinced that it was a mistake—a horrible mistake. It was the same during the interrogation. For two months—beaten, starved, kicked, my teeth bored through, in untold pain—I would repeat to my hangmen over and over again that it was a mistake, a mistake, a mistake. But there came a day when I wasn't so sure any more, and they kept on and on, demanding the names of other people from me. The world turned around in my head. Everything that I thought began to change in a strange way. You see, man is—how should I say?—a conception. Man is the definition of a certain, definite state which has a beginning and an end. Dislocated from this state, man becomes something for which our language has no definition as yet, although some day our universities may come up with one. We don't know how to change animals into humans but we have learned how to change humans into animals. And so, I, an animal, began to supply them with the names of humans, for what ties did I have with *people* then? I, a bloody, beaten piece of meat. It was not I who gave those names. They jumped out of my memory by themselves, precipitated by the twitching of the nerves in my teeth which they had drilled through and through. The twitchings were arranging themselves into names, addresses, and dates.

"I ceased to believe in the purposefulness of nature which endowed me with ten fingers of which each—as if for spite—had three joints to break. As I spat out the names which crowded each other I held onto life as tenaciously as my nails had resisted being torn out of their fingers—though finally they had to give in. Every animal dreads death. I had the right to dread it too, though at that time I dreaded life more. But what could I use to get rid of it?

"All I remember of the trial is the back of the defendant sitting in front of me. A defendant like me. I also remember fragments of the district attorney's speech. He spoke beautifully, using marvelous language and irreproachable syntax. Even when I was in school I could never talk so beautifully. It is a matter of luck. Someone can speak well. Another one is lucky with women, and still another is lucky enough to die before interrogation. I was lucky in none of these ways.

"In the end, I have not been alone. I was one of many who were innocently condemned. . . . Sherlock Holmes, as you probably know, discovered criminals by the method of deduction, and Chesterton's Father Brown discovered them by the method of induction. Of our police authorities it might be said that they discovered criminals by the method of production . . . socialist production, of course. . . .

"But I suppose you want to hear more about the past. Well, you undoubtedly know how they began, in 1954, the liberation and rehabilitation of those 'innocently and mistakenly convicted.' A lot of prisoners were released from my camp. They were given clothes: suits just like you see on me, shirts, ties, shoes, a train ticket, and a food package for the trip. And it was 'good-by, brother, you're free.'

"It's strange, but, would you believe it, many wouldn't go back. A man in a labor camp is a peculiar animal. He becomes attached to one spot and is loath to leave it. After all, you can't just leave a space or time. You have to leave *for* somewhere, to go home, to go to your people. But many, like me, had nowhere.

"It's true, we were assigned to convalescent homes, even offered work. But, can't you see, we didn't quite look at ourselves as humans, and it was not an easy matter to return to human society.

"You know, I can't stand general terms. What do you call

them in Latin? . . . Universalia, that's right. 'Man,' 'People,' 'Society,' 'U.S.S.R.' Things like these don't exist at all. There are no 'people,' just individuals here and there, here in life and there in the camp and the quarry. There are two 'Societies,' one here and one there. There are two U.S.S.R.s, here and there. Don't you think I'm right? You see, you can't just grab an eraser and wipe off eighteen years of your life.

"Here, on the outside, you had war, you were afraid, you were dying, but you were looking forward to new things. And we? All this time we just had the quarry . . . only the quarry. Though to tell you the truth, it was the quarry that had us. I'm telling you this so that you'll understand there are also two versions of history, yours here and ours there. Your history records a war, but ours doesn't. Because wars are conducted by men, not by animals.

"But it's getting late, and I want to finish. So I was set free and told to apply for rehabilitation as a Lenin man. I went to a sanitarium. I had inhaled so much dust that you might say I had a quarry of my own in my lungs and intestines. In fact, in those eighteen years I grew into one with the quarry to such a degree that I took it with me for the rest of my life. I keep carrying it with me, as you do your watch on your wrist or the memory of a girl—your first love—in your heart. After a few months I was advised that I was not eligible for rehabilitation. *I*, understand? *I* was not eligible. I thought that everything would turn upside down again in my mind. And do you know why they refused to rehabilitate me? Because, according to a memorandum they enclosed with their decision, I falsely denounced innocent people during my interrogation. Because of my denunciation these people were convicted, these people who were innocent. Can you grasp it? It was *I* who committed injustice. It was because of *me* that a score of people were arrested, many of whom are no longer living.

"When I read this, I couldn't stand it any more. I ran away from the sanitarium. A few weeks later I appeared before the Party committee which had refused to rehabilitate me. I stood there in front of those clean-shaven, satisfied Party comrades. I, a mistake of history, you might say, a joke of socialism, a living quarry. I showed them my back. The skin had been torn off with a hook during interrogation. I showed them my feet, the likes of which they'd never seen, not even in a zoo. I showed them my hands which they would not shake when I greeted them. 'You, citizen, are not worthy of rehabilitation. It was your fault that innocent men were convicted by court. You made false accusations against them and signed them with your own hand. You don't deserve to be called a Party member. Our society contemptuously turns away from you. No honest man will shake your hand. There's no recourse from this decision. You may leave . . .'"

The man opposite me clenched his misshapen hands. He didn't cry nor did he look shattered. He appeared controlled and collected. He lowered his head, however, and I could see a long scar where he was bald. After a long, seemingly never-ending time, he straightened out and added, "Unfortunately I didn't have enough strength. Then and there I wanted to kill the man who said it. I wanted to crush his nose as they had crushed my hands and feet. But, I had no strength. My strength remained on the stony plates which now support Party palaces, columns, and monuments. I left without a word, and no one paid any attention to me. The downy rugs and leather-covered walls deadened my steps. I understood then that a vicious circle whirled around me. I don't know how to ride the magic merry-go-round of socialism. My survival was the greatest indictment against me, written by those who convicted me and tortured me until I gave the names of other innocent men. I am accused of the imprisonment and death of these people. But I, too, was a victim. Had I died I would have been granted rehabilitation . . . only I wouldn't need it then. But, because I survived, I cannot receive it. So, here I am still with the eighteen years of prison on my torn back because I don't deserve having them taken off.

". . . Eighteen years . . . monstrous work, blood, sweat, an animal life under inhuman conditions. For this the government gave me a suit of clothes to cover my bare back, dental plates to replace the teeth lost during the interrogations, and a pair of gloves to cover my deformed hands. I also have a job. I shall once again be a teacher. 'It's a noble vocation,' I was told when it was given to me, 'a noble vocation. You will teach children truth, justice, socialism, and love for their country. A noble, lofty profession, that of a Soviet teacher!'"

Our conversation was interrupted by the waiter who asked whether we'd permit a young couple to join us at our table. The place was crowded and there were no other tables available. We agreed reluctantly and in a moment a young girl and her escort sat down. There was a moment of stiff discomfort, followed by mutual introductions and handshaking. When my companion extended his hand to the girl, she noticed its monstrous shape and recoiled in horror, withdrawing her soft white hand quickly . . . the orchestra began to play a tango.

Not long after that evening, I met an old Russian professor, a man of great intellectual and personal culture. I mentioned to him the stories of Soviet justice which I'd heard and waited to see his reaction. For a while the professor would not allow himself to be provoked into discussing the subject. Finally, however, after much evasion, he gave a few opinions which were more of a historical rather than of a personal nature.

"Do not forget," he said, "that our criteria are different from those accepted by other societies. Indeed, unpleasant mistakes do sometimes happen, especially in cases when people interested in certain radical ends interfere with the workings of authority. Do you really think that the Czarist police were so ideal? That they were not subject to the pressures of various other powers, including the power of money? That it did not occasionally help in the pogroms of national minorities? Our police traditions are very strong. The passport regime flourished in Czarist times also. You are too young, but I remember those times perfectly. But to convince you, do you remember what Lermontov wrote about Russia long before the beginning of the twentieth century? Do you remember that he called our nation 'obedient to the blue uniform' and to the 'all-seeing eyes and all-hearing ears' of the Czarist police? You see, these are old, old traditions. We have had time to get accustomed to them. Among other ingenious inventions, history will credit our motherland with introducing the first passport in the world. In our country, family, authority, church have always been closely knit together."

Here the professor touched on an essential factor which I faced many times in the U.S.S.R.—the close tie of the secret police to a number of other political and social institutions. These ties were pointed out by W., an engineer.

"The thing is," he said, "that here in the U.S.S.R., especially in the cities, there exists a dialectic mutual tie-up of all the institutions. All these house committees, registering offices, personnel sections in factories and offices, militia precincts, union and Party organizations, Komsomol, and the like, rule over the destinies of men precisely because they are so strictly bound together. If a man is 'through' on one of these fronts he automatically is finished on all the others. As far as the place of the secret police in this 'topography' is concerned, the matter is quite simple. The agents of the secret police are a part of the working staff of every institution, factory, office, and department store. Sometimes they are regular employees, doing regular work to mask their real role. Other times some employees are pledged to collaboration with the secret police. The initiative of such collaboration may be one- or two-sided. The work consists in maintaining a steady contact with the agent in their factory or directly with an office of the secret police and in making as many friends as possible among the workers in their place of employment. Of course, nobody knows of their collaboration. If, by some accident, they are found out they are immediately transferred elsewhere. It may seem strange, but as far as I know they receive no additional pay for this work. The only thing they can count on is possible help from the labor unions when they try to obtain a better apartment, a better hotel for their vacation, a loan, a coupon entitling them to purchase a motorcycle or a TV set at reduced prices.

"Whereas an agent is known to the factory or office management, these collaborators are anonymous. Sometimes they are even unknown to the representative of the secret police in the place where they work. The idea is to have mutual control between these individuals. By this method the secret police receive a more complete picture of what is going on.

"Being a secret police collaborator is not exactly a pleasant task. You must always expect that one day you may be ordered to give testimony against someone close to you, even if you have not been the one to collect the incriminating material. The reason may be to make the case more credible. It often happens that the authority is absolutely certain that someone is guilty of something, but has no evidence. You may then be given the task of arranging a frame-up. Do you understand?

"On the other hand, when I think it over, I come to the conclusion that potentially every one of us is, to a certain extent, a collaborator of the secret police even if we haven't signed anything up to date. Let's assume that today the secret police summoned me. 'We trust you. We know that you are popular among your co-workers and we want you to work for us. Your first assignment will be . . .' Do you think I could refuse? Of course, I could try to refuse at first, giving reasons such as poor health, great excitability, or being a homebody—but I would be told that that is exactly why I'm so suitable for the work, because no one would suspect me. And what then? If I refuse, in a week I'd be sent to work somewhere beyond Tomsk, and who knows what kind of work it would be. Or they might tell me that they have some evidence against me, enough to send me to a labor camp. And they probably do have it at that. I may know that I haven't done anything wrong, but how do I know that all my friends and colleagues are in the same position? A crime committed by one of them may draw me into trouble.

"I'm telling you all this to make you understand the nature of our environment before you try to understand the nature of the men who grow up in it. While I was still at the University, in my section of seventy-five students at least ten of them collaborated with the secret police.

"But you can see for yourself what the final meaning of it all is. Certain concepts assume entirely different meanings with us. The lines between concepts which seem to be opposite to each other are erased. The most important thing is to live in peace.

"But let's change the subject. Don't let's look for trouble. By the way, did you like the ballet I recommended to you? Wonderful, wasn't it? The prima ballerina just seems to float over the stage, doesn't she? Sometimes it seems as if the laws of gravity and motion, to which we human apes are subject, do not apply to her at all."

I would like to quote another conversation that I had with a young lawyer employed in a control commission that inspects the work in the collective farms (kolhozes) and small agricultural colonies.

The young attorney had been graduated from law school six years before, after which he worked in a small town of a few thousand people for a year. After this he was assigned to this control commission. He is completely engrossed in its work.

". . . Sometimes a man from a big city has difficulty in visualizing a small town. These localities are separated by a few days' horseback ride from the nearest hamlet, equally small and forsaken.

"During certain seasons they are completely cut off from the rest of the world. Whenever I visit a place like that—once upon a time you would say a place forgotten by God, now often forgotten by us, the Soviet Government—it makes me think. Do you realize that the Soviet Union consists mainly of never-ending spaces studded once in a while with populated spots like these?

"The U.S.S.R. isn't only the cities marked on our maps by red stars or large circles. The U.S.S.R. also is an uncountable multitude of settlements, villages, hamlets, dispersed over the vast spaces of the countryside. Sometimes I'm sorry that Gogol or Dostoevsky aren't alive to write about them. What a mine of stories . . . and just the kind of topics for them! These places have preserved their pre-Revolutionary character completely. As a rule, their life hasn't changed. They still depend on nature and their own labor. They still raise Czarist generations, though born in the time of socialism. These generations consist of people deeply attached to the soil and to their own customs. For them the world begins and ends with their own community. It is a world still equipped with ideas of divine power, and magic, and old customs and morals.

"But at the same time it is a world under socialist authority, with a Communist Party, a socialist radio whose antenna juts high over the hamlet, and from time to time with a socialist district attorney like me.

"Can you imagine a world made up of the people of Dostoevsky and Gogol, attired in new clothes, playing their old roles as new socialist parts? I suppose I don't have to explain that in these out-of-the-way places the people and the government live in perfect symbiosis, disturbed only occasionally by a commission like the one I'm in. Common law and socialist law tolerate each other and pass joint verdicts.

"These are places where supplies of products for daily life, received twice a year, are distributed in the most feudal manner under the sun. But the lords are not only the priest and his suite, but also the Party secretary with his suite, and the commander of the local militia with his suite. The lives of all the other people are grouped around these three and their followers.

"If someone doesn't like it and reports to us, he's found one day with his head hacked off or an old rusty knife between his shoulder blades, if he's found at all. When our commission arrives, which probably may be only once a year, everything is just fine. The authorities are satisfied with the people. The people are satisfied with the authorities. Everything is in its proper place, and everybody is at his post. The socialist plan of agricultural production for the hamlet has been carried out with a surplus. Compulsory deliveries to the government have been made on time to the nearest delivery point. Conditions in the kolhozes are exemplary.

"But in reality? In reality, in cases where we manage to break through the conspiracy of silence, we find crime, abuses, injustices, terror, weeping, and everybody is involved! That's why nobody can be accused and nothing can be changed. For example, if we tried to change the commander of the militia post, would his successor act any differently under the circumstances? Let me give you some examples we were able to uncover, but which were never entered in our files and about which we could do nothing because we could find no witnesses. The people who reported these incidents to us refused to supply details or name witnesses.

"In a large kolhoze in an agricultural village the commander of the militia and the secretary of the party were building expensive new houses for themselves. They claimed that they had some money saved up. Well, we knew they were using kolhoze funds, but we couldn't prove it. Still, we transferred both to new posts in distant localities. But what good will this do if the situation which made it possible remains unchanged?

"Here's another example. In a large kolhoze a group of young people tried to force the election of a new management, accusing the old kolhoze authorities of abuses. However, before the attempt got off the ground, the two principal leaders of the group drowned 'accidentally' during a swimming party in the lake. A convenient accident, wasn't it? The old management remains unchanged.

"Another example. In a large agricultural colony a militiaman raped a girl. Her parents and a few of the braver men tried to draw up an indictment and forward the case to a higher authority. The commander of the militia forbade them to do it. After they insisted, the same girl was found the next morning unconscious in a nearby forest. She had been raped by several men, probably all from the militia. Her family had been beaten up and were half dead. All the kolhoze knew about it, but nobody dared talk.

"In other places militia and Party authorities resort to theft, sell goods for their personal profit at prices higher than those set by law, and abuse the gray, docile kolhoze community in all sorts of ways. Of course the criminals are never discovered!

"There are many such instances. You could say that in all these lost, dispersed centers of humanity, Czarist Russia has remained inside a socialist frame. There also has remained the nebulous, enigmatic, Russo-Asiatic soul of these people caught between the Orthodox Church and the police post.

"There's one more thing. Don't ever imagine that these villages may become a tinderbox of rebellion against the government. On the contrary. These are communities which have been accustomed to such treatment for ages. They have only known conditions like these. The social organization of these communities is constant. And it is powerful because it is based on common interest and the subjugation of the weak to the power of the strong."

A few days later I visited a newspaperman in the same hotel where Kr. met disaster in his first contact with a modern lavatory. The journalist had arrived in the U.S.S.R. a few months before from one of the Western countries. He was full of praise for the hotel, its service, and cuisine. But with horror he told me of one experience. About a week after his arrival in Moscow, he missed his address book.

"On previous visits to Moscow," he said, "I had made some friends and had their addresses in this little book. I also had the addresses of some people to whom I was bringing greetings from their relatives abroad. I was quite embarrassed when I couldn't find the notebook anywhere. But the next day quite by accident I discovered it right in the desk drawer. But I was sure I had looked there before.

"Anyway, after I found it I began calling the people on the phone. Strangely enough, not one person was home. Invariably, the person who did answer the phone said that the person I wanted to talk to had left town or could not be reached. It was quite frustrating. Finally, one day I deliberately took a taxi to the address of a woman whose parents, emigrants, had begged me to see her.

"I knocked at the door and she opened it. But when I told her my name, she began to tremble. Frantically she kissed my hands and begged me to leave immediately, saying, 'They have already asked me where I met you, why I didn't tell them about our acquaintance myself. I didn't know what they were talking about. Please go . . . go!'"

"I couldn't give her half of the message sent by her parents. I won't even be able to tell them how she looks. It was too dark in the corridor. Isn't it awful?"

I can remember my own amazement when I was told that if I didn't have the present address of anyone I knew in Moscow, or even if he had ever lived in Moscow, I could get his address at special information offices throughout the city. I was glad to hear this, for I had the names of various soldiers and officers of the Soviet Army with whom I had become acquainted during the war and whom I was anxious to see.

I went to one of these information offices where a courteous girl clerk gave me a form to fill out with places for my name and the name of the person I was looking for. After I filled out the form, the clerk took it and went to the telephone. After five minutes I had the address of a friend. He lived in Tbilisi, capital of the Georgian Republic, at the other end of the U.S.S.R.

"Five minutes to find a man . . . in a country with two hundred million people," I murmured overwhelmed.

"Find?"—laughed the girl. "But he was never lost!"

I must admit that all those stories about control in the U.S.S.R. left their mark on me. More and more often I found myself carefully watching my every word and question. Sometimes I would see everything I did from the viewpoint of a prosecutor in a Soviet court. The feeling that I was never alone grew ever stronger in my mind.

One afternoon when I was walking with a charming girl who was a student at some institute, I couldn't help looking around and watching the passers-by, trying to detect the "plain-clothes comrades."

We walked along the crowded streets and then in the park. My companion noticed my anxiety and my nervous alertness. She nestled closer, her soft, scented blond hair touching my lips and cheeks temptingly.

"Whom are you looking for?" she asked. "Tell me. Are you supposed to meet someone, and am I in your way? Tell me. Is it a he or a she? I'm jealous. Tell me."

We continued our walk in the falling darkness. Human faces faded in the shadow and disappeared. My fears faded. Only the awareness of a young woman close to me remained.

The next day, early in the morning, the phone rang by my bed. Half asleep, blinded by the daylight pouring into the room, I groped for the receiver. It was Volodia, a close friend. He was highly excited, wanted to see me at once, somewhere in town.

I had to take the subway, then a bus to reach the appointed place. Volodia was waiting, very worried. He came close to me and said in a low voice, "Listen carefully; a man I know saw you with a tall, pretty blonde yesterday. You walked towards the park. Be careful, she is . . . well, you know what. She has been working with them for a long time. Be very careful. Don't ever tell her what I told you, and in general don't talk much. Remember, you'll leave here, but we'll stay."

I remembered then, and I still remember. Don't worry, Volodia!

8

REPUBLIC OF
SCHOLARS

THE TOWN WAS LOCATED NEAR NOVGOROD AND IT COULD NOT HAVE had a population of more than 5,000. I had notified a friend of mine, a Polish newspaperman who happened to be touring the U.S.S.R., of my arrival and he was waiting for me at the station. I moved to the house of a worker's family whom he had befriended, and almost at once I found myself in the midst of a problem which had been occupying the minds of the family and all their acquaintances for several days. In fact, it seemed to me that the whole town spoke of nothing else and attributed great importance to the matter. The problem was indeed unusual. The fifteen-year-old son of my hosts, after having passed qualifying preliminary examinations, partly in the local school and partly in Novgorod, had left three or four days ago for Leningrad to take part in the first stage of the Mathematical Olympiad. If he passed the Leningrad semi-finals he would qualify for the All-Soviet Mathematical Olympiad in Moscow with other young and talented mathematical students from all over the U.S.S.R.

I talked with the mathematics teacher in the local grade school, a young level-headed woman. "He is a very capable boy, especially in mathematics," she said. "In our local contests in mathematics, chemistry, and physics last year he took third place in mathematics. This year he took first place. In Novgorod, in the elimination contest between districts, he took fourth place which qualified him for the semi-finals in Leningrad. If he does well there, in a few months he will go to Moscow for the Mathematical Olympiad. In this way, each year the most gifted

students in various fields are selected. Emphasis is placed on
the sciences where natural capabilities are particularly important.
These selected students are surrounded with special attention
by school authorities. They are exempt from various social tasks
and are taught the habit of working independently and crea-
tively. Of course, all expenses connected with the trips to the
Olympiads are paid by the state. Incidentally, expenses connected with all learning are paid by the state.

"You can imagine that such yearly selections from all over
the U.S.S.R. yield an excellent crop of the most capable individuals, sometimes a genius who may never have been discovered otherwise."

After this I, too, shared in the excitement of the town, waiting
for the return of the talented young mathematician. When he
did come back, he was greeted by all the young people in the
town and its vicinity, by the school authorities, and representatives of youth and Party groups. The boy had passed the Leningrad tests, taking third place. As a result, he would take part
in the Mathematical Olympiad in Moscow.

His parents were very proud. "If you continue like this," his
father said at supper, "you'll be a great man some day. You'll
study in Moscow at the Lomonosov University. You'll live in a
fine dormitory, go to classes in beautiful halls. Later, after you
graduate, you'll be a great scientist and even the members of
the Central Committee will talk to you with respect, because
I'm sure they know nothing about mathematics."

The boy sat and listened to his father's praises quietly, gob-
bling up the third plateful of soup put in front of him by his
mother who hovered solicitously over him. On the bureau,
awards received by the boy from school, youth, and political
authorities for good marks in school and success in the elimination contest were displayed. They consisted of a beautifully
bound set of Gorki; Lermontov's poems; a large finely illustrated
album about the history of inventions made by Russians; an
album with color photographs showing the life of students at
"the most beautiful university of the world," Lomonosov University, Moscow; plus other smaller gifts such as a pen-and-pen-
cil set, a leather briefcase, and a notebook with a leather
binding.

After supper we thumbed through the album about inventions. The book was beautifully painted with many photographs, reproductions, and drawings. It bore a mark signifying approval by educational authorities for use as supplementary material in the schools of the U.S.S.R. We learned from it that almost all of the fundamental inventions were made by Russians. However, some were stolen from the Russians by cunning Western industrialists and their agents. Russian inventions included the radio, the telephone, the electric light, the airplane, the internal-combustion motor, the steam engine, the pneumatic hammer . . . page after page listed the discoveries, with the portraits of the inventors and pictures or diagrams of their work.

The mother of our young mathematician stroked his fair hair. "See, Grisha, you'll be in this book some day. Other boys will read about you and your inventions. Maybe they'll even write about your mother and father in some book. Who can tell? You're a Russian, and we Russians are a clever people. Look at all these inventions, all by Russians."

In the evening the Polish newspaperman and I went out for a stroll. "What do you think of that list of Russian inventions?" he asked. "Isn't it a disgrace to distort history like that? Soon they'll be claiming that the first man who tried to fly like a bird was not Icarus, but a Russian called Icarenkov. It burns me up . . ."

Two weeks later I was back in Moscow to spend time at the University in connection with my work. The professor in whose organization I worked took me around Lomonosov University. Its size impressed me. It was monumental, especially when compared with the average Soviet building. As our elevator was carrying us to the top floor, we passed groups of tourists visiting the University.

They were walking up and down the wide stairways following guides. I heard a snatch of the talk by one guide, "This university was built by Soviet engineers and Soviet workers for Soviet scholars. It is the largest and most modern university in the world. Which is as it should be, since it serves the most advanced learning in the world and educates the greatest scientists of our era, the scientists of the U.S.S.R. To the generations educated in this University will fall the honorable and responsible mission of leading the victory over imperialism and the building of world socialism."

During my work at the University I became quite friendly with a student of philosophy, Nikolai A. K. Nikolai was eighteen and a freshman when I met him. Born near the city of Kirov, he was graduated from the local tenth grade school. As a shock worker, he was admitted to Moscow University. It was a great distinction.

He had a small, cozy room in the University dormitory with all comforts and a lovely view. Nikolai was an activist in Komsomol and expected to become a teacher of philosophy, provided, of course, the results of his studies warranted it, and provided he could get himself assigned to such a post.

He kept a diary and had been doing so for two years. He said that he wrote it for himself. When we became friendlier, he let me read it. It was most interesting, an accurate record and evaluation of all the more important events in his school life.

Upon my request, he loaned it to me. I selected the following excerpts which dealt with Nikolai's first contacts with University life.

Monday: At last! My dreamed of goal, the University! The monotonous chain of class—recess—class—recess which dragged on through ten long school years is a thing of the past! All the end term exams, class compositions, reviews, class meetings belong to the past!

I can hardly believe that I'm here. Citizen Nikolai A. K., eighteen, admitted to Lomonosov University, the pride of the U.S.S.R. and the envy of the whole world.

I'm not conceited, yet I suppose I can congratulate myself first, then my Komsomol groups in school, then my teachers, then my parents. Ten years of school! How much work, emotion, nervousness they represent. How many renunciations of beautiful afternoons that I spent poring over books, notes and homework. How many hot days when my mind was really full of the beach, water, and sun.

But there was nothing else I could do. Want to be a man?

Then study. Want to go to the University? Then get good marks. Want to get good marks? Then study systematically. Want to study systematically? Then work in a group. Don't let yourself be torn away from your group. So I worked for good marks. I studied systematically. I was active in Komsomol. For it all, I received the title of Shock Worker in Science and Social Work. After graduation, I was allowed to enroll in the University. I was sent to Moscow University, the best of the best. As a shock worker, I was exempt from the entrance exams which are far from easy. About 30 per cent of the applicants are eliminated by the examinations. They must go to work, and after a year may try again, provided they have proved themselves deserving. So, I'm beginning a new life. . . .

Wednesday: Goodness, what a fantastic place this is! What corridors, rooms, columns, statues! A fairy tale palace couldn't look better than this! Marble, precious stones, elevators that climb up noiselessly with doors that shut by themselves.

When you are on the top floor, all Moscow lies at your feet, Citizen Nikolai. Or you could say that all of the U.S.S.R. looks up towards the tower of my University.

Crowds of students from all over the U.S.S.R. move to and fro. There are many foreigners, Chinese, Koreans, Arabs, even some from European countries. Opening ceremonies, splendid, most impressive with an interesting speech.

Friday: Today we had a meeting of all freshmen majoring in philosophy. There were about two hundred persons, with a slight majority of men. We were divided into student groups with about twenty-five persons to a group. My group consists of students living in the University dormitories. I think it's a very good group. Most of us are Russian, but we also have two Ukrainians, one Uzbek, one Tatar girl, and three Chinese. The scholastic level of the group seems to be about even. Perhaps we'll have to help the Chinese a little to bring them up to our level.

We met the men from the teachers' group, the Party organization, the union organization and Komsomol who will be the advisors of the freshman class. They were very nice people, and seemed energetic and strict. So much the better. We'll do better work.

Monday: Today we had a Komsomol meeting of the freshman class. With the exception of about eighteen people, mostly foreigners, we were all members of Komsomol. We were divided into groups, which are the same as the student groups. In my group only the Chinese didn't belong to Komsomol. But I'm sure they'll attend the meetings of our Komsomol group.

The lectures are already well under way. I have an average of forty hours of lectures and seminars weekly. The lectures are attended by the whole first year, the seminars by two groups at a time. In the seminars we discuss the topics we learned in the lectures. We write papers and answer questions. We learn to apply materialistic analysis and Marxist dialectics to concrete historical and economic situations.

In each group, one person has been appointed to check attendance at the lectures. In the seminars, attendance is checked by the professor. The study discipline is very severe, even though it's only the beginning of the year. All absences must be excused by the University authorities. An absent student must bring an official certificate from a doctor in the clinic of the University. Or, if his absence was caused by a summons to some office, the office must give him a certificate.

For unexcused absence, the student must appear before the disciplinary committee of the department. The committee is composed of the representatives of the University, the Party, Komsomol, and of the students' group of which the accused student is a member. For three unexcused absences, a student may be expelled from the University charged with 'trespassing against socialist study discipline!'

If the student has a scholarship, and almost all have, he loses it and the University Committee for Work Assignment gives him a task for which his incomplete studies fit him.

Lateness for lectures or seminars falls under the jurisdiction of the students' group of which the student is a member. If the group decides that tardiness was due to neglect, the case is referred to the disciplinary committee along with the opinion of the group. The students' group even has the right to request that a student be expelled from the University if he violates some principle of communist morality outside the University, despite the fact that as a student he may perform all his duties.

Wednesday: Today, at a meeting of our students' and Komsomol groups, we elected group officers. Until now everything was temporary. But now that we know each other sufficiently, permanent authorities can be elected.

The oldest and most capable of us, Mishka V. V., twenty years old, was elected secretary of the students' group. He distinguished himself right from the start. He speaks very well. He is always prepared at the seminars, and is the first to volunteer when the professor calls for someone to answer a question. He has an excellent background. His father is a worker and a devoted Party activist. Mishka himself is a member of Komsomol and worked for three summers as a voluntary harvest helper.

After we finished the students' group elections, we began to elect officers for the Komsomol group. A girl was elected secretary. Her name is Vala C. B. She is a well-known Komsomol activist in the Moscow district. She graduated from the tenth-grade school five years ago, then worked in the Komsomol field organizations. Only this year was she delegated to study. She is very energetic and probably will have a strong hold on our group. Maybe it's better that way . . .

I was nominated for treasurer of the Komsomol group but somone else received more votes. That's all right. Unfortunately I don't have as much talent for influencing people as some of my colleagues. Perhaps I'm too slow. I imagine a good speaker and agitator must be very quick. He must be impressionable. The atmosphere surrounding him must infect him. He must be sensitive to the vibrations, changes, moods, of his surroundings. I don't have this talent, and that's why it won't be easy for me to stand out in a group. Others will do it much sooner . . .

Monday: Gosh, we have so much work. We're all ticking like well-wound clocks from lectures to library, from library to seminars, from seminars to a meeting of youth or Party. I can hardly catch up. I'm behind in my reading on the political economy of capitalism and on the history of human thought.

I have two or three meetings every week: the students' group, the Komsomol group, the reviewing circle, the Society for Sino-Soviet Friendship.

From time to time special meetings take place, such as the Review of Current Political Events at Home and Abroad, debates, group visits to a theater or movies. My time is full as never before in my life. And it's going to get worse later. Before the exams we'll review our material in groups.

Thursday: I can hardly believe that the first three months of my University years have already passed! It seems like a week, at most. Still, in this time everybody in our section has become so well acquainted with each other that it seems as though we've known each other for years. It means a lot to be together, work together, have the same interests.

In the students' group or Komsomol meetings we all take part in discussions of the personal affairs of each of us. If we know each other so well now, imagine how well we'll know each other in four years!

Now I understand the principle of the group as I never understood it before. Only through the group can people get to know each other so thoroughly. In a family the parents can never get to know their children so well, especially since they are never with their family in the daytime but only at night when everybody is asleep.

Saturday: My report on current international events met with very serious criticism by the class. Several people accused me of giving a schematic list of events without dwelling on their causes, without evaluating them or showing their significance in dialectical historical processes.

Some criticisms were very strong. One colleague, for instance, said that "from a student of philosophy, which is, after all, the science of the Party, and from a Komsomol member, one would not only expect evaluation of phenomena from the Party viewpoint and a Marxist-Leninist analysis, but also Party fervor, enthusiasm, and curiosity."

It's easy to say. But after all, I didn't want to repeat what anybody could read in the newspapers. Those who crave 'Party

curiosity' can reach for a copy of *Pravda*, to which we all sub-
scribe, or *Izvestia*, or any other paper.

Just the same, I wasn't right. My next report on current international events will be swimming in ideological gravy, and that
should make them happy for a while.

I wonder whether this unsuccessful report will be discussed
at the meeting of the students' or Komsomol groups. We'll see
in three days. . . .

Tuesday: Well, I was right. The matter of my unsuccessful
report was brought up by the secretary at the meeting of the
Komsomol group. There was a brief discussion. A few people
recommended rather casually more thorough preparation of reports of this type.

Vala, the group secretary, said, "Marxism-Leninism is life
itself. It is the laws of life, progress, development. We study
Marxism-Leninism to apply it to daily life, so that we can
think in its terms. These terms are proven by the practice of
our Party and the practice of the international communist movement. Comrade Nikolai should reconsider his relationship to his
report and realize what caused his ideological deficiencies."

I took the floor after Vala and conceded all her points. I
promised to write my next report on current events in a different
and better way. I also volunteered to do the next report in
three weeks. Gosh, I don't know how I'll make it!

Saturday: I can see that the ideological temperature of our
department is rising steadily, though it's mighty cold outside.
There's real icy Moscow weather.

Yesterday, at a dialectics seminar, three students attacked
Professor S., who is in charge of the seminar, for, as they said,
"overestimation of the scientific contribution of the scholars
of other European countries while omitting Russian scholars,
and for attributing too much importance to various West
European pseudoscientific theories."

The professor was very much upset. After all, he is over
fifty. But he promised to review his course once more and discuss
it with his colleagues to ascertain whether his teachings really
went beyond the program of the Ministry.

We took the matter up at the meeting of the students' group, but opinions were divided. Some people thought that the professor, who was not a Party member, may have indeed lost his sense of proportion in favor of the bourgeois countries. Others said that this was not true. All the professor did was to lecture on some views of bourgeois scholars too objectively, without proper evaluation. The matter will be decided in a few days, at the next seminar. We'll see then where we stand.

Thursday: Ideologically, it's getting hotter and hotter. A combined meeting of the students' and Komsomol groups is scheduled for tomorrow to discuss 'personal affairs.' There's great excitement. Nobody knows whose personal affairs will be brought up. We were informed of the meeting by Vala, the secretary of the Komsomol group. Mishka, the secretary of the students' group is also very upset. He doesn't know what it's all about either. We'll see tomorrow.

Saturday: Well, it's all over. The meeting lasted from 4 P.M. to 1 A.M.

The 'personal affair' concerned Mishka, the secretary of the students' group. Who would have suspected it? And it was some affair.

The meeting was attended by Assistant Professor K., the faculty advisor of our group, and by the Komsomol secretary for the entire department. Mishka's affair was presented by Vala, speaking for the Komsomol organization.

The charge concerned his relationship with one Olga L., a clerk in some office or distribution center, whom he had known for two years. Mishka severed his relations with Olga after two years, claiming that her intellectual standards were incompatible with his, especially now that he was a University student. He had discovered new horizons that she would never be able to find. We all knew that the truth of it was that Mishka had become friendly with a girl in our department.

In her accusation against Mishka, Vala said among other things, "Comrade Mishka V. V. has proven himself two-faced, hypocritical, and unworthy of being a socialist student. In his relationship with comrade Olga, whose Komsomol organization referred her case to us, he spoke of her 'intellectual level.' However, at the same time, he himself never as much as mentioned Olga's existence to his new friend in our department. On the contrary, in our interview with this new friend it came out that Mishka had cynically assured her that she was the first close friend he had ever had.

"Comrade Mishka stated that he has the right to arrange his private life as he pleases. That is not true, comrade, not true at all. Your private life does not take place on a desert island, not even in a bourgeois, capitalistic island. Your private life takes place in a socialistic society and by grace of this society. That's why your private life is subordinated to the life of this society, just as your person is subordinated to our students' and Komsomol groups which in a moment will pass judgment on your behavior. Comrades, please speak up."

Almost every one of us had something to say. Mishka's behavior was naturally condemned. He made a feeble effort to defend himself, but only harmed himself more because he was then charged with obstinacy and conceit, excessive ambition, and defiance. In conclusion, Vala spoke once more, and after her the advisor of our department.

Someone moved that Mishka be reprimanded and the reprimand recorded in his personal file. In the voting that followed two students abstained, but all the rest voted for the motion. Next, I made a motion, which was logical, that Mishka be removed from the office of secretary of the students' group. The motion was adopted unanimously.

Mishka tried to fall back on self-criticism, but the effort failed. He lost all his self-confidence, and it sounded like an oration. So he promised to reconsider his attitude, thanked the group for its sincere criticism, and that was the end of the personal portion of the meeting.

In a special election, we elected a new secretary of the students' group. Mishka's fate lifted my spirits a bit. He had been so influential, popular, brilliant. Yet after one group meeting nothing was left except the record in his personal file that on such and such a day, in his freshman year of philosophy,

Mishka V. V. received a reprimand from the Komsomol and students' group for. . . .

Monday: We are all working like horses. Everybody's cheeks are flushed from feverish study, note-jotting, cramming, endless reviewing. We have formed review teams to try and help the weaker students. The point is that the combined marks of our group must not be inferior to those of other groups. To lose in this competition would be a great disgrace. All the members of our group live in the University dormitories and have scholarships. We have, therefore, the best possible conditions for study.

Friday: My report in the history seminar was a success. The professor didn't have many reservations. The only severe criticism came from Andrey B. W. who said that it lacked "any originality in concept and the author limited himself to traditional repetition of traditional arguments in traditional sequence."

Andrey is the best history student in our department, but I think he overdid it this time, because he gave no convincing arguments to support his judgment.

Tuesday: We were given the schedule for our mid-term exams. I hope I'll be ready! Now I even study while riding in the elevators and while eating. At night I dream of my economics book, about historical data, about discussing and defending my views. . . .

Wednesday: At the meeting of the Komsomol group I pledged myself, along with all the others, to pass all my exams with the best marks possible. The delegates of our group, together with the delegates of the entire department, have worked out a plan with the professors to allow us to repeat exams in case any of us don't receive the highest grades.

We study without rest. A group of three students is in control of our whole life. They have been appointed to check on our state of preparedness, on the list of books we read, the way we make notes in the lectures, our proficiency in seminars and in discussions.

Tuesday: I'm so busy I can hardly find time to write a few sentences in my diary. I passed three exams very well. They were very stiff. The professor covered the entire material of the course.

I have four more exams left, two of them based on the economics and history seminars. In a week, the students' and Komsomol groups will meet to appraise the results of the exams. Some will be scolded, I know. Not all the students were as prepared as they should have been. There'll probably be a change in the Komsomol officers. Vala, our secretary, received poor marks in two exams and will have to answer for that. So, busy weeks lie ahead of me again. I'll have to give up my diary for the time being.

So, let's leave Nikolai to his own affairs. He is very busy indeed, and spends most of his time in the excellently equipped University Library, or at the various meetings which absorb him as much as study.

Let's now turn to other aspects of Soviet learning.

An Assistant Professor of International Law in the Law Department of Lomonosov University, an acquaintance of mine, told me that after 1953 vital changes were made in, as he put it, "the distribution of emphasis on the various branches of learning."

"You see," he said, amplifying the statement, "from the time of the 1917 Revolution until Stalin's death, humanistic studies, especially philosophy, political economy, and history, were so closely knit with the policy of the Party and the U.S.S.R. that they became the most important areas of Soviet learning.

"This does not mean that the natural sciences were left behind. They did develop, but without the hubbub and applause which accompanied each new work by Lenin, Stalin or Kalinin, and Zhdanov, or a collection of articles by Molotov or Vishinsky.

"The humanistic studies were reserved, in those years, for the politicians, and they constituted, as the phrase went, 'the weapon for the struggle with bourgeois thinking.' Hence all the debates and purges occasionally taking place in humanistic studies and through them in the theoretical parts of the natural sciences.

"In those years only 'politically reliable' persons were admitted to humanistic studies—persons who were going to take up a political-administrative career or a scholarly career which was on the same level as a political career and which could lead to a distinguished position.

"After 1953—to be more exact after the Twentieth Congress of the Party—the situation changed radically. First of all, the international situation forced an intensified armament and technological effort upon our country. Aside from that, the realistic policy of Khrushchev's new Central Committee, which attacked the so-called cult of the individual, resulted in a downgrading of the humanism in which that cult flourished. Humanism was accused of falsifying history and economics, of making myths of reality, and of other similar errors.

"To the natural sciences, especially physics, mathematics, and chemistry, was now given the role of repairing the errors made by philosophy, economics, and history. As a result, the criteria for judging the importance of a scholar changed also. First place was given to the representatives of real sciences, mathematicians or physicists. These sciences were to convince the Soviet people and the foreign followers of communism and the U.S.S.R. of the superiority of the socialistic system over the capitalistic system and of the superiority of the military power of the U.S.S.R.

"Present theory proclaims that capitalism will not collapse by itself under the pressure of political economy, but will collapse due to and through the power of Soviet Russia. The power of the U.S.S.R. is said to be the result of the polytechnicalization of the Soviet society, and not of its continuous political growth.

"That's why we expect our school system to be radically reformed in the near future. This reform will be based on the premise that the fundamental element of socialist schooling is preparation for an occupation, for a concrete occupation in a definite branch of industry.

"Academic studies will be made possible for gifted individuals, especially in the natural sciences to which the future belongs. Some of us teachers believe that fields such as political economy, philosophy, law, and history will be reduced to small departments which will educate teachers primarily, or will be attached to Institutes of Agricultural or Industrial Economy to educate cadres of experts to organize and manage production.

"In this way, the reform of the school system of the U.S.S.R. will become the most revolutionary reform of its kind carried out anywhere in modern times. Even considering the size of the U.S.S.R. and the wide-spread educational system already in existence, such a reform would change the face of Soviet education in a few years.

"Certain substantial changes in the organization of research work in the sciences were already introduced as far back as 1946. Then the first large centers for theoretical and practical research were organized outside the universities. They operated in complete independence from the official and open academic scientific centers.

"In any case, I have no doubt whatsoever that the present Central Committee of the Party considers its first task in education to be the carrying out of a gigantic reform that will lead to the polytechnicalization of the entire educational system and that will base the entire new structure of Soviet learning on polytechnicalization."

I talked to an old professor of mathematics who had retired in 1957 because of his age. The professor was proud of many of his former students who had become leading mathematicians and physicists. We talked about the teaching of mathematics and physics in the Soviet universities.

"It's true that much has changed recently," the professor said. "Formerly, in Stalin's time, we students of science suffered from a kind of inferiority complex. We were underprivileged because of the lack of political elements in our sciences. But, probably because of this, we were also free of those periodic upheavals inflicted upon the humanistic sciences. Not a few times, these storms struck prominent scholars who became silent for many years as a result. Though the students of history and economics kept company with the gods as if on Olympus, they were compelled by these gods to mechanically repeat the theories given them to believe. Somehow, in mathematics, we succeeded in escaping this. It is true that some attempts were made against certain theoretical premises in mathematics and physics as well, but it all ended in a few unimportant articles condemning one thing or another.

"Now the situation is different. Politicians listen humbly to the scientists because they realize that it is the scientists who are building their political power. It is also true that large scientific centers have been organized, although they suffer from the unavoidable shortcoming that they are completely cut off from the rest of the world and they still work on the old principle of strategically important goals.

"However, from the viewpoint of a scientist these centers are as nearly ideal as they can be. The state equips them with the most ultramodern equipment and sets no limit to expenses. They have an absolutely free hand in experimentation, tests, and plans. The staffs of these centers, often numbering several thousand, are composed of the best specialists from all over the country, and frequently from abroad also. The best possible conditions for work and recreation are provided.

"You could call them little islets cut off on all sides from any contact with normal society. Every person who works there is, in fact, a 'lifetime worker.' They will always remain within the scope of their speciality and will mostly work in such isolated centers. But then what more could a scientist ask for?

"At first, science students may not like the idea of working their whole lives in these 'cages for birds of paradise,' as they call them, nor the fact that to their families they'll remain only a post-office number for life. But in time they will get used to it. Especially since these centers often become the size of small towns where they can always find interesting friends and acquaintances. Yes, young man, a new era is coming in science. The place of society in science has changed, but so has the place of science in society."

The principles under which each scientific organization operates in the U.S.S.R. were explained to me briefly at Moscow State University by the secretary of the Party organization in one of the departments.

He said, "Socialism is a system in which the principal role is played by technical and scientific workshops. Preparing cadres to work in these workshops is the primary duty of the Party and the government. That's why the real ruling body of the universities and of the entire educational system is the Party.

"In the University, the Party organization includes the students through a tight connection between the students' groups, the Komsomol, the students' union, and the members of the Party executive committee. It includes the faculty and the administrative staff through labor unions and through training and political work. The University is a factory producing scholars.

"If you were familiar with our factories and then saw our University, you would see what little difference there is between them. At the University and the factory, the group is the main principle. Like the worker, the student works and lives in groups. He belongs to them, and to a decisive extent they shape his attitudes and make his progress possible. In the University, no student or worker is left out of the group principle, and all these groups are interwoven tightly. Students' groups include the members of the Party or union cells in the department, and faculty members are also members of these cells.

"Each affair of the students' group finds an echo in the Party or union organization, and through them reaches the professors and scientific workers who are responsible for the progress of the students' group. Thus nothing can escape the Party's attention and in this lies the Party responsibility for the University and for the production of scholars.

"The responsibility is grave. For instance, if a students' group receives worse marks at the examination than other equivalent groups, the fault may be that of the professors, assistants, and the Komsomol, but it is mainly the responsibility of the executive of the Party organization who failed to see in time why the group's work was inferior and neglected to correct this state of affairs.

"Say a professor should raise or lower the standards of his examinations regardless of orders. To us, the Party, falls the duty of investigating the matter and, if need be, having the educational authorities arrange for new examinations. And so, as you see, everything centers in our Party executive committee which is the heart and brains of the University.

"Naturally the University is organized to facilitate, not hamper, this work. All the responsible and key positions are occupied

by Party members who control the fulfillment of party instructions. Besides this, the Party organization is tightly interwoven with the trade-union organization, with Komsomol, with
training and cultural organizations and so on. No individual in
the University can avoid being in one of these organizations. And
as soon as he belongs to one, you understand, he belongs to all
of them. From this viewpoint, there's no difference between
the rector of the University and the janitor, between a professor
and a student. But as proven by the history of the U.S.S.R.,
only this type of social, political, and professional organization
of science results in complete success and assures that progress
takes place throughout the country."

This concept of scientific collectivity is not embraced enthusiastically by all scholars. I remember meeting a professor from
one of the satellite countries of Eastern Europe. The professor
worked in the field of mathematical computers and came to the
U.S.S.R. for a scientific consultation. He had just taken part
in this consultation when I met him. These consultations are
carried out in the U.S.S.R. for the scientists of satellite countries
under the pretext of 'co-ordination and guidance in the direction of scientific research.'

This professor told me, "Certain fields of scientific research
were included in the so-called strategic plan for exchange of
scientific experiments, directed for all the satellite countries
by the U.S.S.R. and its research centers. From the viewpoint of
the U.S.S.R. the matter is quite simple. The idea is to take over
results of the research of scientists in the satellite countries and
to use this research in the Soviet science centers which have
financial resources at their disposal that are much greater than
the resources of the poor and neglected centers of the satellite
countries.

"To us, however, the scientists of these countries, there is
another side to the matter. Every now and then we must go to
the U.S.S.R. for these consultations. During them a Soviet professor, or several professors, are assigned to us to become familiar with the direction and achievements of our theoretical-ex-
perimental work. Because this procedure is being carried out on
the basis of that so-called 'strategic plan' the data and information we give must be very accurate and complete. It is later

checked with the appropriate authorities in our countries. Therefore nothing can be concealed.

"But this is not the point I want to emphasize. The point is that in this way many of us are forced to divulge the results of our work, sometimes our whole life's work, to an anonymous team of Soviet scientists. Very often our work concerns matters that are not directly related to their strategic plan. But where there's the desire, anything can be made a part of 'strategically important matter.' Afterwards, it's not unusual to come across the results of our research and experiments printed in Soviet scientific periodicals or in reports from conventions and scientific congresses as a 'new victory of Soviet science' or to find them simply signed by certain Soviet scientists as their own. Well, no matter how great our indignation and resentment, we can't do anything about it. We must continue to attend 'consultations.' That's why you see me here."

We talked about the organization of Soviet knowledge and scientific research, which is called by some people a genuine 'kingdom of scholars.' The professor laughed bitterly at these words, "Get on, with your kingdom of scholars—it's simply a socialist republic of scholars, that's all!"

The professor thought that, like the organization of the rest of Soviet society, the organization of Soviet science will become more tightly controlled in the future. In his opinion, the long-term goals of the U.S.S.R. outside the country require an iron social organization within the country, an organization capable of repelling any possible shock from without which the U.S.S.R. may have to reckon with. Therefore, the professor felt, the future would only bring more perfect and more severe forms of organization.

"Communism," the professor said, "is principally organization, a way of management, of control over society and production. It is a certain method of political and economic authority. Ideology is a secondary factor, and explains nothing. On the contrary, it muddies and complicates a clear understanding of the substance of the matter. Who knows, maybe that's its purpose?"

We walked through the wide corridors of the University. When we reached the rotunda, paved with marble, we suddenly lowered our voices. There was a strange acoustic phenomenon here. The lowest whisper was echoed and intensified by the walls and ceiling. It resounded for a moment around us, to die out afterwards in the corridors, corridors radiating in all directions filled with light, marble, and silence.

9

A TRIP ABROAD

WHILE NEAR LENINGRAD, I PAID A VISIT TO AN INDUSTRIAL PLANT where several scores of workers had just returned from a visit abroad. One group had visited France, another Italy.

There was a discussion of these organized tours at a special meeting of the Party group at the factory. Almost all the employees were in the great factory hall. The meeting was open, which meant that workers who were not Party members might attend also.

On the front wall facing us hung the traditional transparencies and slogans. On either side of a large portrait of Lenin were portraits of the secretaries of the French and Italian Communist Parties, Jacques Duclos and Palmiro Togliatti.

The secretary of the Party organization opened the meeting. He talked about the necessity for continually raising the ideological and political standards of the Soviet workers. One of the ways to raise this standard was, in his opinion, by means of trips organized by the Party and the government for the most deserving Soviet workers to leading capitalist countries.

The secretary was followed by the man who had guided the tour to France. He was secretary of the factory labor union. "The organization of our tour," he explained, "was executed efficiently and according to plan. The comrades who took part became familiar with everything that makes up present day France. During their sight-seeing tours, in their frank talks with the people of the French cities, towns, and villages, our Soviet comrades came to know not only the beautiful scenery of the country, but also the basic problems of French capitalism, the exploitation and misery of large masses of workers, the French proletariat.

"On their first trip to a capitalist country our comrades consolidated the ties of fraternity and friendship with the French Communists, the best part of today's France. In discussing the organizational side of our trip, I want to emphasize the fine discipline of our comrades who adhered strictly to group sightseeing, which protected us from the ever present danger of being provoked by police or by fascist and pronouncedly anti-Soviet elements.

"The only serious lapse in discipline—and I'm talking about Comrade M.—did not disturb the unity of our excursion. Comrade M., willfully and on his own responsibility, separated from our group for one whole day. He exposed himself and all of us to unforeseeable consequences and trouble which could have resulted from his action. Comrade M.'s case will be the subject of discussion at a session of the executive board of the Party organization and will be taken up by the mixed Party-union commission as well.

"In closing, let me once more express my honest socialist thanks from the depths of my heart to our Party and our Soviet Government for having organized this trip for us . . . a trip which once again confirms the righteousness of the road we are following. Long live our Party . . . long live the great U.S.S.R., the haven of world peace and socialism!"

We left the crowded meeting. I had never been in France or Italy so I naturally was anxious to hear what the travelers would have to say. Nor had I ever toured in a group, so I was curious to hear about the organizational side of this successful trip to one of the most interesting countries of the old world.

I saw the secretary of the union begin to leave the suffocating atmosphere of the hall, wiping perspiration from his forehead. A few friends and I caught him and invited him for a well-deserved dinner.

A short time later, with the tasty meal helped along by strong wine, he began to enliven our conversation with information about the organization of tours abroad. Comrade Secretary swallowed the last bite of his dessert then, loosening his tie, he began. "You see, comrades, the organization of a trip abroad is a very serious thing. There's no good trip without good organization. Without proper organization, the trip would never take place at all.

"I had to take a special course before taking over the leadership of our tour of France. One of the instructors explained that it's no trick to organize the trips of foreigners visiting the U.S.S.R., but it's quite a job to organize a trip abroad from the U.S.S.R., especially to capitalist countries.

"The excursions which come to the U.S.S.R. have a long tradition and have won the good will of hundreds of thousands of tourists from all the capitalist countries. But now we must create a tradition of trips from the U.S.S.R., and we must try to live up to the standards of those other excursions. You might wonder what the most important thing is in a trip abroad from the U.S.S.R.

"Well, I'll tell you. The most important thing is group organization. What does that mean? It means that from the moment it leaves the U.S.S.R. the entire excursion group is one body, and it is the same body that it was in the U.S.S.R., in Soviet life. Why? Because in this way we don't really leave the U.S.S.R., but only go look at another country. That's why we make the excursion in the same group that exists in the U.S.S.R. in our factory. A stronger discipline must be observed in an excursion group than anywhere else.

"Comrades—tourists must bear in mind that their behavior during an excursion abroad is a test of their political training in the U.S.S.R. Our tour has a rigid program for seeing the country which we visit. Everything is ready, waiting for us—busses, hotels, guides. Meetings with personnel at factories which we intend to visit have been arranged. In order to assure the success of our excursion and give us a maximum of opportunity to observe various fields of life, the employees of our diplomatic missions have planned and prepared everything well in advance of our arrival.

"If any one, for instance Comrade M. of whom I spoke at the meeting, breaks away from the program which was arranged for our own good, what does it prove? It proves that he really was alien to the organization of our life in the U.S.S.R., since he broke away from it as soon as he found himself abroad. It proves that deep in his heart the ideals governing our life are alien, that he does not feel compatible with his fellow Soviet workers, that he is a stranger among us. It also proves that he was anxious to see something special in that foreign country and the Soviet excursion group interfered with this private interest of his, so he had to break away from our group.

"But forget about him. His case will be taken up by more competent people. So, as you see, our excursions are organized, you might say, dialectically. Thanks to such organization, our workers get to see the various sides of life in a foreign country, frequently opposite sides. This helps them to come away with the proper view of the whole thing. But you'd do best if you talked about it with the people who made the trip. They'll tell you what they saw. They'll show you pictures and souvenirs."

Yevgenia was the wife of a factory engineer and worked in the same section as her husband. She was selected for the excursion by a woman's organization in which she was a volunteer social worker. Yevgenia was a university graduate, had read a lot, had a keen mind with well-balanced, thought-out views on most matters.

She gave us her impressions from the tour of France with great animation. Her impressions were still fresh in her mind, though they already had been put into a frame of reference and co-ordinated with what she thought she knew about France before her trip. A pile of pictures taken by Yevgenia in different places in France lay on the table. Most of them, of course, were of Paris.

"Paris," Yevgenia glanced through the pictures, "what a lovely city! I must admit I had imagined it to be quite different. When I had read Balzac or Erenburg, Victor Hugo or the historical novels of Tarlé, I received quite a different picture of Paris. The French films I had seen didn't tell me much.

"When we arrived, everything was ready. We were given guidebooks, specially printed for us, and albums with photographs. Look how well printed they are. Busses took us everywhere; we visited the most interesting places. It's such a big city, you know, but we were still able to see a lot.

"Once we went to see the sections of the city where the bourgeoisie and the capitalists live. We saw how they live, on the

Rue de Flandre, the Rue du Faubourg-St.-Honoré . . . you know, near the Place de la Concorde. We saw their palaces and villas. I tell you their apartments must have ten or more rooms, with big windows and balconies. In front of the houses stand rows of cars, very strange. Some are very long with tails, and some are small, multicolored, and flat . . . like children's toys.

"And the women who live in these houses and ride these cars . . . goodness!" Excited, Yevgenia got up and started to pace the room with a heavy, almost manly, step. "They look like caricatures. They have colored hair, would you believe it? Green, blue, and red the color of brick. They paint their faces in different colors. Eyes, cheeks, lips, each item a different color. They put on false eyelashes like our actresses when on stage. Would you believe it? And looking like that they walk right down the street in the daytime! They meet your eyes shamelessly and have the nerve to smile at you.

"And the way they dress . . . my gosh!" Yevgenia wrung her hands, overwhelmed by the memory of her astonishment. "They wear huge hats with wide brims, or tiny caps low on their foreheads, like the ones that were worn here by the wives of Czarist officers before the Revolution.

"And their skirts are ridiculously tight, like those of dancing girls, or so short that they hardly reach their knees, or slitted on the side so that you can see positively everything. They all look as if they had just escaped from a circus, or something.

"The jewelry they put on their necks and ears! Earrings that hang down to their shoulders!

"Then the men, goodness! They're sleek, like dolls, with pointed shoes like those worn by circus clowns in our country and trousers as narrow as possible. I don't know how they can get out of them, unless they sleep in them, they're so round.

"They kiss in the street without shame and hug and touch each other. They don't care if there are people around. You know, our guide explained it very wisely. 'The bourgeoisie,' he said, 'separated from the problems of everyday life and work, and being basically anti-national, loses its last vestige of morality. It doesn't see any future in the dying capitalist world and therefore looks for forgetfulness in debauchery, degeneration, and abnormal activities. Declining capitalism creates a morality of de-

cline. Devoid of any ties to the wide working masses, which it
exploits, the bourgeoisie emphasizes the lack of this bond by
degenerate fashions and the disappearance of the last family
ties.' "

Yevgenia was genuinely moved. Nervously, she thumbed
through the photographs to find the one she wanted to back up
her words. She found it finally, and triumphantly pushed it under
my nose.

"Here, see for yourself how they look. I took this picture.
Look here, a long American car with a colored chauffeur, see?
And here she stands, no shame at all. Almost naked, the shoulders, the bust, you can see everything. And look how im-
pudently she smiles.

"Or look at this picture. A girl wearing pants with a young
boy wearing a beard like Marx or Engels. They have absolutely
no moral inhibitions. The girls walk like the dancers used to
walk in Moscow before the Revolution. You know—they wiggle
their hips, curve their whole bodies. They simply climb on these
bearded boys. I'm telling you, they just plain and simply push
themselves between their legs, if you don't mind my talking like
that. Anyway, it's the truth. And you should see how they dance.
It was more than we could take. Finally one comrade moved
that we leave, and we all got up deliberately and left the
restaurant."

Sergei, a twenty-eight-year-old worker promoted to technician was another member of the touring group. She, too,
showed me her pictures. They were carefully numbered. Each
was provided with a caption and pasted on a separate page of
an elaborate album. The cover said in large letters, "FRANCE
—1957."

Sergei pointed out one picture. Before looking at it, I read
the caption artistically printed in white India ink. "A Slap in
the Face of Soviet Citizens—Scene in Front of a Bourgeois
Night Club."

In the greatly enlarged photo I could make out the front
of a night spot with its characteristic neon sign. In the doorway
stood a very large doorman, surrounded by easily recognizable
figures of Soviet tourists. At the very front was the familiar hat
of the secretary of the union, with his face in shade.

Sergei explained, "Our guide, who was a Frenchman who talked Russian as though he had been born here, took us to this club. We were very hungry after our day of sight-seeing and ready for a big dinner. But"—Sergei was obviously irritated and nervously lighted a cigarette—"but just imagine, that doorman saw that he was dealing with Soviet tourists and wouldn't let us in. Imagine it, Soviet workers were not let in!

"He said that it was because we were not suitably dressed. Our guide explained to him that in the U.S.S.R. we don't follow the bourgeois style of dress and that he had a touring group of U.S.S.R. citizens before him. But nothing doing. He wouldn't let us in, and that was the end of that.

"What do you think of it? Refusing us, citizens of the most powerful state in the world, admission to a restaurant. Can you beat that? We, deserving citizens of the U.S.S.R.—and just because we didn't wear their clownish bourgeois clothes. Our comrades were stricken dumb. Such an insult! It just proves once more that the bourgeoisie and capitalists defend themselves as well as they can from contact with the masses. That's why the capitalists have their own clubs, their own way of dressing, and their reserved admission. But, they well know that there is no escape from the verdict of history. History is not afraid of reserved admissions and will enter wherever it pleases without wearing an evening dress or a tuxedo. It will enter, wearing a plain soiled shirt and torn workers' overalls, like mine." Here Sergei pointed nonchalantly to large greasy stains on her blouse and to the frayed cuffs on her slacks, which were too wide and too long for her.

In a factory news sheet posted on the wall appeared a number of photographs from the trip to France. On them were titles such as, "Living Conditions of the French Proletariat," from a series called "Contemporary France." The pictures showed houses of workers which were old and falling into ruins—dilapidated houses with wooden balconies running the entire length of the walls, laundry hanging in the courtyards. Others showed a few children playing in a huge puddle of collected mud in a depression of the street, small boys playing ball among garbage cans, a ragged old woman and a bearded old man begging at a street corner. The last picture showed the interior of a cellar. There were straw sacks scattered under the pipes of the central heating. In the right corner a woman lay on a straw sack with three children. On the left a half-naked emaciated man peeled potatoes. In the back a young woman, showing thin legs naked up to above the knees, smiled in a toothless grin.

The chairman of a women's organization, comrade Olga S., commented on the pictures with emotion. "Just look at how these workers live! Crumbling holes, damp cellars, stench and filth and unbelievable destitution. I have no words to describe it. Some of them have been out of work for a year. They beg, they are without food, without medical care. There is no state assistance. No nothing. The comrades from the French Communist Party who were with us told us that more than half of the French working class live in similar conditions. And only an hour away from this, in the Rue de Courcelles . . ." Olga verified the name of the street on a map that she had made, "yes, that's right, de Courcelles—it's near Parc Monceau— the unrestrained bourgeoisie spend hundreds of thousands of francs on their shameless orgies . . . the blood and sweat of those thousands of people. We saw them, hideous capitalists with big bellies and balding pates, with their bought young wives hanging on their arms, as they drove up to a night club in huge cars bought from American capitalists. The place was called"—and Olga again consulted her notes—"Lido or something. It made us think of Engels who said that the bourgeoisie treat their wives as tools of reproduction. Nothing has changed since then.

"The worst experience, however, was when we were taken to see a bridge. There, under the bridge—not on the bridge, but under the bridge—slept the unemployed sons of the French laboring class. Do you understand? Under the bridge, while whole houses, palaces, even districts are occupied by the bourgeoisie. This was the subject of a talk at a meeting of French communists to which we were invited. They spoke of the horrible exploitation, destitution, and debasement of the French proletariat. They spoke about the debauchery of the fascistic bourgeoisie, of rule by capitalists, and about the philosophy of existentialism, which is the most rotten of all the bourgeois ideologies. They also spoke of us, the Soviet people and our happy life. In France they can only achieve this life by fighting. The same conditions existed in all the cities we visited. Everywhere it was the same—exploitation of the proletariat, poverty of the masses, and a handful of exploiting capitalists."

Lonia was twenty-three and an apprentice in the machinery section. She had three years of polytechnical school and was included in the excursion group as a reward for good work. We sat in a park and Lonia told me with great feeling what impressed her most.

Like Yevgenia, she was disturbed by the appearance of the "French bourgeois women. In their daily life all these women of the bourgeois environment concentrate only on calling people's attention to themselves. They spend all their time in unwholesome pastimes, in the company of people exactly like themselves." With a stick, Lonia drew some figures and shapes in the sand. "Even women and girls of the proletariat are infected by this pattern of behavior. I remember we went somewhere —I think it was in the Place Pigalle—where the entertainment disturbed our comrades to the quick. Imagine! The girls take off all their clothing . . . and they do it very slowly with bright spotlights playing on them. They remain absolutely naked . . . in front of men. Their breasts are never covered, even when they are fully dressed. Just think what they are coming to, these classes which are completely separated from society and the laborers."

Wolodia worked in the sales department. He was thirty-five, married, and the father of a little girl. He was a passionate lover of water sports. He took part in the excursion as an activist in labor unions. At the time of our conversation he was preparing an application for membership in the Party organization.

"In the summary of my application," he confided to me with excitement, "I said that my trip to France strengthened my faith in the righteousness of the path tread by our nation under the leadership of the Communist Party. I now fully understand the essence of decaying capitalism and the morality of the capitalist world. You know, such an excursion is a much better school than the best ideological training. Here is an example. In our ideological training class we studied bourgeois morality, theoretically, with examples. But, on our tour of France, in Paris or

in Marseilles, for instance, we saw actual examples at every turn.
When we were walking in the streets we were accosted by
women. You know, the kind who take money for free love. They
pulled us by the hand, patted our cheeks, hugged us . . . and
all this right in the street, before passers-by, without shame.
Young girls who couldn't possibly be more than eighteen years
old . . . why here girls of that age are still in school. A comrade
from the French Communist Party told us that because poverty
and unemployment prevail in workers' families, the wives and
daughters of the proletariat earn their living in this way. Some
of these women swell the ranks of the proletariat by becoming
prostitutes, and the men resort to stealing and murdering. We
heard this from the lips of our French communist comrades.
They see these things every day with their own eyes. When I
returned I said to myself, brother, now you've seen everything.
You've seen the anti-humane character of capitalism. At last you
have a real argument for joining the Party right away."

One of the factory engineers, a white-haired, tall man of about
fifty, told me of an incident which surprised him greatly. "As
you probably know, we also visited the French Riviera, which
has beautiful scenery and a wonderful sea. But, I saw shocking
scenes there. There were modern hotels of glass and concrete;
parking lots overflowed with the most expensive cars. Women
were luxuriously dressed, and men spent money like water. One
of the hotels was on the program of our excursion group so that
we could see the way the French bourgeoisie relaxes. We were
taken to the beach which the hotel maintains. We were not
dressed properly, for we did not have bathing trunks or beach
clothes. It was a sultry day. On the beach hundreds of men and
women were lying on the sand. They were tanned to a golden
brown. There were colorful beach chairs, umbrellas, sailboats,
motorboats, yachts, canoes. It all looked very nice. In the midst
of all this were waiters, buttoned up to their necks, serving re-
freshing drinks, tropical fruit, and ice cream. When they saw
us—I imagine they must have heard that an excursion of Soviet
tourists was visiting the hotel—this half-naked brown mob surrounded us as if we had fallen from the moon. They started to
photograph us from all sides. They made fun of our comrades
who had taken off their outer garments and were resting on the

sand. True, their long trousers and shirts were not very appropriate for the beach. They were sweaty and exhausted by the heat and a long sight-seeing tour. This mob made faces at us, tried to imitate us, made fun of our women. Many of our comrades understand French, even though they can't speak it, so we understood their vulgar comments. Yes sir, it was a good lesson, no doubt, a good lesson."

I had another conversation. This time it was about an excursion to Italy. Peter, a young man of twenty-two, talked to me. He was an activist in the local Komsomol organization and well-liked by the young people. He had graduated from a trade school and his plan for the future was to work in the Party machine in the field of ideological training. He said with conviction, "I would send all our members of Komsomol on these tours. In my opinion, Italy is especially suited to ideological education. But the excursions must be organized so that all that which has the greatest ideological impact could be packed into a short time. That's how our trip was organized.

"I remember that we were shown the wedding of a Roman patrician to an American movie actress. The wedding cortege crossed the whole city, there must have been at least three hundred cars . . . and what cars! I was told that they were the most luxurious cars built in Europe and America. The guests were dressed regally. And all around these untold riches were ragamuffins, begging children, who were literally throwing themselves under the cars to catch the coins thrown to them.

"On another day we were taken to a beautiful church. As we were leaving it a comrade Italian communist, who was one of the men who took care of our group, pointed out a nearby . . . you know . . . a house where peasant girls and working girls must sell their bodies.

"Two days later we took an express train to Sicily. There we saw the living conditions of the peasants. The agricultural workers were striking at the time, and there were many police all around. We heard the Italian communists address these workers and saw the enthusiasm of the audience. When the peasants learned where we came from they simply wanted to kiss our feet. There was no end to their enthusiastic shouts and demonstrations.

"Good organization of a tour is really the most important thing. You can explain the real truth best to your comrades by using a black and white comparison. Bourgeoisie on one side, proletariat on the other. Here capitalists, there communists. It's the best way!"

Shortly before I left the U.S.S.R., I came across a journalist from Poland whom I had met before in Moscow. He was deeply shocked by discussions he had had with members of a U.S.S.R. group which had just returned from the United States.

"Would you believe it," said the worried Pole, "they returned deeply convinced that the U.S.A. is a country of poverty and exploitation, that it is rapidly heading into a crisis, and that a swiftly expanding fascist movement threatens to put an end to all democratic freedoms. I thought I'd drop dead when I listened to this nonsense. When I argued with them I almost got into a fist-fight.

"They told me about their visit to New York. First they were taken to Wall Street to see 'the machinery of anonymous, imperialistic capital in operation.' Then they were shown offices on Madison Avenue to observe 'the operation of the apparatus for mass stupefaction of the working masses.' Then they went to Fifth Avenue to see the 'aristocracy of office workers and labor —the bought portion of the working class.'

"In Harlem they saw 'the typical section of the city inhabited by the American proletariat and the living conditions of American workers.'

"Would you believe it . . . all America was shown to them in this same way, white and black, the principle of contrast. Here riches, there misery. Exactly as your young Komsomol member was shown Italy.

"And since they only tour in groups, and the span of a tour is limited to about two weeks, they succeed in showing every country in the same way. Besides, you must remember that the Soviet tourist comes to the United States with his mind made up in advance. It's easy for them to adjust their impressions and observations to conform to their preconceived ideas, which no particular incident is able to change.

"For example, when a Soviet tourist sees the tremendously high standard of living of an American worker . . . what he

eats . . . what he earns . . . the car he owns . . . he immediately puts him into the category of 'working class aristocracy,'
the 'bought' section of the proletariat who seek mutual agreement with the capitalists. Did you read, by any chance, the reports and articles written from the United States by Russian
artists and sportsmen who appeared in American cities? They
were the most dramatic descriptions that I read for years. . . .
The image of America that emerged from them was unbelievably
horrible.

"The Soviet tourist has hundreds of qualifying terms in stock.
For instance, prosperity can be 'imperialistic robbing of the resources of other nations,' or 'expansion of capital which sub-
jugates other nations and temporarily raises the living standard
in its own country' and so on *ad infinitum.*

"Two collective-farm workers who recently returned from a
tour made by Soviet collective-farm workers to the U.S.A.
reasoned it that way and were deeply convinced that their reasoning was based on 'objective truth.' Of course they toured
the U.S.A. using the familiar method of 'dialectical contrasts.'

"Their guide explained the lack of a rural proletariat to them
by blaming it on 'the poverty which forced the proletariat to
look for work in the cities.'

"In support of the theory of 'degenerate American imperialism,' a theory that they had been indoctrinated with in advance,
the Soviet tour leaders showed them magazines with pictures of
naked women, a strip-tease act in a burlesque hall, and race riots
in Virginia.

"Of course all these exhibits were arranged in advance. This
means that the tour program worked out beforehand included
all these carefully chosen 'elements of objective reality.' Those
who planned the tour you mentioned before, planned in advance to take the tourists to the night club where they knew
that all customers had to wear evening clothes. They deliberately
forced the doorman to refuse admission to the Soviet tourists
because of their unsuitable attire.

"But the most important point, in my opinion, is the fact
that the Soviet citizen and the Soviet tourist is not interested,
even subconsciously, in changing his views, which are already

shaped. There is nothing to force him to revise his opinions. On the contrary, everything discourages him from it.

"In his world outlook, the evaluation of capitalist countries is closely knit to his relationship with his own country. Any overstepping of the accepted and established appraisal of a foreign country interferes simultaneously with his evaluation of his own country and his entire life in the U.S.S.R.

"On the other hand, we must admit that one of your informants was correct—the one who said that Soviet tours abroad, as well as tours of the U.S.S.R. by foreigners, are organized for the greatest propaganda value. To effectively show France, Italy, or the United States in terms of the schematic Marxism of the nineteenth century is a great achievement, my friend. Just as great a trick as successfully showing the U.S.S.R. to foreign tourists in terms of the technical progress and humanistic social organization of the twenty-first century."

The Polish journalist smiled sarcastically and concluded, "One of my Russian acquaintances told me, as I was leaving his country, 'We Russians have learned to let only that which consolidates our strength in the U.S.S.R. out of the boundaries of the U.S.S.R., namely, Sputniks and tourists.'

"These are our 'boomerangs.' And boomerangs, as everybody knows, return. You would do well to remember this."

10

PRODUCER'S MARKET
AND GOOD WILL

THE EXPLANATION OF THE TITLE OF THIS CHAPTER WILL FOLLOW later. In the meantime, let's say something about the rules of supply and operation of the Soviet merchandise market. Information about this subject was given to me by an inspector in a large commercial center in Moscow.

"Like everything else in the U.S.S.R., the Soviet market and its supply differ fundamentally from the markets and laws of supply in contemporary capitalist countries. We, the economists, call our type of market a producer's market. This means that the only producer, the state and its individual establishments provide the market with merchandise and dictate its prices. In this way the state regulates the supply, quality, and price of merchandise in relation to demand, production possibilities, and amount of money in circulation. The state controls both production and consumption through the amount of goods it puts on the market and their price. This mechanism is quite simple. The consumer can buy only that which the state makes available, and as the state adopts the principle of making supply lower than demand, there is never any danger that some merchandise may remain unsold.

"Why do we have this type of market in the U.S.S.R.? What are its advantages? First of all, this type of market promotes industry by creating ideal conditions for it. The best example that comes to mind is TV. First, the state builds television stations. This, of course, creates a demand for TV sets. Our factories begin to manufacture about five types of sets, and thousands of them are put on the market. But the thousands of purchasers waiting for the sets exceed the number of sets on the market by a large number. Our state takes advantage of this situation by introducing *talons* (coupons) which entitle the receiver to buy a set outside of the waiting list. These coupons are issued by the Party and unions to employees as a reward for satisfactory work or as prizes. The producer gains from this system because it provides him with an uninterrupted turnover.

"The producer's market permits a quick expansion of the production cycle. The goods are sold at once, and the profits serve to continue the expansion of production by bringing out new models or new merchandise for the market. Once in a while prices are reduced or wages increased slightly. This speeds up the turnover of goods even more by increasing the purchasing power of a number of purchasers, which in turn leads to an increase in production.

"In recent years, for example, the state has begun to produce gigantic quantities of TV and radio sets, cameras, refrigerators, toys, record players, tourist equipment, and household appliances. All these articles are produced as a side line from by-products of heavy industry. The demand, of course, is tremendous. The prices are low—in some cases ridiculously low. Why? Well, when these products find their way to the consumer, they again accelerate production and money turnover. The money paid to the population in wages returns to the state. New funds are invested in heavy industry which again, within the framework of side production, will produce the same articles, and so on in a circle.

"In capitalist countries such a market is, of course, impossible. There they have a consumer's market. The consumer, the purchaser, decides what he wants to buy, and thousands of producers of the same articles compete with each other. The fate of a producer depends on the decisions made by consumers. It's a recognized fact that this system harbors, from its very inception, inflation and economic crises, even leaving out such factors as the millions of people who work in non-productive fields such as advertising and sales. In time, you will learn for yourself the social value of our system for the state and its citizens."

And, indeed, I was soon to see the value of this system. One day the couple with whom I was living for a few days asked

me to do them a great favor. They wanted me to take advantage
of my privileges as a foreigner and buy a Rubin-102 TV set for
them. It was one of the most expensive sets, with a wide screen
and twelve channels. There was a huge demand for these sets,
but they were put on the market rarely and in small lots. My
friends had been trying to buy one for three months, but couldn't
get it. They had no hope of ever receiving a *talon* from the
factory where they both worked and with which they could purchase the set directly from a central warehouse. They warned me
that I'd have to give a considerable bribe to somebody. In the
case of a Rubin-102 TV set the bribe could amount to almost
one fifth of the price of the set, which was 2,200 rubles at that
time.

"Look," they pleaded, "we have the money. We saved for
more than a year, both of us together. It's important that we
get the set before fall, because in autumn more people buy
things and it will be that much harder to get. You see, the Anniversary of the October Revolution is coming, and that's when
many workers receive *talons* and cash bonuses. But mind you,
be very careful about the bribe. Pay it where no one can see you,
otherwise the manager of the store may think you're a planted
witness or an inspector."

Armed with these instructions and 2,700 rubles, I went to the
store they suggested which sold TV and radio sets. The store
was terribly crowded, stuffy, and hot. Pushing my way through
the crowds, I kept my hand on the money in my pocket. I had
been told that there were a lot of pickpockets in crowded stores.
Finally, I reached a salesman. He told me point blank that the
TV sets were completely sold out and the new shipment was
not expected before the end of the month. But, following my
friends' instructions, I asked the salesman to take me to the
manager. At first he refused. Only after I insisted, explaining
that I was a foreigner on a visit to the U.S.S.R. upon the invitation of some high officials who were my personal friends,
and showed him some letters I carried in my wallet was he
impressed enough to take me to the manager.

The manager was a very pleasant, middle-aged man. He used
all possible arguments to convince me that he had no TV sets
left in the store. But I would not give up. I used the same

arguments and mentioned my highly situated friends. Finally he scratched his head, looked in his notebook, made a telephone call, and told me to come back at 7 P.M. and he'd have a set waiting for me.

I let him understand that I was perfectly aware of all the trouble I had caused him, and that I'd be only too glad to add the price of his trouble to the fixed price for the TV. The manager did not pick up the subject, but with an embarrassed, coy smile, he assured me of his friendship for me, for my country, for its brave Communist Party, and for its heroism.

I returned to the store at 7 P.M. sharp. The TV set was waiting for me in the manager's office, nicely wrapped. We were alone in the office. I counted out 2,200 rubles, the price of the set, then added another 100 rubles, figuring the manager's good will was worth just that to me. I took the receipt and the printed instructions, said good-by, and went home overjoyed at the prospect of my hosts' delight with the set and by the rubles I had saved on the manager's 'good will.'

My friends were really delighted. But when I handed back the 400 rubles they were nonplused, "Do you mean you really gave him only 100 rubles?" the woman demanded.

I answered yes, still proud of my flair for business.

"But that wasn't fair. He went to special trouble to get a Rubin-102 for you. He probably had to promise a tip to someone at the warehouse too, and yet you gave him only 100 rubles. No, that wasn't fair at all. Do you understand the risk he was running? First, you intimidated him with your talk of high connections. He was afraid to offend you, for fear you would report him and he might lose his job. Then he gets you the set, and you give him only 100 rubles. Don't ever do such a thing again. You mustn't take advantage of people."

I must admit that I was amazed by this speech. My friends were educated people, and I was sure that their views reflected general opinion. I decided to investigate the secrets of the producer's market more thoroughly.

My strolls in the streets took on a new interest. Now the stores became what the factories and Party committees had been before, part of my education in the elements of Soviet reality. I started to search for a chance to penetrate behind the counter, to get behind the scenes in the act of sale and purchase, to become acquainted with the machinery of bribes and customs, the penalties and consequences attached to them. It was not easy. For a long time I couldn't find a way. When I was on the brink of giving up, discouraged, I suddenly saw an opportunity. In a store selling electrical appliances, including small radio sets and table record players, I noticed that the manager was a pretty girl who habitually sat alone by a window in the rear of the store. The rest was easy. I introduced myself and told her that I passed by the store every day, that I'd noticed her face in the window and that I'd admired her loveliness. I quoted a few lines from Pushkin about the beauty of women, and my store romance was on its way.

At first Zoya, which was her name, was very suspicious. "Listen," she said on the third day of our friendship, "if you want a record player and can't find one, be frank about it, but don't fool around with me."

I denied her implication indignantly, and to prove that nothing was further from my mind told her that as a foreigner I could buy anything I wanted regardless of the waiting line. I mentioned the TV set I had bought, but I omitted to mention the bribe. Zoya listened with interest, and when I had finished asked how much I had paid for the set. I said 2,200 rubles, which was its official price.

Zoya walked for a while in silence, then asked casually, "Didn't you give him anything for his trouble?"

"No," I said. "I didn't know I should." Then I added, "And how much do you think I should have given him?"

Zoya thought a while, asked again for the brand of the TV, the year and model, then said, "Around five hundred rubles."

"Five hundred rubles! My goodness," I exclaimed in feigned surprise, "that's a lot of money! If he gets that from every customer he must be a millionaire!"

Zoya went on to explain that in these transactions the manager takes an enormous risk and he must share the money with other co-workers who help him or just watch him. That's why bribes are so high.

We talked no more about it then. But a few days later, when we were more friendly and Zoya no longer had any doubts about me, I decided to reopen the subject but from a different angle. A two-day holiday was coming up, and I suggested to Zoya that we make a rather expensive train trip to a nearby summer resort. Zoya agreed, and we made definite plans.

The next day I casually asked Zoya for help in a little matter. Three of my close friends wanted to buy a record player, and one of them the latest model of a typewriter. These articles were very hard to find in the market at that time, and Zoya knew it. I told her that my friends felt that as a foreigner I could get these items easier. They would give me the money necessary, including the amount required for 'good will.' I asked her for advice, hinting that perhaps she could arrange the transaction through her store.

Zoya thought for a long time, then very matter-of-factly explained the usual procedure to me. At a given time, she would tell me when, my three friends would have to come to the store separately, as absolute strangers to each other. They must ask for the record players and the typewriter as regular customers. However, fifteen minutes before they arrived the warehouse would deliver the articles. Zoya would then sell them to my friends at the regular price on a first come, first served basis just as though it were an ordinary transaction. Then I would give her the 'good will' money.

Zoya said that she would have to give the lion's share of it to the manager of the central warehouse who would have to upset his delivery schedules in order to deliver the three record players and the typewriter to the store at the established hour. The next day I returned the money to my friends, keeping the portion allotted for 'good will,' and passed along Zoya's instructions.

Later I learned that everything went off smoothly according to plan. My friends entered the store separately at intervals of several minutes and Zoya informed them with a sweet smile that they were unusually lucky, because some record players and a typewriter had just been delivered from the warehouse and she'd be happy to sell them to them. When a fourth customer appeared, attracted by the sight of the record players being carried out, Zoya was extremely sorry to disappoint him but the last one had just been sold.

And so everybody was happy: my friends because they had at last succeeded in buying the articles they wanted; Zoya, because she had some extra money; the warehouse manager for the same reason; I, because I had helped my friends and because from then on, I was an 'initiate,' an accomplice, to whom Zoya didn't hesitate to pass on interesting information.

A few days later we made our trip as planned, and in the two days Zoya told me a great deal about the complicated tie-up between the 'producer's market' and the 'good will' of the salespeople and other employees.

"You see, these payments are limited primarily to the network of smaller stores. As a rule, they don't exist in department stores and in the larger stores. Bribery is punishable by a long prison term. It is considered an 'economic crime,' one of the most serious in the U.S.S.R. Naturally, a certain number of salespeople and managers are willing to take the chance. In time, they succeed in organizing a 'chain' running from the warehouse through the store to certain regular customers who resell the articles on the black market. Of course they are playing with fire, or rather many years of a labor camp, but some people are born gamblers. They protect themselves every possible way. You see, in this business you have to mind your p's and q's. Never allow any witnesses at your private talks. You must be sure of your control over the intermediaries and others. And yet, in spite of all their precautions, they often find themselves in jail before they succeed in making a fortune.

"Here's an example of how it works. A store expects a delivery of new radio sets. The first step is to have the purchasers already lined up before the truck reaches the store. If you're caught holding merchandise under the counter it means an indictment under a bribery charge. Therefore, at the moment of delivery the line of would-be purchasers is already at the counter. All of them had been notified in advance and are willing to repay the courtesy by paying a few rubles above the regular price. Frequently the surcharge is paid to the manager even before the shipment arrives, in exchange for the promise that the donor will be remembered at the proper time. Although the money changes hands without witnesses, the person receiving the bribe always has a ready explanation for the payment; it is a deposit on account or some other legitimate transaction.

"Well, when the radios are in the store they are sold normally, as if nothing irregular had taken place, to the line of waiting customers. When the uninformed customers who have joined the end of the line reach the counter, the radios have all been sold out. So they leave empty-handed, hoping for better luck next time.

"That's the simplest procedure. But there are other methods. The manager, in agreement with the salepeople, holds a number of articles such as radio sets under the counter. He makes out fictitious sales slips, paying for them out of his own pocket, or even letting the sales personnel share the investment. He puts the payments through the cash register. An inspection will find nothing wrong. The radios have been sold and the money is in the cash register. In the meantime, the manager slowly and with the utmost caution looks for customers among his friends and his friends' friends who are willing to pay a premium price. This type of operation is necessary when a shipment arrives unexpectedly before the line of customers can be prepared. In a case like that, a certain number of sets will be sold normally, and a certain number of lucky people will be able to buy them at the regular price. The remainder goes under the counter to wait.

"There's another scheme. The store manager may be in steady contact with the manager of the warehouse which supplies merchandise to a network of stores. The store manager regulates the flow of merchandise to serve his 'customers.' But this method requires a 'chain' for efficient organization of the operation. Other links of the chain may include a member of the inspection commission who, in exchange for an 'unrepayed loan' received occasionally from the manager, warns him of an impending inspection or if some doubts are being aroused in the commission about the honesty of the store staff."

Zoya laughed and added, "After all, the most a member of the commission can get as a reward for reporting a store manager is some praise, but just a little effort invested in collaborating with the store manager can triple his monthly income. Show me the man who under these circumstances would prefer to be a socialist hero of labor and ruin the source of his best, truly socialist income."

After hearing this explanation of the complicated secrets of "good will," I sought opportunities to do all kinds of difficult errands for the people I knew. Some probably suspected me of being a large-scale speculator. My information about the stores, sales personnel, and bribery increased from day to day. It was a pleasure to use my information for practical purposes for a change.

The department store was the biggest problem. The large number of salesmen and customers in a small area made the "personal touch" extremely difficult. But a personal contact was essential for a successful purchase.

I worked out a few ways to convince salespeople of my good intentions, which would be reflected by payment for their "good will." I remember when I once tried to buy a refrigerator, the best, for a friend of mine. Very few of them were being produced. Shipments *did* reach the department stores occasionally, but they were only sold for *talons* made out by name to shock workers and deserving employees.

My friend, a well-paid engineer, had promised his young wife a refrigerator for her name day. I promised to take care of it, though I was mystified as to where they'd find space for it in their overcrowded room. The engineer earmarked up to four hundred rubles for "good will" and, pocketing this generous sum, I didn't think I'd have any trouble.

I didn't have any luck in the department stores, but a salesman advised me to go directly to the central warehouse and under some pretext try to talk to the manager of the shipping department. I followed his advice, and made a trip to the warehouse at the other end of town. I was lucky. The first person I asked pointed out the manager, who happened to be in the corridor. I introduced myself and told him frankly about my difficulty in getting a refrigerator. I let him understand that I was willing to cover "all extra costs" up to 40 per cent of the price. The manager seemed to fail to understand me, and said that it would be extremely difficult to get one for me. Then he walked back into the warehouse where I saw him confer with some other employee. He came back and hesitantly told me that he had found a solution to my problem. The refrigerator would be delivered the next day to a midtown store. I was to call for it at a certain hour. The manager "will know all about it."

I was ready to thank him and leave, thinking that the "tip" would be paid to the store manager, when I remembered that he hadn't given me the address of the midtown store. He was quietly studying the tips of his worn and soiled shoes. I understood immediately. Putting my hand in my pocket, I cautiously took out the "good will" money and held it in my closed fist. The manager cordially extended his hand to say good-by, and adroitly transferred the contents of my hand into his. Then, just as cordially, he waved his arm mentioning the address of the store.

The next day, in the store named, I approached the counter and asked for the store manager. He appeared without delay. In a whisper, I gave my name and asked for the refrigerator. The manager smiled brightly and congratulated me loudly on my luck. A refrigerator, just one single one of the make I wanted, had just been delivered by the warehouse. By a mistake, it had been left out of a previous shipment. I received a receipt, paid the cashier, and my friend kept his promise to his wife.

Zoya gave me examples in which high officials of the Department of Supply were bribed by store and warehouse managers. It even happened with high members of the inspection groups. She said this occurred much more frequently in remote small towns where, as they say in the U.S.S.R., "the authorities really get along with each other."

When I once discussed these things with an official in the Department of Supply, he said, "We can't take it for granted that bribery disorganizes our trade. Actually, it just results in a percentage of merchandise being sold at higher prices, and in some people earning a little more money. Those who pay more for the articles they desire just increase the speed of the turnover of money in the market. In the final analysis, it doesn't change anything."

As mentioned before, a certain number of workers and people working for the Party, unions, and government receive special talons with which they can buy rare articles at special points of sale or in regular stores. These talons, bearing the name of the owner, are distributed as rewards or as special bonuses. They are usually distributed on state holidays, anniversaries, and political-social celebrations.

As a rule, an automobile or heavy motorcycle can only be purchased with a talon. If a person who bought a car or motor-cycle with a talon wants to sell it, he can do it only by returning it to a special central store. Thus the authorities bar speculation in this merchandise. Nor can articles bought with talons be sold in the free market. Special inspection teams look for this kind of "illegal trade" carried on by speculators.

One day a man approached me in the street in Leningrad. He wanted to know if I would sell him my suit, which I had just picked up at the cleaners and which I was carrying on my arm. The price he offered was very attractive. For the money, I could buy the latest model of a Zorky-4 35mm camera with two extra lenses. I agreed.

We entered a nearby doorway to complete the transaction. The suit was already on the arm of my "customer." Just as he was putting his hand in his pocket to get out the money, a man came up to us and, showing his inspector's card, asked to see our papers. We handed them over docilely. On seeing that I was a visitor in the U.S.S.R. and hadn't been there long, the inspector returned my passport without making any notes.

He said, "It's time you learned that street trading is against the law in the U.S.S.R. If you want to sell your suit, there are special clothes-purchasing stores and commission centers set up for this purpose by our government. There's no shortage of merchandise in the U.S.S.R., and everybody can buy whatever he wants in stores."

My unfortunate customer did not get off so lightly. The in-spector copied the personal data from his passport and left. For a moment we stood in the doorway together. My casual friend looked very sad.

"In a week there'll be a Party group meeting on my case," he said. "Right after it, I'll appear before a special court which deals with trading in the streets. Really, it doesn't matter any more. Give me your address, and I'll come tonight to get the suit, eh?"

But I was in no mood to agree, and thus went my hopes for a new camera.

But illegal trade does exist in the U.S.S.R. It includes almost any article under the sun. Clothes and custom jewelry are the most popular items. During my stay in the U.S.S.R., the illegal market price of a medium quality man's suit, used, wool, was as much as 700 rubles. The price of a white shirt about 100 rubles. Women's underwear sold from 40 to 80 rubles. (The average monthly earnings of a factory or white-collar worker were 800 to 1,000 rubles.) Tourists from Poland and Czechoslovakia, many of whom were touring the country at that time, would buy excellent cameras, radios, and TV sets, even refrigerators, from the proceeds of the sale of their clothes.

In addition to the network of regular stores open to the general public, there are special stores where only certain groups of administrative and political–social employees and their families are permitted to buy. Zoya told me that a friend of hers who works in one of these special stores talked enthusiastically about the large and excellent stock.

"To buy in these stores you must have a special pass and be eligible," Zoya explained. "You must be a high party official, or an official of some institution, or a scholar in a high post. You can buy anything our industry produces, and imported goods as well. But the main difference is not in the kind of goods but in the fact that these people can buy them in full assortment without standing in line or searching from store to store, without the 'good will' of the salesmen and store manager. From time to time they can also buy goods specially produced for exhibitions abroad and withdrawn at intervals. . . . Such goods are not to be found in the ordinary stores. They are mostly elegant television sets, like TV Temp-9, Admiral, Symphonia, Beylarus-8, or radio sets like the radiophonograph Teika or Latvija-2. . . . Once I saw them all in a catalogue of the Soviet pavilion at some foreign exhibition. God, they were really beautiful! And how big—how much place, do you think, is needed for such a Krystall-Stereo radiophonograph, for example?"

One of Zoya's colleagues, in whose presence we discussed the special stores, volunteered the following opinions. "You know, the government never tried to make a secret of these special stores. Why should it? After all, these high officials and dignitaries don't have the time to spend on regular buying that we do. They are people in responsible positions who work very hard. You can't begrudge them slight privileges like special stores and rest homes in the most beautiful places in the U.S.S.R. Their work has to be rewarded somehow, doesn't it?"

Although the U.S.S.R. has not succeeded in eliminating speculation and illegal trading, in recent years the state has been trying to adjust supply and demand more closely, especially for articles in daily use. This adjustment can be attained sometimes in large urban centers, but only rarely in the provinces. One of the arguments for decentralization is the need to co-ordinate distribution and control over the market in the provinces, in small towns, villages, and settlements all over the U.S.S.R.

But there is another aspect of the producer's market—the needs of the population. These needs, which have been shaped from the time of the Revolution, are the real expression of the influence exerted by this type of market on the tastes and wants of the public.

In an effort to obtain an approximate picture of these wants and tastes, I made my own miniature poll at the Moscow University and in a factory in the vicinity of Moscow. I asked a number of questions of 85 students (38 of them women) in their last year of study in various departments, and of 85 skilled workers (29 of them women).

Given below are the questions and answers:

QUESTION I	Students		Workers	
	M	F	M	F
In your opinion, how often should a person be able to buy:				
A. A New Suit (Dress)				
1) Four times a year	1	5	-	1
2) Three times a year	3	9	-	8
3) Twice a year	13	18	6	18
4) Once a year	20	-	19	3
5) Once in two years	7	-	16	6
6) Once in three years	3	-	5	3

B. A New Overcoat

1) Twice a year	-	12	-	8
2) Once a year	7	23	4	16
3) Once in two years	29	1	28	8
4) Once in three years	7	1	8	7
5) Once in four years	2	-	2	-
6) Once in five years	1	-	4	-

C. A New Pair of Shoes

1) Four times a year	3	6	-	4
2) Three times a year	3	19	2	6
3) Twice a year	27	4	12	25
4) Once a year	10	8	28	1
5) Once in two years	4	2	4	2

QUESTION II

If someone offered you a gift of
a new car or a beautiful apartment, which would you choose?

1) Car	38	22	41	19
2) Apartment	9	16	5	10

QUESTION III

What article of daily use, not
counting furniture, would you
consider most essential in the
present U.S.S.R. apartment?

1) Radio	16	9	19	12
2) TV	13	9	17	10
3) Refrigerator	2	8	3	9
4) Telephone	5	1	-	-
5) Vacuum Cleaner	4	4	4	2
6) Washing Machine	3	5	3	6
7) Record Player	4	2	-	-

QUESTION IV

From the standpoint of mass production
of articles for daily use, is it better to
concentrate on development of heavy or
light industry in the U.S.S.R. today?

1) Heavy	39	36	28	21
2) Light	1	2	6	-
3) Both	6	-	10	16
4) By-products of heavy industry	1	-	2	2

QUESTION V

In your opinion, in how many years
will you be able to buy a car?

1) In a year	-	-	4	2
2) In two years	11	4	4	3
3) In three years	21	16	6	4
4) In four to six years	13	15	20	11
5) Never	2	3	12	19

I must admit that I was amazed by the minimal wants of
the persons I interviewed. But I was told that these attitudes
on the part of Soviet citizens had been formed in years gone by.
Then the material condition of the whole nation was poor. The
continuity between the low standard of supply in the times of
Czarist Russia and in the times of the U.S.S.R. lasted until 1939.

After the war, a radical change took place. Soviet industry
began to develop very quickly, though more extensively than
intensively. This growth brought about a change in the producer's market and in the wants of the population stimulated by
that market.

It's difficult, however, to tell to what extent this market is
catching up to the needs of the entire population.

An economist with whom I spoke in Minsk, a member of
the Academy of Sciences, gave me the following estimates for
U.S.S.R. production in 1960: about 750,000 motor vehicles will
be manufactured, of which 125,000 will be passenger cars; about
5.5 per cent of the population will be able to own a car; about
85 per cent–90 per cent of these persons will have to use *talons*
for the purchase of their cars;

Soviet industry will manufacture about 7.5 times as many
electric washing machines and refrigerators in 1960 as in 1955,
and about 11 times as many electric razors;

About 34.5 yards of cotton goods will be produced per person
compared with 26 yards in 1955 and 20 yards in 1950;

The shoe industry will produce about 2.8 pairs of shoes per person as compared with 1.57 in 1955.

"We also estimate," said the economist, "that labor's interest in production will gradually grow, and that the productivity of the Soviet man-hour will reach about 50.3 per cent of the American man-hour in 1960, as compared with 8 per cent to 12 per cent in the 1922 to 1925 period. The expansion of the market to include household appliances and luxury articles is meant to serve this very purpose. But production of clothes will still lag far behind. The U.S.S.R. needs engineers, technicians, and skilled labor in heavy industry and cannot afford to spare even a small portion of them for light industry. We do not build factories for light industry because that would lower the tempo of the development of our heavy, strategic industry which underlies the power and growth of the U.S.S.R.

"Up to now, the producer's market which the U.S.S.R. has been the first state to introduce, has passed the test in terms of the entire country and is still passing it. In this field, as in many others, confining our socialist society within the boundaries of our country and cutting it off from the influence of capitalist countries was an essential measure. Like the organization of our social condition, the organization of our economy proved to be better and more effective than that of the capitalist countries. Within a period of forty years, this organization made backward Russia into a powerful state. It proved to be suitable for the requirements of the socialist society, the administration, and the Army.

"Someone might say that it succeeded at the cost of the unsatisfied desires of millions of people for food, clothes, and rest. My answer to this charge is that it is not true. Not because our society had everything it wanted—we all know that it didn't. But because the U.S.S.R., cut off from the capitalist world, formed different criteria for evaluating its situation, different criteria for determining its wants. By his very nature, man is a practical creature. If, for instance, a citizen of the U.S.S.R. considers it a luxury to own three suits of clothes and is content with two, while a citizen of West Germany can afford to have ten, this does not mean that our citizen is less happy than the

German. A Soviet citizen goes through life thinking in terms of Soviet standards. Only these exist in his life, and only these have any meaning to him. He doesn't know any other standards, and there's no need for him to get to know them.

"Besides, experience has shown that even if he does get to know other standards, they are alien to him. He does not approve of them. He considers them as unnatural and degenerate. What do you expect after forty years! It's almost an era.

"Some Western 'experts,' especially Americans, think that the moment the standard of living of the U.S.S.R. will reach a pretty high level our people will acquire a 'bourgeois' outlook and will ask for 'capitalist freedoms.' What nonsense! Is it not clear that, the more our workers and peasants will get from the Party and the government, the more they will earn, the easier and more agreeable their lives, the more closely they will feel linked with our authorities, our Party, our trade unions, our Komsomol—and with our ideology—and the more they will be afraid to lose that link? It will be then not only a professional and political link, but a many-sided complete link—the strongest possible link between the people and their government. Don't you think so?"

One day I was strolling along a wide street in a Soviet city. A great state holiday was soon to take place. The streets, store windows, and houses were being decorated. I stopped before a large window in a department store. It was brilliantly lit and displayed many articles for daily use. In the center were two big TV sets with large screens. The window trimmer had pasted portraits of Khrushchev and Mao Tse-tung over the screens. A little to the rear, on the left, a portrait of Marx sat atop a refrigerator. And to the right, Engels stood on top of an electric washing machine. The display was dominated by a large portrait of Lenin, the plan for the electrification of the U.S.S.R. in his hand.

A couple stopped in front of the window. The wife carried a baby in her arms. Their silhouettes, reflected in the window pane, were clearly delineated against the melting contours of the display. They looked enviously at the attractively displayed radio and TV sets, the electric kitchen gadgets, refrigerators, and washing machines. The girl sighed with delight at the sight of ladies' lingerie.

They pointed out various items to each other, and commented in low voices on the prices. Brief fragments reached my ears, "See there, to the left of Marx, those trousers. . . . No, no, on the other side, back of Engels, the panties. . . . You mean that big saucepan under Lenin. . . . Those blue socks, opposite Mao Tse-tung, aren't they something?"

I proceeded with my stroll, realizing that this was the first time I had ever heard the names of the leaders of socialism in these associations.

Above, a big inscription "Forward to Communism" hung over the display. Gay red and blue electric bulbs winked at me roguishly.

11

THE HERO OF
OUR TIMES

I MET DYMITRIJ ZAKHAROVITCH G. IN 1950 WHEN HE CAME TO
my country to attend a youth conference. At that time he was
one of the youngest members of the Soviet delegation. His
dynamic and enthusiastic speeches were fresh and animated.
They relieved the monotony of the conference sessions. Dymitrij was a born orator and he knew it. Both the sense and the
form of his addresses were aimed at arousing a spontaneous reaction from the assembled youths. Bent over the red-covered
pulpit, holding his chin with his broad hand, he looked like a
hero of the 1917 Revolution, someone right out of the primitive,
mass-produced propaganda posters pasted all over the walls and
fences of the city. His speeches condemning the invasion of
northern Korea by American aggressors made a strong impact
on the audience. His colleagues from the Soviet delegation forecast a brilliant future for him. At the invitation of a university
students' organization, of which I also was a member, Dymitrij
stayed on in my country for three weeks after the conference.
He happened to stay at the same rest home in the mountains
as I, and we became great friends. At this time I was just beginning to be initiated into the principles of communist ideology, whereas Dymitrij was already an experienced Marxist. This
led to discussions which we carried on passionately and earnestly
during our mountain excursions. Dymitrij was, of course, my
superior in the art of debating. My role was often reduced to
criticizing his formulations.

I met Dymitrij G. for the second time in 1955, in Poland,
when I attended the youth festival in Warsaw. He was one of

the principal organizers of the festival and a leader of the Soviet delegation. Though five years older, he had hardly changed. His forehead was higher, his hair sparser, and there was the addition of a new gold tooth in the front of his mouth, visible every time he smiled. By then he was extremely popular with the leaders of communist youths of various countries, especially in the people's democracies to which he was often sent on duty. He was surrounded with respect bordering on servility. I heard his speech condemning the policy of the imperialistic aggressors in the Middle East. It was the best-rendered oration I heard at that time. Dymitrij spoke with power, and convincingly, as in 1950, though his arguments did not deviate from the traditional tricks of Soviet propaganda.

Just as five years before, we took rooms in the same hotel. In the intervals between receptions or celebrations we found time to exchange our views. And again, as before, we differed basically in our conclusions. Dymitrij was still faithful to his previous Marxist–Stalinist formulas, while I had already parted from Marxism and Stalinism for good and tried to build up some practical Minimalistic philosophy applicable to life. In our discussions I now had the superiority because of my change in opinions. Dymitrij listened and attacked them from all points. After 1955 we lost contact with each other. I returned to my scientific work, Dymitrij to his political work. Once in a while I saw his picture or name in Soviet youth periodicals published in the U.S.S.R. or in satellite countries.

On my visit to Moscow I was anxious to look up Dymitrij. I wanted to renew our friendship and again exchange views. I knew that he now had a high position in the management of the youth movement in the East European countries. After a long search I succeeded in finding his office telephone. I rang up. After being switched from one extension to another I was finally told by a secretary that Comrade Dymitrij Zakharovitch G. was on the wire. He recognized my voice at once and sounded very glad that I was in the U.S.S.R. He was extremely well informed on the work of the scientific institution in which I was employed and was glad that my work was so successful. He asked whether I could come down to his office.

Fifteen minutes later I entered a large, impressive building which was only a few years old.

The militiaman on guard at the entrance verified my papers and kept my identification card in the drawer of his massive desk. He called the secretariat of Comrade G. and told them that I had arrived. He gave me a pass, and his assistant took me along a carpet-covered corridor to the elevator. The elevator, lined with mahogany colored wood, zoomed noiselessly upward. The elevator man, in a gray-green uniform, looked at the rubber soles of my shoes with interest, as if he had never seen such shoes before.

The secretary, a pretty young girl with a Komsomol badge on the lapel of her sports shirt, examined me and my pass critically. She wrote the exact hour of my arrival at her office on the pass and disappeared behind a leather-covered door. In a minute she was back, saying that Comrade Dymitrij Zakharovitch G. was waiting for me.

The next moment I was sitting in a deep, soft easy chair in Dymitrij's private office. The walls were covered with a light brown material that contrasted pleasantly with a red strip extending around a part of the main wall, where portraits of Khrushchev and Lenin were hanging.

Behind the wide desk sat Dymitrij, wearing a smartly tailored suit. Again I noticed that he had changed very little since our last meeting. The hair on his temples and above his forehead was thinner, making his face look still broader. Three telephones were on the desk, and since I had come in the red lights on them had not stopped signaling. From the other room came the hushed voice of the secretary taking the calls and asking the callers to phone later as Comrade G. was in conference.

From the start, our conversation was extremely interesting. Dymitrij was completely familiar with all the facts about the scientific situation in my country. He told me several anecdotes from his recent trips to the countries of the people's democracy. I decided to leave after a short while, for I did not want to disturb Dymitrij in his work. As I was on my way out, Dymitrij invited me to go on a sight-seeing tour of Moscow in his official car. It was then that, in one corner of his office, I noticed a large colored globe with a wide scarlet-red sash tied in an intricate bow around it. The secretary put down the time of my departure and a seal on my pass. The elevator man was no longer interested in my shoes, and the militiaman handed me my identification card with one hand while taking the pass with the other.

In the afternoon, after nearly a three-hour drive, we were left off in the center of the city and found a relatively quiet corner in a crowded restaurant where with a bottle of good wine on the table we continued our interesting conversation.

We discussed our personal plans and what we were aiming for in our lives (each of us for himself). I spoke first. I explained my views on my life . . . past and present . . . and my future intentions. I purposefully emphasized the *private* character of my goals, my (as Dymitrij called them) bourgeois tastes, and separation from any socially active life. I accented my interest in science and dislike for collective life, for politics, and political and social organizations. It was a candid, intimate conversation. My personal and professional standing warranted this boldness in manifesting my purposes so opposite to those which were Dymitrij's. We were almost the same age—he was two or three years my senior. We belonged to the same era, to the same generation, the generation of identical hopes and disillusionment, lofty ideals, and their hypocritical distortion in real life.

As the evening drew to an end, Dymitrij suggested that we go to his apartment. We entered a building in a picturesque square. His apartment consisted of a very nicely furnished room with a private entrance from the corridor. Telephone, radio, record player along with a modern tape recorder, a large-sized TV set, a small refrigerator—Dymitrij proudly showed me these products of modern Soviet technology.

A fresh bottle of French brandy appeared on the table. Dymitrij drank with relish. He expertly filled the glasses, then sipped the brandy, holding the rim of the glass to his lips for a moment. Suddenly he emptied the glass and put it back on the table.

From the radio came light music, followed by a Czech singer, then came melodious, nostalgic army songs which had been sung at the front.

I asked Dymitrij to tell me about himself. It was not a fluent narration. Possibly it was the first time Dymitrij had spoken about himself extemporaneously. I realized then that whenever I had heard him previously he had spoken in well-polished and prepared statements, delivered by a good speaker. But now, the *man* was speaking. He stuttered, repeated himself, broke the continuity of his story. What he said, however, was extremely interesting and characteristic.

Dymitrij was born in an extremely poor workers' family in a town near Moscow. Both his mother and father were laborers. The father worked on roads, the mother in a dress factory. "My childhood," said Dymitrij, "was probably no different from the childhood of hundreds of thousands of my contemporaries. At an early age I was completely absorbed by school collectivity. For instance, at this moment I remember my schoolmates better than the faces of my mother and father at that time. And I'm an only son. Strange, isn't it? My father died when I was nine, and Mother went to live with her sister in the Urals. She is still there. I was left in a boarding school, with my school-mates, completely integrated with my surroundings. During that time I learned to think of myself in terms of my environment. This means that I tried to see myself as others saw me. The concept of a collectivity which directs the individual's life became very close to me. I realized that my fate, my value, and my future depended only on me. Even then, as a teen-ager, I was a good speaker. I was always chosen to talk at youth assemblies, celebrations, and anniversaries. I spoke calmly, correctly, without nervousness—even with pleasure. I had serious altercations with other students equally talented and equally pushing. These quarrels often occurred during our ideological debates or group meetings. The most dreaded competition was from children of educated families. Sons and daughters of lawyers, doctors, teachers, and engineers surpassed me with knowledge learned at home and in their ability to use good language. Their syntax was better, their vocabulary richer, they learned more easily, they had better marks on their tests. What I had to attain by tedious work, poring over books, and many hours of cramming, they had known before from home. Perhaps it was then that I acquired a resentment for men of sciences—

especially humanistic sciences—for polished expressions, clear-cut definitions. Their language was not the language of Lenin or Stalin, simple, understandable to all, strong in argumentation. Nor did they look like the leaders of the proletariat. They were well-groomed, always clean, pedantic, with a false smile, cringing before themselves and before others of whom they were afraid."

Dymitrij filled his glass and with silent concentration looked at his huge hands, which were worn, red, and rough. The light seemed to bother him suddenly, and he pushed away a lamp with a pretty shade. He continued.

"I realized then that our Party gives people like me a certain life credit by considering them, people of workers' origin, the most valuable. It is, I might say, a compensation for the lack of certain values not brought from our family environment. My workers' origin is a kind of head start which makes it possible for me to outrun other competitors and be the first at the winning post of life.

"I saw that all the social, scientific, political, and administrative institutions were open, first of all, to the likes of us, people with proper class origin, devoted to the Party and to the cause of the U.S.S.R.

"This became my signpost. I was uncompromising to myself and even more so to others. From then on my speeches purposefully imitated the workers' speech by being unpolished in form. I emphasized my origin and used it to hit my competitors on the head.

"High school strengthened the conviction in me that man lives amidst other people, that he is born thanks to them, and he may die thanks to them. That was one thing. Number two was that to become something in life you have to take advantage of your environment, affect it but allow it also to affect you.

"I obeyed all orders I received. During vacations I harvested to 'help the nation.' I reported the hostile attitude of one of my schoolteachers who was dismissed as a consequence, 'on behalf of the working class.' I frequently criticized myself 'for my own good.'

"In 1941 when war broke out I was in the last grade in high

school. I volunteered for an auxiliary unit and since I was physically well-built and developed and since my record in the Komsomol and school was excellent, I was accepted. After a period of digging trenches and transportation work I was transferred to a regular unit.

"It was hard getting used to army life. It took me a while. There were many bad moments, hungry days, and nights which seemed endless. After a short time, however, I discovered the same social mechanism in my regiment: a collective, meetings, debates. It did not take me long to become an activist in my regiment, a sought-after speaker, agitator–communist, the right hand of the commander and of the political commissar.

"Towards the end of the war I made up my mind to seek a Party-political career. You smile. 'Career' is a bourgeois work, isn't it? Well, anyway, to my mind, at that time it was the best road to an interesting and creative life."

Dymitrij rose and began to pace the floor in a hard, almost military step. "Right after the war I enrolled in a Party course, giving up the idea of university. The university was not for me. It was school all over again and it lasted too long. I considered it a pure waste of time and that I was too old to start. In the Party school I was the best student. Only I know at what cost to myself.

"After graduation I was delegated to work in Komsomol. I toured practically the entire territory of the U.S.S.R. I spoke in many places: factories, schools, prisons, labor camps, universities. To actors, to workers, to peasants, professors, doctors, prisoners. I set up youth organizations and dissolved those whose work was not satisfactory. I was a lecturer, agitator, and propagandist, and sometimes, when necessary, even a prosecutor. As I told you, I was uncompromising. Twice I broke up nationalistic trends in the Komsomol: in the Ukraine and in White Russia. Several times, as a result of my inspections, a number of people were tried in court, many were convicted. These were the times when the success of the U.S.S.R. and of Comrade Stalin turned the heads of many people. Here and there they began to trifle with organizational discipline, to loosen the bonds between the youth and the Party. So I always had my hands full. I was already considered one of the best speakers the Komsomol had. When I took the floor at a meeting, I knew I could hold the attention of every single person in the audience. I learned how to accent certain words and how to use them according to these accents. I knew when to start building up tension and bring it to a climax, when the audience would burst out in frantic applause, and when all would rise and begin to shout with enthusiasm and conviction for the slogan I'd suggested.

"I was always delegated to the most difficult meetings. I was entrusted to speak on matters hard to prove, or not very well documented, especially in cases concerning the dismissal of a person from the Party or the Komsomol. I don't think there was a single case where I didn't succeed, or that there were ever any doubts or questions left in the audience. Everything was always as clear as a child's tear.

"It was then that I learned Stalinist logic in presenting matters and analyzing cases, in ascribing motives and purposes to the accused as well as to the accusers. I knew that when I spoke the audience had the reactions and the conclusions that I wanted them to have. I also saw how those whom I accused broke down, though they still could have defended themselves or answered the questions put to them. I saw them try in vain to collect their thoughts and then I saw them panic.

"I wish that you could understand it from my viewpoint. To me, this type of work is the most magnificent thing there can be. Our whole life prepares us for this work—except that everyone cannot learn it. If I don't act in this way others will, and I will be the one who will be hurt. To be always attacking others, to bring to life the Party line, and at the same time not to come into conflict with that line is the most difficult game. I think that I have been able to maintain it.

"In 1949 I was permanently assigned to Moscow to handle communist youth movements in the countries of people's democracies. I was in Czechoslovakia, Hungary, Poland, and Rumania several times. On my visits as a representative of the Komsomol I met the most important Party and government dignitaries of those countries. I also met scientists and social workers. My position was becoming more stabilized, growing stronger. And I was becoming more popular. I don't understand your questions: Do I feel the need for a different life? To marry and have a family? Tell me, can any other life furnish me with so much excitement as the life I have now?

"Can any love replace the kind of passion and activity required by work for the Party? Work which absorbs you entirely and makes you completely forget all other matters? Did you see our youth? What do you think absorbs and attracts them most? Girls? Sports? Personal life? Scientific laboratories?

"Well the answer is no, no, and no! Our young people thrive on social interests. They find their outlet in social organizations —at school, in the student Komsomol, and, when employed, in the labor unions. In these activities our young people find all the interests and passions required by their age: the hazards of satisfying ambition, fighting competitors, struggling to hold their own position, or trying to capture a position occupied by someone else. All other interests such as study, sports, private life, love, are secondary to these social activities.

"You see, all of you from outside the U.S.S.R. have to understand once and for all that it isn't our ideology that forces us into this kind of life. Nor is it necessary to search for five members of the secret police behind every average Soviet man who lives this way. You people from outside the U.S.S.R. might sometimes prefer to think it so, but it really isn't. The organization of our daily life forces us into these activities. All the parts of our life are closely tied to them. If a man wants to live—and what man doesn't—he must change as his surroundings change. Each of us is a small wheel in a large machine, and there is no way out of it. You can change places with another wheel, but you can't change the machine itself. And you can't live outside the *organized group*.

"But let's come back to my own story. After the split with Yugoslavia I understood that trying to spread communism by ideological or Party influence was a thing of the past. Suddenly all the theoretical illusions and abstract formulas which I had been taught and which I used to believe, fell off me. I became politically mature. I understood that under the new politico-economic conditions, the U.S.S.R. and the Communist Party had to play a new role, and it couldn't be otherwise. Now it is a military-political role, not ideological-political as it used to be. I understood that during these present years, at this very moment, a new history of the world is being shaped, and this history is being written by the U.S.S.R., the greatest power of the modern world.

"I realized that I was living in a different era, an era during which the face of the whole world is being changed. And this change is being made by my Party, our Communist Party.

"To my surprise, Stalin's death and later the Twentieth Congress of the Party were not as great shocks to me as I would have imagined. In fact, there was only a rather superficial feeling that something that I always carried with me was no more. I had delivered many successful speeches about Stalin and thus made a considerable contribution to his cult in the U.S.S.R. My personal view of Stalin? I will give you an evasive reply. It is possible to change religion without changing God, isn't it? Well, I personally believe that it is also possible to do the opposite. Stalin was undoubtedly a genius. To a genius much is forgiven— even the lack of genius. . . . He was a great popular leader; more than that, he was a true political hypnotist of the masses. . . . It is not necessary for such a hypnotist to look the people in the eye."

Dymitrij laughed openly and stopped pacing the floor. He refilled his glass, looking through the window at the people strolling in the square, and then resumed.

"In my practical life, what counted was not Stalin, but the Party. Stalin was gone, but the Party remained. I think the Party became stronger for want of Stalin than it was with his presence. Khrushchev's speech about the terrible results of the cult of the individual convinced the nation that these results would not be repeated. Especially one basic result . . . unpreparedness for war.

"Our Party swore never to repeat the Stalinist phase of its history. There remained the strong and compact group of the Central Committee. Perhaps I'm wrong, but I think that the Central Committee's policy will change the political map of the world more than it's generally believed. At any rate, since the Twentieth Congress I've been driven by one clear-cut purpose —that is to occupy a position high enough in the government or in the Party to assure my remaining in it for good, a position inside the Central Committee which will permit me to have a personal share in changing the face of the twentieth-century world. The man who climbs to the top of the social ladder often forgets why he climbed and who sent him to the top. I will try not to forget this. This is my purpose and my goal. I'm convinced that I've been following the right track up to now. I'm convinced that I'll achieve my goal, unless stopped by some unforeseen event."

Dymitrij was impressed by his own words. He took off his jacket, though it was cool in the room, and wiped perspiration from his forehead. He looked like a man who was suddenly stricken by the revelation of his own goals, like someone who has seen himself for the first time.

"At present, I'm still far from it," Dymitrij said hastily, as if afraid of his boldness, "very far. But a man's life is a process of becoming somebody. You may wonder what qualifications entitle me to dream of holding a place in the Central Committee. Well, I'll tell you. I am a political leader, an organizer, a propagandist, a man devoted to the cause of the Party and the U.S.S.R. by profession. In our time, and even more so in years to come, this sort of man will be more needed than engineers, doctors, or teachers.

"Why? Because the period we live in is the period immediately preceding the world victory of socialism. In political terms, it means the defeat of the capitalistic U.S.A. by the U.S.S.R. and People's China. The process of this defeat began after World War II and is now entering its decisive phase.

"Why only the U.S.A.? Because militarily Europe ceases to count as soon as the coming war breaks out. Even the German divisions armed with American weapons won't change this fact. So certain is this, that the near future may see amazing changes in our policy toward Germany. Our only remaining opponent is American imperialism.

"In my opinion, there are two alternatives that could lead to the military defeat of the U.S.A. The first and more probable is the break-up of the U.S.A.'s military and economic strength through war. In this war we'll take advantage of our entire modern military technology which will lead to a quick victory

with a minimum of losses on our side, perhaps even no losses
at all.

"Of course of prime importance here are the different
strategic concepts of the U.S.A., which lag far behind the requirements of such a war. The organization of American research
into the techniques of modern war has not changed since 1953.
In addition, you must remember the complete unpreparedness
of their economic and political system for such a war.

"The other alternative is a systematic and persistent build-up
of decisive military superiority over the United States, accompanied by efforts to blackmail the U.S.A. dangling before its eyes
the possibility of another war. Americans are in mortal fear of
war, and they will probably never decide to start one.

"What will be the results of this alternative? First, as soon as
we force the passage of a disarmament resolution in the U.N.
the U.S.A. will experience a chronic and insurmountable economic crisis. In time this will degenerate into an internal political crisis which could lead to the formation of a government
which will give in to all the political terms dictated by Russia.

"Second, after a short transitional period, free elections will
be carried out under the strict supervision of the U.S.S.R. This
will put political power into the hands of a Communist-leftist
government which will proceed to change the socio-economic
face of the country.

"By this time, the U.S.A. economy will probably be incorporated into some broader economic grouping, according to the demands and requirements of an international market which will
be formed after the defeat of the U.S.A. These events are, of
course, far in the future. But both alternatives have one common
political-geographical element. Asia and Africa must fall within
the sphere of the political influence of the Soviet-Chinese block
before the ultimate defeat of the U.S.A."

Dymitrij talked slowly and with conviction, though sometimes I felt he was repeating ideas he had heard somewhere
else. My obvious disbelief in the future world he described,
though certainly plain enough on my face, didn't stop him.

"When the U.S. ceases to count as an imperialistic power,
the second historical mission of the U.S.S.R. will begin—the
organization of world socialism, the building of world socialist

societies, reorganization of the world economic market, the setting up of new international institutions and organizations.

"And don't fool yourself . . . these problems may be more difficult than the victorious ending of the third and last World War. Our experts in all fields, especially political organizers, will be sent everywhere. They will build new economic and social institutions. They will occupy leading positions in the Central Committees of all the Communist Parties.

"The problems of possible counterrevolutionary forces will have to be worked out, as well as the problem of strict control over the very large political and national groups such as Germany in Europe. Our armed forces will have to remain in such places for a long time. The U.S.S.R. and Communist China will together carry on in the great task of building a new world order. By that time the world will realize that the new history began with two communist revolutions: the revolution in China and the revolution in Russia. At present we are still inclined to see the great significance only of the Russian revolution.

"But to return to me and my generation. Can you imagine the power each of us will have? We, the proven, schooled men bound to the cause of Communism for life or death? We who will be the core of the Communist Party?

"Don't smile so sarcastically. This isn't some wild dream. The conquest of the United States will come within ten or fifteen years. This isn't just my opinion. It's the opinion of our experts, primarily our military experts. By that time our technological-military potential will be able to defeat the imperialist armies while successfully protecting us. We'll be able to attack the U.S. from all possible sides, from underground and on the ground, from under water and on the water, and from space with the use of interplanetary platforms. We'll be able to crush the U.S.A.'s military forces to dust by using all available means—atomic, chemical, radiological, and bacteriological. And there will be no force that can oppose us.

"Then the next historical era will begin. And I'll only be forty-five or fifty years old! Or let's even say sixty. It doesn't matter too much. With the new methods for prolonging youth and life, sixty will be when man is in his prime. Or even before his prime. I'll still have twenty to thirty years of active political work before me. Think what a fascinating life it will be!"

Dymitrij was exhausted by his monologue. He sat down opposite me, staring at my face searchingly, then asked, "Tell me, what do you think of all this? Do you think anything else can happen? Do you think that historical forces can be stopped? Do you think that the thousands and hundreds of thousands of people like me can be mistaken? If you do think so, then tell me where you see any other social forces which can create and crush as ours can? Where? Where is there a technology that can oppose us now, at this moment, let alone in fifteen years? What social system has managed to achieve so much in so short a time? What other system has shown so much resistance to defeats and failures and such a capacity for working towards victory?

"There are no other forces, there is no other social system, there is no avoiding history, and there is no escape from the future. Once, perhaps ten years ago, these words may have been only slogans. Now they are processes obvious to everybody who will look. Well, what is your opinion? Where do you want to see yourself in the coming years? Where do you want to spend this period of 'storm and drive?' And do you really believe that there is a way out?"

I didn't want to start an argument with Dymitrij. I was afraid that if I disagreed with his "historiosophical" prediction our conversation would degenerate into futile argument. I was anxious to hear more of Dymitrij's views. Therefore, I told him that he was right, and that if history did follow the path he expected an extremely interesting future would be open to him.

The topic of our conversation somehow changed to the personal life of the individual. It became obvious that here too we differed greatly. My ideas were, as Dymitrij said, more antiquated. His ideas were "dialectic" and conformed "to the spirit of the time." It's strange, but it never occurred to Dymitrij that his opinions might differ from those of *all* his friends and acquaintances. He quoted examples to prove that all Soviet youth reasoned in the same way, and that their daily life prepared them for such reasoning, no matter where they lived.

I must confess that Dymitrij knew how to analyze his environment correctly. I had noticed on several occasions that he was a keen observer, sensitive to the surroundings which played such an important role in his life. So, though the hour was late, I continued listening to him. I listened attentively, recording every word in my memory.

". . . A man changes continually," Dymitrij said, picking up a thread in our conversation. "Often it happens without his knowledge. Our environment permeates our consciousness so strongly that we fail to recognize certain changes going on in us, if at the same time they go on in our environment.

"Let me give you an example. I had a very close friend. Our friendship started during the war. To me it looked like a friendship that would last until death. I won't tell you his name. No use to, he isn't around any more. Let's call him Stenka.

"Well, Stenka was a lot like me. We looked at life the same way. Both of us clawed at life with our nails. We knew what we wanted of it, and what we were willing to sacrifice in return. Stenka was in the Party school with me. We got the same good marks, except he wasn't a good speaker. A hall full of people made him nervous. But he was an excellent organizer and, like me, was given a relatively responsible position. His specialty was the problems of the people's democracies. He visited Albania and Bulgaria. We went together to Rumania and Czechoslovakia. We loved each other more than brothers. We had many common interests and always a lot to talk about and often got into stormy debates. You could say it was a genuine, deep friendship.

"Anyway, sometime around the middle of 1952 we were together in Czechoslovakia. I was invited by some youth congress and Stenka was assigned there on some business by the Party authorities. At a Party meeting, Stenka met a girl and fell in love with her on the spot. She was a Czech Party activist, closely connected with the highest Party circles in Czechoslovakia. After two weeks they were married. Incidentally, I was a witness to the wedding. She was scheduled to come to the U.S.S.R. to join Stenka shortly thereafter. Personally, I approved of Stenka's choice. His wife made a very favorable impression. She was well-educated, clever, had a high Party standing, and was quite good-looking. All in all a valuable wife.

"Meanwhile, Stenka and I returned to our country and to our work there. Our close friendship continued. However, one day I was summoned to a meeting of the executive committee of the Party organization of which Stenka was a member. When I arrived, I was told that 'Stenka's case' was being considered. The case was simple. Stenka's wife had been arrested by the Czech security authorities upon the motion of the Party Central Committee for her collaboration with so-called 'Slansky group.' Interrogation proved that she was undeniably guilty, and she was due to be tried with Slansky and his associates.

"The Party organization of which Stenka was a member made an investigation of its own, and decided to expel Stenka from the Party for 'connections with the reactionary Slansky group.' One of the most damaging arguments against Stenka was the fact that during his visits to Czechoslovakia he and his wife often visited people backing Slansky. The Party instructed me, as Stenka's closest friend, to make the charge against him based on the material they would supply. The idea was to make the Party's case appear stronger by having me, his closest friend, seem convinced of his two-faced and hostile attitude.

"Go on, ask whether I was really convinced of Stenka's opposition to the Party." Dymitrij stopped talking and fell silent for a few moments. He held his glass up to the light and watched the brownish rays reflected through the brandy. The silence was broken only by the shrill soprano singer wailing on the muted radio.

Dymitrij put his glass down, and his resonant voice boomed forth once more full of determination and conviction. "Actually, I think that it's of no importance whether or not I believe the charge. Just as it was of no importance whether Stenka was really two-faced and had acted to the detriment of the Party. In other words, it doesn't matter what a man really is. A man is only what others think he is, nothing more. Especially under conditions where the value of uselessness of a man is evaluated by an organized group. This is certainly true in the case of a Party member whose fate is wholly dependent upon the reputation which he manages to gain in the Party. From the moment the Party began to regard Stenka as an enemy, he became an enemy regardless of any other considerations.

"To return to Stenka's story, the meeting was scheduled for ten days later. And all this time, when meeting Stenka, I had to pretend that our friendship was unchanged. Those were my instructions. Stenka was not to suspect a thing. He did not even know that his wife had been arrested, though he was quite upset by the fact that he hadn't received any letters from her and that no one answered the telephone when he called her.

"While listening to Stenka's worries, I was already drafting my coming accusation against him, putting it into a logical form. I framed the questions I would ask him, ones I was sure he would not be able to answer. I thought up implications in the questions which he could not comprehend, but which would be perfectly understandable to the meeting, and other implications which the meeting would not understand, but which would disconcert Stenka completely and utterly disorient him.

"Finally the day of the meeting arrived. Once again I was warned to make my charges against Stenka as convincing as possible, so strong that they would not leave any doubt in the minds of Party members about his collaboration with Slansky's group. I was warned that I, myself, was partly responsible for Stenka's actions. Didn't I know his wife and attend their wedding?

"My part of the performance was perfectly planned and executed. First, I went into an exhaustive self-criticism. I reproached myself for neglecting the principles of alertness in regard to sectarianism and revisionism in the Communist Party of Czechoslovakia. Next I intimated that, blinded by my friendship for Stenka, I had shut my eyes to his gradual drift away from our Party and our ideology and therefore was implicated in a way with his case. Next, insinuatingly, I brought the meeting's attention around to the fact that perhaps Stenka and his wife were taking advantage of me as a screen for their hostile, anti-Party work. I then went on to outline Stenka's treacherous actions, basing my accusation on material received from the Party's executive committee.

"Stenka went completely to pieces during my indictment. He was so deeply affected that any answers he gave to my questions only served to involve him further. In the voting that followed, Stenka was expelled from the Party and dismissed from his position.

"I'm not sure, but if I remember correctly the case was later referred to some special commission of the Central Committee that was formed after the trial of Slansky's group and the death sentences that followed it. Stenka's wife, I believe, was sentenced to fifteen years in prison. And that was the end of my friendship with Stenka. . . ."

Dymitrij paused and looked at me with clear eyes. "What did you expect? Our Party knows what it's doing. In any case, it's not up to the individual to judge its actions. The Party has its own criteria and its own ways of carrying them out. The best thing an individual can do for himself is to adopt these criteria and ways as his own. What else is possible?"

It was very late. The square outside the window was deserted. Dymitrij showed me his calendar. The coming day was full of meetings, consultations, and conferences. It was to be a full and fruitful day, one which, according to Dymitrij, would bring him closer to his goal.

At this moment I happened to notice the portrait of a white-haired, handsome old man hanging on the wall. The old man's face was tanned and wrinkled. His eyes were the clear eyes of a child, but they peered from under bushy brows. Noticing my interest in the portrait, Dymitrij laughed and explained, "I'll bet you'll never guess who that is. He is one of the principle Czarist generals and a court dignitary. Imagine, still alive and a model in the art school! You may see him sometime in the streets of Moscow. He must be eighty-five, but he's still very sprightly. Funny, isn't it? Some of the bourgeois revolutions didn't even spare the relics, but ours not only spared the works of art but that model to boot. I was given this picture by my students in an ideological course that I taught."

Dymitrij fixed a glass of warm milk for each of us. While we drank the milk, we listened to the latest news on the radio. Then Dymitrij started to stock his briefcase with notes, papers, and books. I noticed some of the titles: two pamphlets called *Propagandist i Agitator* (Propagandist and Agitator), one copy of *Krizis amerikanskoi voenno-teoreticheskoi mysl'i* (The Crisis of American Military Theoretical Thought), three or four copies of the periodical *Voennye Znaniia* (Military Knowledge), and a book in a red binding, *Sredstva i sposoby zashchity ot atomnogo oruzhiia* (Ways and Means of Defense against Atomic Weapons), which had several colored bookmarks between its pages. When the briefcase was almost full, Dymitrij telephoned for his official car to take him to work saying he would drop me off in midtown Moscow.

While Dymitrij was busy, I drank my milk and looked over the titles of the books on his night table. There was a fat book, *Sovremennaia voennaia tekhnika* (Contemporary Military Technology), an English-Russian dictionary of idiomatic expressions, Mayakovsky's *Poetry*, and Lermontov's *Hero of Our Times*. Dymitrij, putting on his coat, said, "My favorite authors. I know almost all of them by heart, but I keep on reading them. And the English may come in handy in the future."

We went outside. Dawn was breaking in the street. The new day rose slowly. A polished, shiny car waited in front of the door. Dymitrij greeted the driver. Seeing his inquisitive glance directed at me, he explained hastily, "This is the comrade you met yesterday, remember? We talked too late, so he stayed for the night."

The driver smiled at me vaguely. Soon we were driving through the wide city streets. Workers, men and women hurrying along the sidewalks, cast curious glances at the elegant ZIL-III limousine, trying to see the faces of the passengers.

Casually, Dymitrij pulled the cerulean curtain across the window and stretched out lazily with a yawn. Outside, the morning mist, a white-gray haze, roamed among the houses, forming a halo around lights in the windows and outlining the figures of people moving around inside.

Suddenly, in the rear-view mirror hung above the windshield of the car, I noticed the driver's cold and suspicious eyes staring at me in concentration. I responded with a rather weak smile.

12

THE CHOSEN PEOPLE

"THE COMMUNITY OF SOVIET NATIONS—PRIDE OF SOCIALISM IN the U.S.S.R." was the title of the lecture. It was being given at Lomonosov University, Moscow, for all the students and the public. Lengthy and monotonous, it ran on about the national cultures blooming in socialist form in the socialist commonwealth of nations.

After it was finished, a friend introduced me to a squat young man in horn-rimmed glasses with black, tightly curled hair. Large olive-colored eyes looked at me searchingly from behind the glasses. "I want you," my friend said, "to meet my colleague Chaim Z——baum. He is studying mathematics."

Chaim walked home with me. When we were alone, in front of my house, Chaim said, "You'll be staying here a long time, won't you? If you do, you'll find out that two nations are in extreme positions here. The Russian nation chosen to rule, and the Jewish nation chosen to be hated. You have become acquainted with the Russian nation, I presume. Now you must learn about the other one."

During my visit to the U.S.S.R. I met many Jews, though arranging this was more difficult than I had thought. These people were usually frightened, restless, full of prejudices and suspicions. They talked nervously, their eyes always looking around. I found it hard to persuade them that I had no bad intentions, that I wouldn't repeat our talks, and that I hadn't been "sent" by anybody. Their nervous alertness was infectious. It passed on to me and to everybody around us.

The behavior of these people reminded me of the Jews who were hiding from the Germans during the last war. Inhumanly hunted, they tried to save themselves from death in a crematorium or in a concentration camp, or from suffocation in a common grave which they first would have to dig under the barrel of a machine gun. They carried an inhuman fear in their eyes which paralyzed their movements, penetrating their hearts and brains. Death was around them, but it was already in them too.

When I visited the U.S.S.R. it was twelve years after the war. I must admit that during the first part of my visit to Russia I couldn't understand the tragic mood of the Jews I met. I was inclined to attribute it to the ordeals that they had experienced and that had robbed them of their loved ones. I thought that they still could hear the screams of their murdered people, they could still see the black smoke curling from chimneys of the crematoriums.

But sooner than I would have thought, I learned that it was not the past but the present that was the cause of this mood. Chaim Z——baum was right. The Jews remained a chosen people in the U.S.S.R. also. There was no room for them in the "Socialist Community of Nations," though there was space for them in the U.S.S.R., space sealed off and surrounded by hatred.

There were four members in Chaim Z——baum's family. When I met them, they looked at me apprehensively. We were seated at a round table. The father was fifty-three and worked in a publishing house. The hair of the mother, forty-eight, was completely white. Chaim's sister, fifteen, had black hair braided at the top of her head.

I talked at length about myself, while their eyes stared at my lips. While I talked, Chaim's mother went to the door twice to make sure that nobody was listening. The family lived in one and a half rooms on the sixth floor of a large building. The remainder of the five-room apartment was occupied by other people. The kitchen, the hall, and the bathroom were used by all the tenants.

At the end of my introduction, I showed them my documents proving that I was a foreigner. Chaim's father verified them

carefully. Staring at me closely, he asked, "So you won't stay
here for good?"

I assured him that I wouldn't and that I would be going back
to my own country soon where my parents and my work awaited
me. I would go, and all I had learned about the U.S.S.R. would
go with me. If I wanted to learn, it was only for my own sake.
I was anxious to know the truth, that was all.

I won't quote everything that the Z——baums told me. The
story of this family since 1927 certainly deserves to be recorded,
though it undoubtedly is the story of all Russian Jews. I'll tell
only about the present.

Until 1948, Chaim's father was a university professor. He
taught evolutionary psychology. However, in 1946 a fierce drive
began against Jewish scholars in all realms of science. It was
carried out under the guise of a "struggle against cosmopolitanism in science." Critical areas included philosophy, political
economy, psychology, statistics, mathematics, and physics. Old
Z——baum showed me periodicals from 1946–49. Nearly every
issue contained new reports in these areas. The most frequent
argument used against the Jewish scholars was "cosmopolitanism
and an inferior attitude towards bourgeois science."

A few score professors and cultural and scientific workers
were ousted from their posts. Almost 100 per cent of them were
people with Jewish names. They were transferred to other oc-
cupations and deprived of the opportunity to do scientific work.
Among them was the psychologist Z——baum. In looking
through the present lists of scholars at various universities I see
that practically none of these people have returned to scientific
work in their field.

So Z——baum worked in a publishing house for scientific
books. Almost all of his co-workers were promoted, but not he.
He was a good, conscientious worker, knew his field well, and
loved books.

On his passport, on the line for nationality, the word "Yevrei"
(Jew) was written in large letters. This line was not abolished
by Soviet socialism, and Z——baum had to bear all the consequences of being Jewish.

And yet, from the point of view of the "objective theory
of the socialist nations in the U.S.S.R." this line was a paradox,

for the Jews were the only "nation" without land in the U.S.S.R. This became especially important in 1948, when the cultural commissar, Andrei Zhdanov, sentenced five hundred Jewish poets, writers, journalists, scientists, and artists to professional and even actual death for "turning their backs on socialism."

"They did so," said Zhdanov, "because they have no permanent ties with socialism. They are a nation without land, and therefore in Soviet terminology *they are not a nation*."

Thus Soviet anti-Semitism gained new arguments, and at the same time got rid of those who could fight it through their talents. The situation was aggravated in 1947 when the Jews regained their motherland, Israel, which became the mainstay of the Western world against the communism inundating the Arab countries. Mass dismissals of Jews from all authoritative posts in the Soviet Union followed. Three million Soviet Jews had no legal representation. The basic reference book, The Achievements of the Soviet Regime in Forty Years Given in Statistics, did not even mention their existence.

Z——baum held the book in his hand. "You see," he said, "we have been erased from the Soviet reality for which we must work. There are about thirty thousand Jewish scientific workers, mostly in mathematics, physics, chemistry, and statistics in the U.S.S.R. now. Many of them are old professors, the original organizers of scientific institutions, inventors, research workers, but you won't find their names mentioned anywhere. The results of their work are published anonymously, or—and this happens quite often—under the name of a non-Jewish scientist. During the war, of the eleven thousand soldiers and officers in the Soviet Army who received the title of Hero of the Soviet Union, about 530 were Jews. But they have been forgotten. Though publications about Heroes of the Soviet Union list various nationalities, they never mention the Jews.

"You have to understand that under these conditions the word Yevrei becomes one more reason for persecution. In my office it takes various forms. Three years ago half a room was taken away from my family, though I was entitled to it because my wife has tuberculosis. They said that 'as a typical Jew' I wanted to have more space for my family than a Soviet citizen would have wanted. Such accusations are not unusual. Look

at this 1957 issue of *Pravda Ukrainy* (Ukrainian Truth). There's
a short story on the first page. The main character is a Jew,
Moisei Chaimovich Liubich, a notorious forger of documents
and official papers. He gains riches dishonestly to add to his three
bank accounts, in which he already has 100,000 rubles. This
type of story is meant to foment hatred for Jews and point
out their non-socialist character.

"Here's another paper, the *Sovietskaya Litva* (Soviet Lithuania) of August 11, 1957. Here, in another short story, the
villain is also a Jew. This time he's the manager of a textile
factory. His name is David Naumovich Rubinstein. The factory
is located near Vilno and the manager has his official residence
in the city. But he isn't interested in the factory at all. He
never visits it, but doesn't hesitate to collect *per diem* and expense money from the Flax Trust to cover his alleged trips
there. He has another apartment in Vilno, and he systematically bribes inspectors and his superiors and anyone who could
cause him trouble. The moral of the story? Jews are not fit to be
appointed to leading posts in industry.

"Another example, this time in *Sovietskaia Bielorussia* (Soviet
White Russia) of August 25, 1957. Again a short story in a
prominent spot. The main character is a young Jewish doctor,
Moisei Ruvimorich Chernov, who takes advantage of his position to dishonestly collect two salaries. Through some crooked
trick, he manages to avoid being sent to a post far from his
family. He ends by building himself a luxurious villa with his
ill-gotten money. The moral? Jews shouldn't be allowed to study
medicine for they're fundamentally an untrustworthy people
inclined to cheat and will take advantage of their position for
private anti-national purposes.

"Please note that each of these stories was printed in a different republic. One in the Ukraine, another in Lithuania, and
the third in White Russia. In looking through magazines and
books published in the U.S.S.R., you'll find that 90 per cent
of the villains are Jews, and that they're always branded as individuals opposed to socialism and the U.S.S.R. If you care
to delve deeper into the problems of Jews in Russia, you'll discover other interesting facts in connection with the present
policy of Russia in the Middle East."

While traveling in the White Russian Soviet Republic, I came across the problems of the Jews at almost every step. In Minsk I met an assistant professor of Russian literature in Minsk University. His name was David F——man. He was twenty-seven and had been living in Minsk since the end of the war. All his family, and that of his wife, had perished during the war, murdered by the Germans. In the White Russian Republic there are a great number of Jews who had lived there before the war and who returned to their old cities and towns after the war, despite their utter destruction.

In F——man's opinion, there were about 45,000 Jews in Minsk, out of a population of about 450,000. In Bobruysk, out of about 155,000 residents, seventy thousand were Jews. In Mogilev, out of 110,000, about 11,000 were Jews. In Gomel, with a population of 150,000, there were more than 14,000 Jews.

F——man said, "If there is a list of Jewish unhappiness anywhere in the world, the Jews of the White Russian Republic are in first place. A great number were murdered by the Germans and by the Ukrainian-Tatar Mercenaries serving in the German Army. They were shot like animals. They were hung up by their hands and feet. Their tongues were torn out. They were burnt alive in barns set on fire. Soldiers raped wives before the eyes of their husbands, and daughters before the eyes of their parents. Driven by fear of the German troops, some of them managed to escape. However, everywhere they were looked on as aliens, everywhere spat at, beaten, humiliated. They wandered through strange republics, woods, steppes, tundras, and mountains. When the war ended they slowly began to return to their former homes and were greeted by rubble and graves. At this moment, the Jewish population is roughly two per cent of the total population. A large portion of them are educated people with a high standard of education, culture—and suffering.

"At Minsk University where I work, a kind of quota system has been in operation for Jews for many years, though nobody calls it that. I'll give you examples. Last year, in my history department, in the graduating class there were 215 White Russians, 75 Russians, 39 Ukrainians, and 6 Jews. In other departments, especially those of literature and philosophy, the percentage of Jewish students is even smaller. In university life, the few

Jewish professors and students are openly discriminated against.

"For example, it's absolutely impossible for a Jewish student to become a shock worker of science. The other students just wouldn't allow it. A Jewish scientist has practically never become the head of a research group. A Jewish scholar can't publish a work solely under his own name. There must always be another name, usually of a Russian scholar. It's done under the pretext of supporting the 'collective of Soviet scientists,' but Russian or Ukrainian scientists are allowed to publish their scientific works individually.

"In recent years anti-Semitism in the U.S.S.R. has been strengthened on a new front by the alliance with the Arab countries. On every occasion the 'imperialistic character of international Jewry' is emphasized, and prominent Jews in capitalistic countries are slandered. Jews are placed in embarrassing and humiliating situations. For instance, my colleagues tell me that when Arab politicians and scientists study in Soviet universities, Jewish students and instructors, if any are left, must be removed.

"In the Minsk Academy of Sciences we had a scientific meeting in honor of some occasion or other, at which a few Egyptians who were touring the country were expected. All Jews were excluded from the sessions, including two aged professors, one a mathematician, the other a physicist, to whom Soviet science owes a great deal. The secretary of the Party organization just 'asked' them to be absent in the name of the university authorities. Toasts offered at the celebration included such as 'Down with Israel,' 'Down with international Jewry.' But the climax was an address by an Egyptian, I think the chief political instructor of the group, who said that, 'Hitler was the first to understand the danger of international Jewry and knew how to fight it, setting an example to his successors.' This sentence was uttered in Minsk, twelve years after a war in which millions of Jews perished, including hundreds of thousands in the U.S.S.R.

"Just a few kilometers from the spot where this celebration was taking place and where these words were uttered there is one of the mass graves of murdered Jews. But don't think that this speech was unpopular. Oh no. As soon as the Russian interpreter finished reading the text of the address, the auditorium, filled to the brim, burst into uproarious applause. Cheers of

'Long live Egypt,' 'Down with the imperialistic U.S.A.' 'Long live Egyptian–Russian friendship,' and 'Down with Israel' rang out.

"My wife is a chemist. Somehow she managed to graduate from this university. Of the 60 or more Jews who applied to study chemistry, only 12 were accepted, of whom 5 were dropped during their studies for various 'ideological' deviations. Thus, of 349 graduates last year, 224 were White Russians, 82 Russians, 39 Ukrainians, and 8 Jews. As you see, the Egyptian seems to have the right idea. Anti-Semitism has its usual forms here. I could give you many more details if we had more time.

"How about coming to see us next Saturday afternoon? Our co-tenants are going to some reception and we'll have the room to ourselves. My wife promised to cook a good dinner. Maybe we'll be able to get some more people in. It'll be fun. Can you make it? Fine, see you there."

In my many talks with Jews in various parts of the U.S.S.R. I always found the same theme. Unlike the Russians or Ukrainians, these people thought of themselves as shut inside of a world to which they did not belong, which hated them, but from which there was no escape. With what envy they spoke about Polish Jews, a number of whom managed to emigrate to Israel! With what terrible sorrow they lamented that their children would have to live in the same "society-prison" forever, always alien to it, bearing Jewish names inherited from their parents (in the U.S.S.R. name changing is forbidden), their heritage an intensified hatred on the part of the authorities and the surrounding world. These were really hopeless talks with people who had lost all hope.

One day on my visit to a factory I saw a wall newspaper with a column entitled 'Idlers.' In it there was a large caricature of one Abram Katz, a worker who was described in the newspaper as a loafer and idler, whose head was filled with thoughts of 'distant hot, imperialist countries' which didn't leave him any time to perform his work. Emerging from Katz' head in the caricature were four little houses with the inscription, 'here we don't work. Kibutz No. 6,' which, of course, was a reference to Israel.

I decided to find Katz and have a talk with him. I met him

after work in the workers' canteen. He was about fifty, short, slightly stooped, bald, with full lips, round features, and the remnants of black hair on his temples. Abram worked as a locksmith in the repair shop. He was a very strange man.

First of all, he was deeply religious. He always carried a Hebrew Bible with him, which he reportedly had received from his father, who in turn had received it from his father, a rabbi. Abram Katz lost his wife and children during the war. He himself managed to survive in a most unusual manner. Put in a concentration camp by the Germans, he waited patiently for death which took hundreds of Jews every day. However, one day, in his daily work, Abram Katz by himself pulled a stump out of the ground that three men hadn't been able to move together. Katz's unusual strength caught the attention of the guard, who reported the incident to the camp commander.

The commander showed his interest in his own peculiar way. He organized weekly wrestling matches between the strongest Jews in the camp. These fights were for life or death. The loser was sent the next day to help dig mass graves into which the diggers were tossed after being murdered. The victor won a week of life, after which he had to wrestle a new opponent. Katz fought a great number of matches, and was always the winner. A tie was impossible. They were horrible fights. Katz told me that he never attacked. He was always on the defensive. He won, not by damaging his opponent, but by exhausting him with his defense.

"A man has the right to defend himself," Katz said, "when he is attacked.

"The camp commander added stimulants to my opponents' food. During these fights, they acted more like wild animals than people. There were no restrictions in these fights—anything went. They were great entertainment for the guards and the camp commander."

Katz survived the annihilation of the entire camp. The Germans used him for pulling out cars and field kitchens stuck in the mud. One day, when the guard wasn't looking, Katz broke his neck in one blow and escaped. The retreating German units were too busy with their own troubles to bother much about him. After a few days of wandering around he came upon some Russian partisans.

For a while, after the war, he enjoyed the religious freedom permitted the Jews and worked in a Jewish community in White Russia. However, 1948 brought a wave of anti-Semitism, and the religious life of Jewish communities ceased to exist formally. He was sent to work in a factory.

His religious way of life made him the object of steady persecution in the factory. Since 1949 he had been sent three times to labor camps for being 'a loafer and an idler.' The penalty really was for refusing to work on Jewish religious holidays.

In 1952 Katz received a letter and a package of books from Israel. Of course they were not delivered directly to him. He received a notice from the post office informing him that "the XY section of the post office notifies citizen Abram Katz that a consignment has been received from Israel. The parcel contains printed matter and religious pamphlets propagating *American imperialism and backward ideology.* If, in spite of this, citizen Katz wants to receive the consignment, he should call at this office between the hours . . ."

Katz, however, wasn't afraid to have books with "backward ideology" in his home. Despite the advice of the clerks and the threats of the chief of the post office, Katz called for his package and signed a pledge not to lend the books to anybody.

Thus he became the owner of a considerable religious library and information about Israel. From that time on, Israel seemed like a paradise to him. He spoke of it in words full of worship, pride, and pathos.

A few weeks after receipt of the parcel, Katz was called to the personnel office. The personnel director held a paper in his hand. It was Katz' personal questionnaire completed a few years before. I repeat the conversation that followed, as it was told to me by Katz.

Director: Say, Katz, why did you lie in your questionnaire? Do you realize that giving false information is punishable by a long prison term?

Katz: I wrote nothing but the truth in my questionnaire. I don't know what Tovarishch Director is talking about. Really I don't.

Director: Why do you keep lying, Katz? You wrote in your questionnaire, in the column about relatives, that you had no relatives abroad, outside of the U.S.S.R., didn't you? Is this true?

Katz: Yes, it is the truth. I have no relatives abroad.

Director: Katz, I'm warning you once more, it could end badly. Soviet authority is no joke, and I wouldn't play games with it. You'll be sorry. Now tell me the truth. Do you, or do you not, have relatives abroad?

Katz: Truthfully, Tovarishch Director, I have no relatives abroad.

Director: As you will, Katz. You are digging your own grave. Our personnel section was notified yesterday by the post office that you received a parcel with books from Israel containing imperialistic and backward ideology. Is it true?

Katz: I received a parcel. It contained religious books, but I haven't found anything about imperialism as yet.

Director: The post office also notified us that the sender of the parcel was one Samuel Katz who lives in Tel Aviv, Israel, and who wrote in the letter enclosed, 'Dear Abram, my dearest brother.' Is that true?

Katz: Yes, it's true. He always wrote to me like that, even before the war, when he lived in Poland.

Director: Our investigation showed that Samuel Katz left Poland in 1947 and went to Israel. He has relatives and family in the U.S.S.R. Do you admit that he is your brother or don't you?

Katz: Of course he's my brother. And what a brother! Samuel was always the smartest of us five brothers. That's why he is now in Israel, has a house, children, and a lovely wife, and is rich.

Director: Katz, are you playing jokes with Soviet authority? Do you realize what you're doing? Have you ever heard about Siberia, Katz? If you have a brother abroad in Israel, I'm asking you here and now, Katz, why didn't you include this in your questionnaire? Why didn't you write that you had a brother abroad, eh?

Katz: Have you flipped your lid, Tovarishch Director? I have no brother abroad. It's my brother Samuel who has *me* abroad. I told the truth.

But Katz didn't succeed in convincing the authorities that it was he who was abroad. For furnishing false statements in his questionnaire he was sentenced to a year of hard labor. He built dams, standing in water for hours at a time. He carried stones, until one of them fell on his legs and completely crushed a foot.

He returned to the factory, crippled, still more alone and shut inside himself, carrying the worn Hebrew Bible in the inside pocket of his jacket next to his heart. He seemed to ignore his environment, but the environment wouldn't ignore him. So in the wall newspaper I read under Katz' caricature that he didn't perform his duties.

"Citizen Katz," said the caption under this photograph, "finds time for his religious vagaries, but forgets that if he fails to sweep the shop someone else will have to do it for him, and he may sweep citizen Katz away too."

Katz stood in front of the newspaper with me and smiled skeptically, looking at his caricature, "What do they know about *kibutzes?* What do they know about Israel? My brother Samuel wrote me in that letter that *kibutzes . . .*"

After saying good-by to Katz, I left the factory with Samuel's address in my pocket. I promised Abram to write him.

"Tell him," said Abram, "Israel is not only a piece of land surrounded by water and enemies. Tell him that Israel is something that you carry here, in your heart, right under this book I carry in my jacket. There is my Israel, my *kibutz*, my country. And there it will remain as long as Abram Katz will walk on this earth."

A group of workers that I'd met before stood in the wide doorway of the factory. I greeted them, and one of them asked laughingly, "What did you learn from that stinking Jew, Katz?"

A few days later I talked about anti-Semitism with another Jew, a former university professor in Leningrad. In 1953 he was relieved of his professorship for attributing a positive role in one of the historical periods to Judaism. Since then, he has spent hours in the university library working "for himself," as he put it, and hanging on to life.

The professor said, "Just note how anti-Semitism has changed historically. Until Lenin's death in 1924 anti-Semitism was always anti-communist, because the persecuted Jews in capitalistic countries leaned toward socialism and communism. Now anti-Semitism serves communism because their purposes are identical, both internally and externally. In Stalin's time the treatment of Jews was perfidious. On the one hand, they were given high positions in the Party and in the government. Many Party leaders, among them Stalin himself, married Jewish women. On the other hand, all Party and government failures were blamed on the Jews as an 'alien element' in the Soviet nation and in the national ideology of the Communist Party. There were many Jews among the leaders of the communist movement, especially in the first stage of the existence of the Soviet state. Yet, especially in the thirties, and after the war during the famous trials, the defendants' seats were filled with Jews charged with 'high treason,' and 'servility to imperialism.'

"Khrushchev carries on this tradition. In internal life, Jews are exploited, especially the Jewish intelligentsia. Scholars, mathematicians, physicists, and designers are forced to work anonymously in groups directed by Russians. At the same time, in foreign policy, the nations of the U.S.S.R. are turned against the Jews as alleged 'agents of imperialism,' who try to hinder Russia in its attempt to liberate the colonial and dependent peoples, especially the Arabs, from under imperialistic oppression. Israel is allegedly the tool of the imperialists.

"It also seems that Khrushchev's policy skilfully exploits the fact that you can talk the anti-Semites of the world into anything as long as you use anti-Semitic slogans and fight the Jews. In this way you may even condition them to overlook Soviet actions. We must admit that Khrushchev was right when he replaced the old slogan 'workers of the world, unite' with the new slogan 'anti-Semites of the world, unite.'

"Until recently the anti-Semites used to talk about 'the Jewish Commune'; now the Jews talk about the 'anti-Semitic Commune.' World anti-Semitism paralyzes measures which could be taken by the West to defend the Jews. When they fight against the strengthening of Israel, the anti-Semites promote the Kremlin's policy in Arabian affairs. Their relationship to Israel reminds you of the relationship of racists to Jesus Christ. Because they doubt whether He existed at all, they proclaim to the world that the Jews murdered Him."

"You are right—their situation is hopeless," a Russian said to me about the Jews. He was an intelligent, educated man who worked in a transportation center. "I'm almost sixty. I've changed my job several times, and wherever I've been I've worked with Jews and observed them. My Lord, 'a chosen people!' Those whom I met could only be called 'a tragic people.' Hounded, bullied, oppressed by those around them, their Jewish names and surnames were a stigma for life. To me, personally, the most horrible thing was the fact that, though Jews, these people were usually very good Russians at the same time. They loved Russia no less than we do. They were proud of it. They wanted to help it and demanded nothing in return.

"And they got nothing, neither from the 'old and white' Russia nor from the 'new and red.' They both beat the Jews wherever possible, with whatever possible, and whenever possible.

"And occasions were never missing. And now they are locked in a circle of hatred, in the most frightening prison that can be imagined. Their children are called by vulgar nicknames, beaten, spat at, harassed by other children. Can you understand the sorrow of a father and mother when they see their child bruised, beaten until it bleeds, humiliated and tyrannized, and not able to prevent it? I have children too, and I know I could never stand this. I sometimes see and hear how the Jewish children suffer in school, no one knows for whose crimes. It would seem that the measure of their sufferings overflowed during the war. It would seem that the ordeals the Russian nation went through should have enabled it to understand and be sensitive to the fate of the handful of Jews who survived the war. But no, the people follow the Party and the government policy. This is the best proof that Soviet Russia continues certain traditions of pre-Revolutionary Russia and that the nation believes blindly in its new political and spiritual leaders.

"Have you heard what happened to the Jews who lived in the parts of Poland that were occupied by the Soviet Army in 1939? After being exiled by the Russians to Siberia, under an agreement between Khrushchev and the Polish Government in 1957, they were allowed to return to Poland. Try to get in touch with somebody who took part in the repatriation of these Jews and ask for details. Only then will you be able to comprehend the extent of human evil. If you're interested I'll give you addresses of some friends of mine who are familiar with these circumstances."

I was interested. I talked about it later with many people—Russians, Jews and Poles—all of them had had something to do with the repatriation of the Jews who, as Polish citizens, were allowed to return to Poland. In Poland conditions had changed in the meantime so that those who returned could have hope of being allowed to emigrate to Israel.

It was a trying period for the Polish Jews who had been in Russia since 1939. Many of them had married Russian Jews who were not entitled by law to leave. In many cases the children of Polish Jews, educated in schools which deprived them of any contact with their parents, refused to go back. In cases where the children hesitated, local authorities hastily framed charges of 'imperialistic provocation by international Zionism' against the parents. Provocation, but committed by the authorities not by the Jews, was a daily occurrence. Party and administrative officials organized *ad hoc* charges of espionage against many of the Jews who were allowed to leave the U.S.S.R. under the agreement. Many were arrested and exiled to other parts of Russia. Others, in fear of provocation and of reprisals against their families, gave up any idea of leaving the U.S.S.R. In the case of scientists, especially mathematicians and physicists who intended to avail themselves of this chance to return home, low-grade blackmail was used. They were threatened with arrest and being exiled to Siberia with their families. Many scholars remained voluntarily, rather than be separated from their children.

Taking advantage of the opportunity, local union, political-social and cultural organizations started large scale campaigns against the Jews. The victims were the Jews who decided to leave. Invectives were hurled at them, they were quoted as examples of "cynical cheating of the Soviet authority for many years," "double-facedness," and "results of imperialistic propaganda." At every step they encountered difficulties in completing the formalities connected with their departure. Their complaints addressed to the Polish authorities in charge of the repatriation never arrived. Their applications with enclosures, often the only copies of valuable documents such as birth certificates or pre-war Polish passports, were lost in transit, purposely destroyed by Soviet clerks. The applicants were required to submit all kinds of certificates that were immensely hard to get and whose loss automatically meant a refusal of the application. The Polish Re-emigration Commission, snowed under by applications and not too anxious to fight the arrogant representatives of the Soviet side, yielded wherever the ill but purposeful will of Soviet officials was too plain.

But the exodus of Polish Jews went on. The fortunate ones who managed at last to wade through the hell of Soviet bureaucracy, bribery, provocation, and blackmail took their belongings, paid for their transportation and customs, and departed in the direction of Poland, westward towards the more imagined than real Israel. In crowded trains, perhaps the same trains which a few years ago carried their brothers and relatives to the camps of death, the Jews "returned to life," rode towards the vision of their own country, their own home, and the laughing happy faces of their children beloved above anything else.

They rode but with them human hatred went for a long time. The guide of one of these trains, a Russian, an old railroad man who still remembered the railroad station Dno where the Czar of All-Russia signed his abdication, told me, "I traveled with these Jews as a technical manager of the transport, and I watched them. They were a very unhappy people, I must say. They were frightened, afraid if you as much as looked at them. Just let anyone shout at them or give them a bad word, right away they shrank, became small, their faces pale. The children cried silently and embraced a man's legs. 'Don't beat us' they begged. 'A Jew is a human being too. He can get hurt.' 'Have mercy, don't beat. We didn't do anything wrong.'

"Their luggage traveled in special cars. Some had their radios and TV sets with them, others had pianos and musical instruments, while still others had household articles, refrigerators, washing machines, and other things they had bought with their hard-earned money. When we arrived at the end of the line and the reloading to Polish trains began, everything still seemed in order; but later we found out that perhaps our guards, or the loaders, or probably both together got hold of all these things and, just to spite the Jews, damaged them all. They broke the tubes in the television sets, broke the wires in the radios, destroyed everything. They stuffed filth and rocks into the refrigerators, they broke strings in the piano, stuffed them with sand and poured water inside.

"When I saw it, I thought I'd drop dead of rage. Why? Why do all this to these people? Why take revenge on them, for what sins?

"So I asked a guard. I said, 'Did these Jews do anything to you? Did they make you lose anything? Did they hurt your children? Did they take bread away from your mouth? No, no, and no. They didn't hurt you. They didn't take anything away from you. On the contrary. Since the Revolution they have been working hard with us and by our side. They have suffered more than all of us. Why do you plague them, you evil man? Haven't you had enough trouble during the war? Haven't we got enough left still? Won't there be enough trouble in the future, when the atom bombs and God knows what other bombs fall on human homes?'

"That's what I said to him, and he started to explain that the Jews are the worst foes of socialism and the U.S.S.R., that Israel attacks and murders the innocent Arabs, that Israel is the obstacle to communism among the colonial nations. I just shrugged my shoulders. It seems I'm too old to talk with these people. They are already made over, shaped like a shoe that has been wet, tied, and put on a crooked last. What good is such a shoe? It might be good for kicking but not for walking. I was ashamed to look these Jews in the eyes. I was sweating from shame, but it was too late to repair the damage.

"And so these Jews went from the U.S.S.R. into a different world, perhaps better, perhaps worse, but not the Soviet world. Those who remain will now be persecuted for the departure of those others. And so it goes in a circle, relentlessly. Human hatred is like a serpent. Cut off its tail and another will grow. It must be the law of nature. Such must be our country, or perhaps such is the Jewish fate?"

After some time in Leningrad, I talked with a young Jewish poet, M.V., about Jewish problems in the U.S.S.R. Our talk started with a discussion about an article printed in the September 26, 1957, issue of *Literaturnaia Gazeta* (Literary Gazette), a leading Soviet literary journal. The writer described his impressions of his trip abroad. Among other things he stated that the Russian emigré newspaper in New York, *Novoye Russkoye Slovo*, served the cause of international Jewry by combining the American imperialism of Washington with the Jewish imperialism of Tel Aviv.

The young poet wrote poems in beautiful Russian. Some were printed, and criticized for 'lyricism alien to socialist realism.' Others are kept in his desk and will probably never see the light of day.

"You find it hard to understand," M.V. says, "that a man can write 'for the drawer.' Yet it is so. A poet writes more for himself than for others, just as a violinist plays more for his own ear than for the audience. Officially, I am a translator of oriental poetry into Russian. Aside from that, I write my own poems. As a Jew, I can't expect to be recognized. Even if my poems were perfect, I could never win a prize. The Russians are very sensitive as far as their literature, theater, or ballet are concerned, and would never put up with the fact that a Jew could be a great, recognized poet. They would be ashamed of losing face, especially before the other nations of Asia and the East.

"There has been a long-term process of replacing Jews in various cultural institutions with Russians or even other people with 'full national rights.' In our labor union, which as you know is called the writers' union, Jews are more than unpopular. There are few and they keep quiet. We are probably a dying generation of Jewish creative workers. Conditions now make a creative beginning for young Jews impossible, just as they make literary studies impossible. In recent years original creativity in the Jewish language has almost disappeared."

The poet sat for a while in grim silence. He doodled on a piece of paper with a pencil, then said, "You know, sometimes I think that history may like to repeat itself, but I also think it likes to play tricks. The Jews in Russia, persecuted by the

Czars, tied their fate to the 1917 Revolution from its very beginning, and supported the ideals of communism. The Jewish intelligentsia took its stand at the head of the Revolution and led it during its most difficult period against the current. Involved in the complicated mechanism of the Revolution, the Jews helped to establish its rules and laws, not dreaming that a day would come when these laws and rules would be used against them. The Soviet Revolution, as other revolutions, devoured its children. Later, the Bolsheviks began to talk in the name of nations. But they didn't show their letters of credit for it, and unfortunately no one demanded to see them.

"But back to reality. Did you know that some of our poets and literary men are now being commissioned to do scenarios for propaganda films for Arab countries? These films are very crude. But there's nothing crude about the ideas they carry. 'American imperialism and Israel are identical.' 'Israel must disappear from the face of the globe in the interests of free nations.' 'Jews constitute the greatest evil of contemporary civilization, the future of which belongs to communism.' I saw two or three such films while they were being dubbed into Arabic before being shipped to Egypt. Believe me, I was shocked. Goebbels would not have been ashamed of these films. They reeked with blind hatred. Jews are represented as degenerates, perverts, and reprobates whose only goal in life is to fight communism. The films use all the old and proven tricks of anti-Semitism. You might say that at present world anti-Semitism is an ally of communism, and the anti-Semites a column of the Soviet Army."

We went out together. In the streets people were milling about. A streetcar approached, and we climbed on and found seats with difficulty. The streetcar started and passed through tree-lined streets. Suddenly it braked sharply, throwing the poet against a fat man with a big face which reddened with rage. The man looked at the poet for a second, then pushed him away, shouting for the benefit of the whole car, "Look who you're pushing, you mangy Jew, you. Haven't you enough room? Then go to your Israel. Get out of here, you stinking Jew."

The poet bent his head. The people in the tram laughed loudly.

13

WAR AND PEACE

AT A RECEPTION IN THE ACADEMY OF SCIENCES, I SUDDENLY noticed the figure of a well-known Party leader whom I had met before. I greeted him, and five minutes later we were standing together at a table lavishly spread with food and talking like old friends. When the Party leader asked why I hadn't chosen a military career, I answered that I didn't think I could adjust myself to the military way of life and its limited independence. The Party leader seemed to disapprove and said that in his opinion the future belonged to the military men—at least the immediate future.

I gathered my courage and asked directly, "Do you mean that there will be a war in the near future?"

The official looked at me from the corner of his eyes. "You must answer that question for yourself, my friend," he said with a smile. "Personally, I can tell you that it is my opinion that the Soviet Union will decide to start a war whenever it becomes known that the Pentagon has decided to start one. But of course you are free to have your own opinion."

My own opinion? I had no opinion whatsoever on the subject. But I realized that the question was fascinating, especially in the U.S.S.R. What were the opinions of the average Soviet citizen on the subject? How did he interpret Soviet peace propaganda? How did he fit this propaganda into his own world outlook, of which the Soviet educational system was so proud?

I made up my mind to find the answers to these questions. Pure chance helped me. One day I met a friend, a newspaperman from my country. He and four of his colleagues had been in the U.S.S.R. for several months at the invitation of the News-papermen's Association, and they were working with the editors of various Soviet papers and periodicals. During our conversation my friend told me about what he called "the investigation of the terrain" being conducted by a group of Soviet journalists in various parts of the U.S.S.R. These investigations were conducted in response to the Party's appeal for a "closer approach of journalists and propagandists to the everyday life of the working masses." Primarily it was a question of determining how the current political appeals and slogans used by the press and scientific-popular publications were grasped by the different social levels of the U.S.S.R. Another pertinent element of these investigations was an effort to discover what changes were being produced in the consciousness of society by Khrushchev's new conclusions and formulations and by the activities of the Central Committee of the Party.

"You see," my journalist friend explained, "propaganda is not such a simple affair in the U.S.S.R. People here are accustomed to repeating—or, if you prefer, declaiming—certain appeals, slogans, and formulas. At the present time, those responsible for propaganda in the U.S.S.R. probably want to know how everyday people are reacting to these slogans and formulas, what themes and connotations they give rise to, and what the common people think is behind these slogans. Propaganda is one thing and the way it is understood by the broader masses is another. To the journalist it is the latter which is important; the reverberation of propaganda among the masses. It is impossible to propagandize properly the policies of the government and the Party if one does not know how people are reacting in their minds or what the intellectual context accompanying the reaction to propaganda is.

"In recent times especially, the effort to conduct such a study which would make it possible to grasp the attitude of the masses to current propaganda formulas has become pressing. As you know, many of the accepted theories of government and party policy have been undermined. Many of these have been removed from the official dictionary of ideology and politics. Some are not discussed because one does not know if they are *still* binding. Others are barely mentioned because one does not know if they are *already* in force. Thus in a certain sense there exists a sort of indecision about certain doctrines, all the more so since in the last forty years our society has not had many occasions which called for individual political thinking.

"There is, therefore, a kind of political consternation among the press and propaganda workers who now, as never before, are condemned to personal decisions in their efforts to present a more elastic and flexible government and Party policy to the broad masses in a way that is comprehensible and consequential. This is why it has been necessary to organize these investigations of the terrain to find out 'what is squeaking in the grass.'"

From conversations with journalists whom I met later, I found that they had conducted these investigations in close understanding with authorities of the Party and the Soviets and in close co-operation with both the workers of the propaganda apparatus and the publicists of both the Party and the Soviets. The journalists who took the responsibility of conducting this investigation were representatives of several of the most important Soviet papers and some students of journalism who were acquiring practical experience at various publications. The investigation was conducted in various parts of the U.S.S.R. It was based on selecting typical groups in the various professional classes and holding specially organized meetings.

"In the U.S.S.R. it is impossible to do it otherwise," one of these journalists explained. "Here people are not accustomed to speaking out 'somewhere on the side.' This immediately gives them the impression of a political investigation, and the only thing one would be able to obtain would be the official phrases and slogans, declaimed with stubbornness. Our investigations were organized differently. We call this method 'directed discussion.' It works, more or less, like this: The leader of the discussion tries to draw out contrary opinions from the discussants or to start controversies. During our investigation we very often did this ourselves, for example, by offering contradictory explanations of some thesis of Lenin or Stalin or contradictory explanations of some move by the government or the Party. Then we offered various arguments supporting each of the controversial themes. The polemical attitude quickly affected those taking part in the meeting, and when the culminating point was reached and controversies still continued, we categorized the formulations and conducted a vote. Those who thought this— hand up; those who thought that—hand up. Counting the people who supported various positions was done very quickly, and since at the very beginning we had stressed that no one should refrain from voting, we managed to receive a rather full picture of the attitudes that the participants held towards the problems under discussion.

"At the beginning of each of these meetings we stated that our Party was aware of the fact that in our society there were contradictions when it was a question of understanding certain problems and that a sincere and definite statement of opinion given by all those present would, in the future, allow us to pre- pare better handbooks, better theoretical discussions, and bet- ter articles. Because of this, those present did not tend to regard their lack of decision on certain questions as something negative. On the contrary, they expressed their indecision most energeti- cally, making an effort to show their willingness to correct any mistakes they might be making, their willingness to learn the truth and to help the Party prepare better educational-propa- ganda material. There is no doubt, therefore, that we obtained a picture of how the problems discussed among the participants, at all meetings, were really comprehended by them.

"During the investigation it becomes evident that our society and especially certain segments of it differ percentage-wise in their understanding of certain theoretical formulations con- nected with our foreign policy and some of the practical moves of our government. The greatest confusion exists on questions which concern the war between socialism and capitalism, the possibility of war and the means of preventing war, justified and unjustified war, the reasons why such a war could break out, etc. That this confusion should exist is not strange, if one takes into account all the different formulas that have gathered about the Marxist-Leninist theory, the theories expounded at different times, and especially of the sort which left the gate wide open for differing interpretations of the basis of the foreign policy of the U.S.S.R. In recent times, because of the criticism of the cult of the individual as well as other declarations by comrade Khrushchev, this confusion has deepened. I must tell you that these investigations which we conducted have given me a lot, personally, and I have learned a great deal from them. Why don't you try to obtain access to these results? They are really very interesting."

After this discussion I made efforts to obtain the statistical results of these studies, which, as is evident, could be regarded as a sort of public-opinion poll. The investigation itself had ended in the fall of 1957 when I was trying to obtain permission to see the results. They were at a Moscow editor's, being subjected to an initial analysis of the gathered data. They did not have any specially secret or confidential character. Nevertheless, in Soviet editorial practice any materials that have not been officially published have a rather secret aura. To obtain access to such material one must obtain permission of the highest responsible authority. Since several newspaper friends of mine were then in touch with the same editors, I sought their intercession and for a short time I was permitted to appraise the results of the poll. These indicated the interesting fact that among the main professional classes of the U.S.S.R. there was a specific understanding and interpretation of the official propaganda of the Party and the government. That the broader masses stretch their understanding of propaganda beyond what the propaganda broadcasts literally, is very evident in the example of the attitudes towards peace and war.

However, let us consider the poll itself. The section dealing with peace and war was tested in the U.S.S.R. in 1957 among five socio-professional groups. Each of these groups—workers, intelligentsia, peasants of the *kolhoze*, students, and Party functionaries—occupies a well-defined place in Soviet society. Each is clearly distinguished, historically, culturally, occupationally, and politically. The data concerning war and peace were obtained mainly in the European part of the U.S.S.R., in cities of above 500,000 population among the following groups:

A) 262 skilled and unskilled workers who had been at their jobs for more than three years in factories located at Moscow, Kalinin, Leningrad, Chelyabinsk, Kuybyshev, Stalingrad, Rostov, and Kiev.

B) 198 persons representing the so-called intelligentsia, mostly white-collar workers, administrative personnel, artists, people in the public health service, and primary and secondary school teachers. All of them had been in their profession for more than one year in Moscow, Leningrad, Rostov, Kiev, Minsk, and Vilnius.

C) 153 *kolhoze* peasants from the vicinity of Kursk, Pskov, Vologda, Tambov, Kuybyshev, and Voroshilovgrad, polled for the most part on their group excursions to Moscow, Leningrad, and Rostov.

D) 113 university students in their first three years at the Universities of Moscow, Leningrad, and Kiev.

E) 76 professional Party officials from secretaries of factory or office Party organizations up, mostly in Moscow, Leningrad, and Kiev.

Below are the questions asked in the poll and the answers received, given in percentages of the various groups polled.

QUESTION

1. In your opinion, will a war between capitalism and socialism take place?

2. Do you think there is any possibility of preventing such a war?

3. If such a war were to break out, in your opinion how many people would die in the U.S.S.R.?

4. Should the war break out next year, do you think *you* would survive it?

5. What, in your opinion, would be:
   A) The cause of such a war?
   B) Its length?
   C) The weapons used?
   D) The outcome?

6. In your opinion, has tension between the U.S.S.R. and the U.S.A. grown or decreased between 1950 and now (summer 1957)?

7. Suppose one day all the Soviet radio stations simultaneously broadcast that an atomic explosion had taken place near Leningrad, causing the death of 20,000 people, and an atomic alert is proclaimed over the entire U.S.S.R. What, in your opinion, would have been the cause of the explosion?

It must be specified that the problems connected with peace and war were not the main part of the poll. They appeared rather on the margin, in connection with other questions, such as "The current stage of Marxist-Leninist theory," "The road to communism," "The battle with imperialist powers," etc. Below are the percentage results obtained, grouped according to questions asked. The questions were asked in various order. Only question 7 was always asked at the end of the discussion so as not to avoid disturbing the theoretical character of the first six questions.

Here are the answers and percentages for various groups:

QUESTION 1	Labor %	Intell. %	Peasant %	Student %	Party %
a) "The political situation makes war inevitable."	48	33	2	58	51
b) "Due to objective laws of history and economics, war is inevitable regardless of politics."	18	19	2	36	47
c) "War will come if God wills it."	4	-	28	-	-
d) "It's hard to tell, it may or may not come."	26	32	59	3	2
e) "There will never be a war."	7	16	11	3	-

QUESTION 2	Labor %	Intell. %	Peasant %	Student %	Party %
a) "The war cannot be prevented."	52	53	2	12	-
b) "Imperialism needs war, therefore it must come."	21	19	5	37	56

c) "Hard to tell, who knows." 4 3 29 4 -

d) "The U.S.S.R. can only prevent war by armaments and war and industrial technology." 12 18 4 25 30

e) "Combined action by all nations could prevent war." 9 3 11 7 4

QUESTION 3	Labor %	Intell. %	Peasant %	Student %	Party %
a) "Less than one million would be killed."	26	20	4	49	21
b) "About two to five million would be killed."	23	47	3	22	55
c) "More than five million would die, and as many would be wounded."	3	19	46	3	5
d) "Many would be killed and wounded."	8	2	4	20	-
e) "Impossible to foretell now."	40	12	43	6	19

QUESTION 4	Labor %	Intell. %	Peasant %	Student %	Party %
a) "I think I would survive."	58	28	12	44	72
b) "I would survive because of					

	Labor %	Intell. %	Peasant %	Student %	Party %
certain favorable factors."	11	36	5	27	16
c) "Impossible to tell."	22	19	61	19	2
d) "I would not survive because of active duty at the front."	6	11	18	8	2
e) "I wouldn't survive because of old age, illness, nervousness, etc."	3	6	5	2	8

QUESTION 5	Labor %	Intell. %	Peasant %	Student %	Party %
Part A					
a) "The U.S.S.R. will be attacked by the U.S.A."	39	24	32	41	52
b) "The U.S.A. will take advantage of a local war as an excuse for aggression."	22	32	-	18	38
c) "The U.S.S.R. will attack first, thus thwarting an imperialist attack."	6	2	9	15	2
d) "The U.S.S.R. and U.S.A. simultaneously attack and it would be a world war from the outset."	5	11	-	6	2

e) "Impossible to foresee at this moment."	28	31	50	20	6

Part B

a) "Less than one year."	41	27	-	7	15
b) "Between one and two years."	27	39	5	58	63
c) "Three years."	9	16	7	12	3
d) "Three to five years."	5	8	22	2	4
e) "Impossible to tell now."	18	9	66	21	15

Part C

a) "All weapons, including those of mass destruction."	61	49	77	39	70
b) "All arms, including tactical atomic, but excluding weapons of mass destruction."	26	41	-	45	18
c) "Only conventional weapons."	3	5	-	13	4
d) "Impossible to tell now."	10	5	23	3	8

Part D

a) "The war will be won by the U.S.S.R. at the head of the socialist camp."	54	57	20	50	61
b) "Cornered, Imperialism will surrender to avoid being crushed by the					

military forces
of the U.S.S.R.
and the other
socialist coun-
tries."

26	25	10	27	19

c) "There will be
a treaty under
which capitalism
will remain in
the U.S.A. only.
But the U.S.A.
will be disarmed
and remain under
international
forces led by the
U.S.S.R. and
People's China."

14	10	-	23	20

d) "Nobody will
win, there will
be mutual
destruction."

6	2	37	-	-

e) "Impossible to
tell, the future
will show."

-	6	33	-	-

QUESTION 6	Labor %	Intell. %	Peasant %	Student %	Party %
a) "International tension has grown steadily since 1950."	24	68	-	62	59
b) "Sometimes it grows, sometimes lessens, but on the average it remains the same."	28	13	11	7	27

c) "Tension lessens
for the U.S.S.R.
but grows for

	the imperialists."	25	10	-	30	14
d)	"There is no visible change. As a rule it remains steady."	13	6	10	1	-
e)	"The average man doesn't know."	20	3	79	-	-

QUESTION 7		Labor	Intell.	Peasant	Student	Party
		%	%	%	%	%
a)	"I would think that the Americans had dropped a bomb on the U.S.S.R."	35	40	29	26	19
b)	"Imperialism had started a war."	28	24	32	41	23
c)	"It was an act of sabotage."	17	20	31	21	18
d)	"I would wait for further information from the radio before making up my mind."	14	7	8	4	21
e)	"A bulletin like that without giving the cause of the explosion would be impossible on the radio of the U.S.S.R."	2	8	-	5	19
f)	"I wouldn't think much of anything at a moment like that."	4	1	-	-	-

On receiving these findings I decided to cross-check them with a number of my friends who would prove reliable references.

As a rule, the majority conceded that the percentages revealed by the poll reflected the opinions and attitudes of Soviet society fairly accurately. However, they pointed out that the poll was made in the European part of the U.S.S.R. and in cities of over fifty-thousand population. In small towns, *kolhozes*, and villages removed from industrial and urban centers, the answers of the population to the poll would be quite different, especially the replies to questions one, five, six, and seven.

Let us begin with the opinion of one of the newspapermen who took part in conducting the study. When I expressed my astonishment at Soviet society's unexpected attitudes towards war and peace, he said, "You are astonished because you have not taken the trouble to think back. You have seen the masses of workers and peasants demonstrating in the name of peace. You have been overwhelmed by the crimson of the placards; their peace slogans. You have heard our leaders appealing for peace, calling for a struggle towards peace. You have heard them on the radio and seen them on television calling for the co-operation of peace-loving nations. . . . Isn't it so? On this basis you have come to the conclusion that the people of the Soviets do not want war, they desire peace and do not believe in war. Nevertheless, the poll indicates quite clearly that our society overwhelmingly *believes* in war. Does this mean that it desires war? In reality, no. One may not wish war personally, and thus one may be inclined towards peace, but at the same time one can believe that one will inevitably be attacked—and thus, to a degree, be pro-war. In other words, the pro-war attitude of Soviet society is a result of a deep belief, constantly reinforced by the government, in the criminal and warlike intentions of American imperialism. This problem is not usually noticed by foreigners, although it is quite obvious. You see, the pro-war attitude of a society can be of two kinds. It can be a result of the desire for aggression—and this is one type which has been realized classically by Hitlerite Germany. On the other hand, the pro-war attitude of society can result from a deep conviction that it will be attacked, that the enemy stands around the corner with an atom or a hydrogen bomb in his bloody paw—just as the United States is pictured here on propaganda posters. This type of pro-war attitude is currently prevalent in the U.S.S.R. You surely understand that with this attitude our society will support every armed action of our government and the Party, deeply convinced that it is merely a reply to the aggressive intentions of imperialism."

He regarded me a moment in silence, smiled, then added, "Thus one can say that the basic paradox is that our effective peaceful politics and propaganda have more influence in preparing our society for war than the ineffective pro-war policy of the United States, which everywhere on earth meets with the opposition of nations frightened by the might of the U.S.S.R. As we say here, a real peace can be achieved only by a final destruction of imperialism, which, doomed to destruction by the laws of history, gropes blindly towards war. This is exactly how our society reasons and that is exactly how it should understand it. It is upon this that the effectiveness, the validity, and the great success of the internal policy of our party and our government depend."

Here is what a man working for a popular scientific publication for peasants had to say about our poll, "Of course our peasants lag far behind the intellectual level of the rest of our society. That's quite understandable and needs no explanation. That's why only 4 per cent of the peasants polled ascribe the inevitability of war to the international situation or to the laws of history. Another proof is their hope that it can be avoided through chance, or the will of God, or on a naïvely conceived treaty between governments.

"On the other hand, their dread of war, their forecast of great losses, and of a multitude of ordeals is understandable, since the peasants bore great losses in the last war and this fear is still alive in them. Note that almost 90 per cent of the peasants felt that losses 'could not be foreseen' or 'would exceed five million.' This is significant, especially when compared with the optimistic—if you can use this word in this context—viewpoint of labor and the students. Our intelligentsia, as always, is inclined to exaggerate. It thinks that it would survive war due to special favorable factors.

"But back to the peasants. Did you notice that as many as 59 per cent say that it's impossible to foresee who will be the attacker in the coming war? Now that's food for thought, but it does agree with our observations in the rural districts. At the same time almost a third prophesys mutual destruction in the coming struggle. Yes, it's true. In our society it is mainly the peasant who is afraid of war and of any violent change in general. This feature of the peasant character, fear of a change in the status quo, is still alive in spite of forty years of socialism.

"Though who knows, maybe it's *due* to socialism, which did not treat our peasants any too well in the thirties. Now look at this, 61 per cent don't know whether they'd survive the war! If we compare this with 2 per cent of the Party officials, it becomes obvious that they, as opposed to the peasants, have the strongest sense of security in our society. Once upon a time we used to say that only work on the soil could give a real sense of security. Strange, isn't it? Yes, our peasantry still remains the eternal mystery."

The next to comment on the results of the poll was an assistant professor of Soviet history at one of the universities. He discussed the views of the university students.

"Our students are real 'children of our times.' Note that 58 per cent consider the war as unavoidable because it will be forced on us by the international situation, and 36 per cent think it will be forced by the march of history. In other words, almost all of them think war unavoidable, according to your poll. But I have some reservations. From my observations of students' debates, it seems to me that a considerable portion of our student group is of the opinion that there will be no war in the sense of military conflict. I have the impression that a very popular belief among students is that the U.S.A. will not risk war and the destruction it would bring. Our students are therefore apt to assume that historical processes are acting to the disadvantage of the U.S.A., and since a war between the U.S.S.R. and the U.S.A. has failed to materialize up to date it will not take place in the future.

"Now in your poll only 3 per cent think that there won't be any war, and 3 per cent are undecided. Well, I doubt if these figures are correct. Maybe the past few months have caused a change in opinions, but I hardly think so. On the other hand it is possible that the 36 per cent who feel that war is inevitable in the march of history consider the present situation between socialism and capitalism as a sort of war . . . a war in politics, economics, and even in local armed conflicts. If so, this would agree with my observations.

"As to the views of the students concerning the armaments of our army and the development of war technology, I must agree with your results. Our students are fascinated and inspired by our military achievements and the growing power of the U.S.S.R. As a rule, they're tremendous optimists. You can see that your poll shows that as many as 49 per cent think that less than a million people would perish here in a war, and 58 per cent believe that the war would end in a Soviet victory in less than two years! A full 27 per cent believe that imperialism will surrender, while 23 per cent are certain of a disarmament treaty favorable to the U.S.S.R. I'm inclined to agree with all of these figures. My observations at the university lead me to conclusions more or less similar to the students.

"But I have one more reservation. In your poll, 45 per cent of the students and scholars believe in the possibility of a war being conducted without the use of weapons of mass destruction. Personally, I think this percentage is much too high. In my opinion perhaps 10 to 15 per cent believe in this possibility. The others think that if war were to come, it would be conducted primarily by weapons of mass destruction. Aren't we building our military power on this assumption? On the other hand it is true that our newspapers, especially the military press, have shown a tendency to emphasize the need to prepare for a war conducted with traditional weapons as well, excluding weapons of mass destruction. But to tell the truth I don't think that this is possible. Even if we wanted it, the imperialistic forces of the U.S.A. would not refrain from using atomic weapons. And so we wouldn't either. What do you think about it?

"At any rate, our students are optimists, take it from me. Especially the younger ones now enrolling. They actually plan to prepare themselves for future positions in France, England, Africa, India. They see themselves as the future builders of socialism in those countries."

A female philosophy student said to me, "Don't be a child who can't understand anything. The matter is very simple and any Soviet citizen can explain it to you. Imperialism is preparing to attack the U.S.S.R. The United States is surrounding us with bases which are ready to fire atomic bombs. Western Germany will soon possess the most powerful army in Western Europe, equipped with the new weapons of destruction. What does this mean? Does this mean peace? No, my dear, that's not true. In reality war is *already* going on. It is a war of nerves, an armament race, a hit-and-run battle. For this war to develop into open conflict is merely a question of time. It is a question of the ability of American imperialism to hold out, and this is already ending; pushed towards war by economic laws. Our society is constantly informed of this, and the more we stress our desire for peace, the more we strengthen the desire of the U.S.A. for aggression against the U.S.S.R. and the countries of the People's Democracies."

Here are some comments furnished by Party officials on various rungs of the Party ladder. An instructor in ideological training belonging to the Party city committee in Leningrad questioned the validity of a number of the conclusions. "While I concede that almost all Party officials are of the opinion that war is inevitable, of course none of them would express it so bluntly in an official interview. But I absolutely do not agree with the conclusion reached in your poll alleging that as many as 56 per cent of the Party officials think that war cannot be prevented because it is indispensable to the imperialist economy and political system.

"This is absolutely incorrect, in my opinion, and I pride myself on quite a good knowledge of the situation in the party. Actually 60 to 80 per cent of the Party officials believe that war can be prevented, by developing the industrial and military power of the U.S.S.R. In your poll, only 30 per cent say this. That's ridiculously low! Furthermore, I don't believe that as many as 55 per cent of our officials think that two to five million people would perish in case of war. This figure is also exaggerated. You see, we don't expect any victims on our side in our victory over imperialism. No one would ever mention so many! Though our army is only four million strong at this moment, in mobilization this number would be multiplied by five. Besides, don't forget that *in our army* we have a powerful ally, People's China with an inexhaustible reservoir of manpower. I say 'our army' because in case of military conflict People's China would enter into the combined socialist army, the main part of which would be the forces of the U.S.S.R. Don't you think so? Anyway, this factor is taken for granted by our entire society, so you might as well concede it also.

"You're probably still baffled by the sense of personal security shown by our Party officials, aren't you? By the fact that the poll indicates as many as 72 per cent are certain of surviving, and 16 per cent more of surviving under favorable circumstances. Well, remember that in case of war our Party officials would occupy important posts and naturally would be better protected than the ordinary white-collar or factory worker. That's why they have a right to assume that they'll survive. Besides, don't ever forget that we believe our power will be sufficient to defeat the forces of imperialism and grind the aggressor to dust while at the same time protecting our country from damage. That is, if the aggressor does not disarm prior to complete defeat out of fear of such a catastrophe.

"Do you realize how rapid the development of our war technology has been and the level we have already reached? Let alone the level we'll reach in ten years! Is imperialism better prepared for an attack on the U.S.S.R. now than it was in 1948? Of course not. But our situation has changed, hasn't it? This is the way our labor and intelligentsia think. Even your poll shows it. It's obvious that our intelligentsia reasons more cautiously, is more critical because it understands more, but these processes are evident to everybody in the U.S.S.R.

"The answers to question number seven, about the atomic explosion and the death of 20,000 people, were interesting. It's curious that not one of the persons polled presumed that the explosion could be due to a simple accident, such as the crash of a plane carrying an atomic load, or an explosion at a military base. The majority thought of a bomb dropped by the U.S.A., or of the beginning of war. The third guess was sabotage, really just another variation of the answer about U.S.A. aggression."

The next person I spoke to was a retired colonel, a fellow-

countryman, who had just recently arrived in Russia. I met him
at a reception in Leningrad given by the university youth organization in honor of some deserving Air Force division stationed
near by. The colonel was conspicuous by his head of thick white
hair and a chestful of the highest Soviet military decorations
hanging from the lapels of his civilian jacket. I learned later
that these medals were worn in the last war when he piloted a
Soviet pursuit plane. For exceptional courage, and shooting
down a great number of German planes, he received the title
of Hero of the Soviet Union.

When I met him, he was in Russia as a guest of the Air Force
division stationed near Leningrad in whose honor the banquet
was being held. He had fought with that division during the
war and experienced his successes with it.

Luckily, in our first conversation we found that we had a few
common friends in our country, some of whom occupied very
high positions in the Party and in the government. This fact
sealed our friendship, and we were soon on the best of terms.
As a reserve Air Force officer, the colonel wrote stories and
articles on aviation and military problems for popular military
publications. Occasionally his Air Force friends would let him
renew his pilot qualifications and fly a new jet. The practice,
he claimed, strongly stimulated his writer's imagination. He
was, of course, an old member of the Party, having belonged
since 1941. He had a fanatic admiration for the U.S.S.R. and
worshipped Soviet military power, especially the Air Force and
artillery.

The colonel liked to talk about the views prevailing among
the higher military and Party officials with whom he came into
contact at receptions and celebrations. With some of them he
had been friendly during the war, long before they occupied
such high posts. He respected them all. However he described
them as determined men, secretive, difficult to live with, always
on the alert, and watchful towards the people around them.
The colonel called them 'the steel generation,' men who held
onto power with their teeth and nails and were prepared to do
anything to remain on top.

"You see," he explained, "they are so high that they always
live in fear of being pushed down again. The ladder on top

of which they sit is climbed very slowly. Sometimes on your way up you grab hold of the legs of somebody above you and pull him down if he's in your way. Often this is the only way you can reach the next rung. But when you reach the very top you have to be careful. For if you start to fall, all those who are still climbing up push you down faster and try to discourage you from trying again."

The colonel told me about the interesting—as he called it—way by which groups in the Party Central Committee, in the Army, and in the government mutually control each other. "It's like a chess game," he said. "They always have each other in check. But, my friend, if you're checkmated in this game you're defeated for life."

The colonel liked to compare the life of the Soviet top officials to that of his fellow pilots, many of whom did not survive the war. "These people are literally suspended in the sky, except that they are surrounded by groups of men exactly like themselves. They don't live a normal life. They don't marry like normal people. They don't know what it is to sleep peacefully and relax in good company. Their life is owned by the Central Committee. The Central Committee gave them life and can take it away from them. The Party can tell each of them as Gogol's 'Taras Bulba' told his son, 'I caused your birth and I will cause your death.' Their wives are usually political workers also. Often they are older than their husbands. Their children go to special schools and are branded by the power exercised by their parents. They take their recreation among their equals. They spend their vacations in special rest homes. They may change the climate, but never the social environment. The nightmare of the collective follows them through their whole life, and there is no escape. None of them can say, 'I've had enough of this game. Leave me alone. I want to be a common little man again. Just let me go away quietly.'

"Have you ever been in the Kremlin?" the colonel asked, commenting on the policies now followed by the U.S.S.R. "If so, you were sure to see that all the rulers of Russia suffered from megalomania, a desire for leadership, for conquest, and expansion. You saw a bell, the largest in the world, which has never tolled. You saw a powerful *car-pushka* (Czar cannon) which never fired a shot. If you ever traveled on the Volga-Don Canal you saw how this same tradition is continued in Soviet times. You see, the present 'rulers' of Russia, as they are sometimes called, are not only the heirs of the cultural heritage of the Czars, but they are also fanatics of cold and consistent calculation. I have the impression that the present Kremlin group firmly believes that it has been assigned the mission of defeating imperialism and beginning 'the era of world socialism.'

"Who knows? Perhaps they are on the right track, or perhaps they are mistaken. At any rate one thing is sure. They move cautiously but surely, taking advantage of every mistake and false step by their adversary. Their political planning is a work of precision, even though stitched together with coarse thread. They constitute a young, relatively monolithic group. They have introduced comparative order into the internal affairs of the country. They did not forfeit Stalin's heritage in external politics, though politics demanded repudiating Stalin.

"Instead of looking at them as individuals, the West should learn from their policies. They are, most of them, repugnant, probably even to each other. Most of them look boorish, have coarse hands with dirty nails, wear unwashed shirts. Their wives are just as ugly and repulsive as they are. Altogether, they look disgusting, are usually badly dressed, have no manners. But they are proud and touchy.

"They don't waste any love on each other, either. They spy upon one another, and inform. They watch each other's every move. You might call them the victims of the system of power they have built. If they are free, it's only of riches. Old Karl Marx said that the proletariat had nothing to lose and the whole world to gain. For these leaders of the Party, government, and unions it is exactly the same. A victorious war with the forces of imperialism would open for them, as men, not only new possibilities of power, but their insecurity would diminish. Their constant fear of being 'assigned' to Manchuria or Mongolia, dread of falling out of the ranks, of being politically 'washed up,' would be less.

"That's probably why the pro-war and aggressive policy of Comrade Mao Tse-tung and his Chinese group has so many adherents in Khrushchev's circles, including Khrushchev himself. They suddenly feel strong as never before. Strong as politicians, as military men, as rulers of the Soviet Union, as international leaders. Their megalomania has suddenly acquired a realistic foundation. Their bells toll. Their cannons shoot. After Stalin's death they became wiser. They finally came to understand that the era of 'jet-propelled socialist ideology' belonged to the past, and that jet-propelled planes and rockets had to be built in its place. The era of pinning labels on other countries had also ended. Instead of a system of labels, a system of economic aid could be used to bind the countries that would accept it. And many would accept it because the American policies didn't appeal to them. In fact, in recent years United States policy has supplied Russia with many willing clients who felt they had been treated badly in Uncle Sam's supermarket and who preferred freshly printed rubles to dollars."

A few days later the colonel was invited to visit a military base not far from Leningrad by the commander, whom he had known during the war. He returned full of enthusiasm. At first he wouldn't talk since what he had seen was supposed to be secret. But at my burning curiosity, then real disappointment tinged with disbelief, he broke down and told me some of the story.

With eleven other high officers he had been driven to the base. The trip took about two hours in Volga ZIS-10 and ZIM limousines. Although it was late at night, the windows of the car were still tightly covered by black curtains. Twice their documents were inspected by officers and "although there were several colonels and two generals with us," related the colonel, "the inspection was as thorough as if we were American spies dropped from planes."

He said that with all his writer's imagination he had never in his life pictured anything like what he saw at that base—fantastic electronic and radar apparatus. Rockets the size of those that had been displayed on the May First parade in Moscow sat on platforms ready to be launched. Most exciting of all were supersonic all-weather fighters of ultramodern design which were displayed in an enormous hangar. The colonel couldn't have spoken more tenderly about a beautiful woman.

He was no less impressed by the long-range strategic bombers, which he didn't actually see but which were shown on a film. They were full jet, turbo-jet, and multi-turboprop. In describing them, the colonel used terms which I did not understand and which I couldn't find in any traditional aviation dictionary.

On several occasions the colonel spoke to me about Soviet war strategy and the military tactics and organization of the Soviet Army. He said, for instance, that in Soviet war plans the heavy long-range strategic bombers would co-operate closely for tactical and strategic purposes with long-range rocket weapons of intermediate and strategic types which now were considered a form of artillery by the Soviet Army.

The colonel thought much more highly of intercontinental ballistic missiles than he did of guided missiles. He once told me that the German scientists took revenge on the United States for the defeat of their country in 1945 by directing U.S. military research towards guided missiles that for decades would continue to suffer from a high degree of vulnerability to electronic interference.

"Now the United States has learned its lesson, but it's too late. In Russia the scientists have been working on ballistic rockets since 1946, and the U.S. will never catch up with us." As evidence of the importance the U.S.S.R. attaches to ballistic missiles he told me that at present all branches of the Soviet Army, Navy, Air Force, and Air Defense Forces have been assigned missiles and rockets, including short-range and intermediate ballistic missiles. The most important unit in the Soviet Army, subordinated directly to the Minister of Defense, is the Long Range Strategic Ballistic Missile Force partially connected with the Long Range Air Force.

"In the Soviet Army guided missiles are not popular. This was the reason why their foremost advocate, the Chief Aviation Marshal A. P. Zhigarev, was discharged from his post at the beginning of 1957. Allegedly, he planned to set up a separate command for Long Range Ballistic Rockets. He was replaced by Aviation Marshal Vershinin. The Long Range Air Force included submarine-launched missiles, ballistic rocket artillery, and long-range bomber forces. And as opposed to United States' policy, it operates as a combined command. The rocket program is headed by the Marshal of Artillery, while command of regular bombers, pilotless bombers, and guided cruise-type missiles rests in the hands of the Marshal of Aviation.

"However, guided missiles do have their place in Soviet strategy. For instance, I read an article by Admiral Vladimirsky recently in which he says that submarines armed with guided missiles having atomic warheads can strike powerful surprise blows on industrial centers, seaports, and enemy bases, thus fulfilling tasks on a strategic scale. I also read somewhere, or perhaps I was told—I don't remember which—that the Soviet Union is doing research on underwater containers holding ballistic rockets. These containers could be anchored by our submarines in many different carefully selected locations. The rockets and missiles would be launched by timed or remote-control.

"In the U.S.S.R., it's the strength of the Army and the final victory that counts. The problem is not how to drop a hydrogen bomb on someone's head. The trick is to be able to stop a hydrogen bomb from being hurled at our heads and to attack the other side at the moment when they intend to do the same."

I must admit that I was greatly impressed by these revelations and even more by my own ignorance. I decided, therefore, to supplement my knowledge of Soviet strategy, tactics and army organization. I started, of course, in the library. However, the attractive chief librarian in the university library informed me that to use "the special catalogue" which lists special military periodicals published in limited editions I needed a permit from a certain military department. In the meantime, I could use the general catalogue.

I decided to try to get a pass. I visited an old professor, a theorist on military affairs and army organization, well-known even before the Revolution. After the Revolution he worked with Lenin and Trotsky and taught in various Soviet military academies. He was one of the Soviet experts on the armament of the Red Army and an advisor in strategy and tactics. After Lenin's death and the downgrading of Trotsky, the professor was removed from any contact with military affairs. He told me he escaped trial and a sentence because of a serious illness which kept him bedridden during the worst period. After his recovery he taught economics but his interest in military matters continued.

The professor was very old. He must have been eighty-five, and lived in a small portion of a room occupied by another family. Two walls of this area were of plywood, supported by piles of books rather than by wooden props. With glasses stuck on his nose, closing one eye, and inclining his white head towards his right shoulder, the professor read, made notes, and was always cheerful and smiling. We talked. First the professor established my exact interests, then tested my knowledge. He examined me in Latin declensions and European history. "My son, before he was killed in the war," said the professor, "always grew angry when I examined his colleagues when he brought them home. All I wanted to know was what they had inside those peasant-worker heads. Unfortunately, I often found nothing."

I told the professor of my newly aroused interest in the problems of war and peace and the difficulties I'd experienced. The professor promised to give me a letter of reference to one of his friends who worked in the editors' library of *Pravda* and who would be able to get me the pass. In turn, I asked the professor what he thought about the chances for war, or for peace, and about the international situation.

The professor laughed. "Do you know who Descartes was, young man? It was he who said: *'larvatus prodes'*—I walk in a mask. I have been walking like that for many years. And here you come and ask me such questions? You, a representative of the new atomic generation which, in this country, has only contempt for us, the old; which hurls at us such adjectives as 'cosmopolitan,' 'bourgeois,' and 'servile toward the West.' At this moment war is no longer a matter of politics. It's rather a matter of economics. And that's where we must begin, with the economy of the U.S.S.R. Don't suspect me of historical materialism or Soviet patriotism. No sir, when a man is almost ninety he has courage, perhaps more courage than that Hero of the Soviet Union you were telling me about. The authority of death is the only truly bourgeois authority that remains in this country.

"But let's go back to our theme. In my opinion, by 1970, perhaps 1975, the Soviet economy will be so highly developed that even if no capitalistic crisis takes place in the meantime, it will be able to afford to make decisive global moves. Of course I mean moves with reference to the United States. But let us talk for a moment about the economy. In 1955 Russia produced more than 45 million tons of crude steel, that means 4 million more tons than Western Germany and Great Britain together. In the same year, 1955, Russia mined 390 million tons of coal while the total output of those other two countries was 36 million tons. In electric energy Russia generated 166 billion kilowatt hours, while the other two countries generated 155 billion kilowatt hours. And, just for the sake of comparison, 25 years ago the U.S.S.R. produced only 35 million tons of coal annually. You could point out that in 1937 the United States produced 444 million tons of coal, 51 million tons of steel and generated 146 billion kilowatt hours. You'd be right. But our tempo of growth is much faster than that of America.

"What were we in 1937 and what are we today? In 1960, the last year of the present five-year plan, our employment in industry and administration, not counting agriculture, will increase from 48 to 55 million. By then we will produce more than 600 million tons of coal, and our steel output will be more than 70 million tons. Our production of oil will be doubled and we will produce about 330 billion kilowatt hours of electricity. But you must bear in mind that these continuous comparisons with the United States don't tell the whole story. The U.S.A. has been losing ground recently in these comparisons. A ton of steel produced in the U.S.S.R. and a ton of steel produced in the U.S.A. are, as a matter of a fact, two different tons of steel. Consider how much steel of the Soviet ton goes into light industry—passenger cars, bicycles, refrigerators, electric stoves, toys, and the like. Very, very little, as you know. The greatest part goes into heavy industry and armaments or is used for the development of the productive resources of the nation. But how much of the American ton of steel is used for light industry and consumer goods? Incomparably more.

"That is why, young man, the prospect of a victorious war by socialism against capitalism, or if you wish, by the Soviet bloc against the American bloc, rests on economics, not politics. And by 1970 to 1975 the U.S.S.R. will be ahead, by several lengths, of all the capitalistic countries taken together depending on how many of them still exist!

"In some respects this is true even today. Do you know, for instance, that by 1960 in the U.S.S.R. there will be more students enrolled in institutions of higher learning and starting polytechnical studies than in all the other countries taken together? In 1965 this generation will already be a work producing machinery and precision apparatus. This is only one of the signs. But we must also consider other signs, including those that appear in the U.S.A. The economic collapse of the U.S.A. could have an enormous significance for the power of the U.S.S.R. You see, when the U.S.S.R. undermines the U.S.A.'s economic power, and by its political actions diminishes the possibility for expansion by the U.S.A., the U.S.A. is apt to suffer a crisis the like of which it has never suffered before. You don't need much to achieve this. Just two things are needed: a continuation of the present U.S.S.R. policy, effective, successful, and flexible; and a continuation of the present U.S.A. policy, entirely ineffective, chaotic, and rigid. Don't you think I'm right?

"One more thing. As you know, our economy is devoted to the development of heavy industry which in large part concentrates on armaments. According to my own calculations, the U.S.S.R. has at this moment at least 35,000 tanks, about 40 to 45 artillery divisions, 150 divisions of infantry fully mechanized, 120 cadre divisions, and in the Air Force about 450 regiments and probably about 25,000 planes, of which at least 2,000 are for long-range use. And there's still the Navy. Do you realize that after the war we built at least 22 up-to-date cruisers, plus 270 to 300 modern long-range submarines? I'm certain, furthermore, that about 300 old sea-going and coastal submarines were rebuilt and modernized. I estimate that the Navy also has about 150 to 200 sea-going destroyers, of which at least 120 were built after 1946.

"And the Army? At this very moment, after all the reductions, we still have a minimum of 4,000,000 soldiers including the units for internal use. Our new plans for economic decentralization have a predominantly military character and include a new distribution of industrial and military centers. So, as you see, much has changed here since 1917. And now let's have a cup of tea."

Three days later I went to see the newspaperman with the letter of reference from the professor. The newspaperman made a few calls, and the next day my permit to use Catalogue "C" in the university library was ready. I must say that I did not find many military periodicals. The most interesting was *Voennaia Mysl* (Military Thought), a monthly published by the General Staff since 1937. It is a periodical for higher officers, but scientists may use it by special permission. I learned later that this periodical is regarded as the best source for military information. Its articles are often discussed in military circles and in the Frunze and Voroshilov Military Academies. Other monthlies are *Tankist*, (The Tank Man), *Morskoi Sbornik* (The Naval Journal), *Artilleriiskii Zhurnal* (The Artillery Journal), *Vestnik Protivovozdushnoi Oborony* (The Herald of the Air Defense Forces). Out of the periodicals which were in general circulation, only occasional copies of military magazines passed the censorship. In general circulation were certain issues of *Sovetskii Voin* (The Soviet Warrior), *Tyl i Snabzhenie Vooruzhennykh Sil* (The Rear and Supply of the Armed Forces), *Voenno-Inzhenernyi Zhurnal* (The Military Engineering Journal), *Voennyi Sviazist* (The Military Signal Man), *Bloknot Agitatora Vooruzhennykh Sil* (Handbook for the Armed Forces' Agitator).

Unfortunately I didn't have enough time to peruse these magazines thoroughly, especially since my interest at the time was to obtain a general view of Soviet strategy and tactics and to get some idea about the possibilities of a third World War. In this respect, the periodicals gave me a lot of interesting material. I thought it rather significant that many articles emphasized the necessity of building a new Soviet strategy and abandoning the old strategic concepts of World War II, and the 1946–53 periods. They recommended that all officers participate in the military science societies which were being set up in various units and military districts. The tradition of these societies reaches back as far as 1920. They not only encourage debates and discussions on current military and strategic problems but stimulate creative thinking among the military and help to discover gifted men whose lack was strongly felt in the Army during the years of "the cult of the individual," the cult of Stalin. But, to my mind, the basic theses of Soviet strategy remain the same. It is still believed that victory consists in defeating the adversary's military forces and not in prior destruction of his industrial centers and populated districts. The idea may be to preserve the industrial centers for their future utilization by the victor or it may be a propaganda trick. At any rate, the trend of the articles in those periodicals was to criticize severely United States strategy for its emphasis on the destruction of such centers by means of weapons of mass destruction. This does not mean that Soviet strategy rejects the strategic bombing of industrial and population centers, but it ascribes only a secondary importance to them. That is why the organization of the Soviet Army always includes such large numbers of divisions of mechanized infantry and land forces.

In one of the articles, I read this quotation from the book *Voennyie Ideologi* (Ideologists of War) by Maj. Gen. M. A. Milsztein and Col. A. K. Slobodenko published in 1957: "It is essential to select targets for strategic air strikes carefully to prevent the enemy from dealing a retaliatory blow." For this purpose the Soviet Army has the Long Range Air Force and the Intercontinental Ballistic Missile Forces and submarine-launched short and intermediate range missiles and rockets. Soviet strategy, as outlined in those magazines, rejects the decisive importance of any certain weapon but puts accent on the co-operation of all types of weapons. According to various authors, no individual weapon can solve the problems of a new type of war. Even the use of atom or hydrogen bombs cannot decide the result of the war.

Not long before his removal, Marshal Zhukov strongly emphasized this principle, saying that one must bear in mind that one cannot win a war with atomic bombs alone and that air power and nuclear power and weapons by themselves cannot determine the outcome of an armed conflict. One of the chief Soviet experts on matters of strategy and armament, Major General Pokrovsky declared in 1955 that atomic and thermonuclear weapons in their present stage of development only supplement the fire power of the old forms of armament, such as artillery, small arms, tanks, aviation, and other armaments which were and remain the basic fire power of the army.

These views were supported by Marshal Zhukov's successor, Minister of Defense Marshal Malinovsky who, in his address to the graduates of the Moscow Military Academies in November, 1957, said, among other things, that considering that victory in combat must be achieved by the combined efforts of all the arms and components of the Armed Forces, we must give special importance in our training to combined operations by the ground and air-borne forces, the Air Force, Navy, rocket formations, and air defense forces in various types of operations.

When I read these views I began to understand the structural principles of the Soviet Army about which the colonel had spoken. The Soviet High Command is the organizational expression of these principles. Thus the unified Ministry of Defense directly controls the chief administration for the various armies and special units. That's why there are first deputy ministers who serve as commanders-in-chief of the ground forces, naval forces, air forces and air defense forces. There are deputy ministers who head the rear services and the long-range air forces, tank troops, air-borne troops, and artillery. The Army and the land forces have the strongest representation in this command.

Going back to strategy, all the periodicals I read denied the idea that a war could be won by a so called blitzkrieg, or a surprise attack, and called it a fantasy. One of the Soviet leaders said that "blitzkrieg can lead only to blitz collapse." The conception that a war could be won by a surprise attack or blitzkrieg was one of the most frequently criticized concepts of Western war strategy. As Marshal of Aviation Vershinin said in September, 1957, in the opinion of Soviet strategists, the possibility of a lightning annihilation of the Soviet Union by air attack is excluded, not only because of the Soviet defense forces and the almost simultaneous attack on the U.S.A. which would follow, but also because of the fact that the U.S.S.R. is not an island or a point on the globe.

Many articles pointed out that a war between the U.S.A. and the U.S.S.R. would be very long and would require many military campaigns and operations on an enormous, global scale.

They stressed, therefore, the importance of large armies and tremendous quantities of arms, conventional as well as atomic and hydrogen, and preparation of the national economy for unceasing production of these materials regardless of the duration of the war. A number of authors emphasized the need for preparing military and administrative cadres to be used for immediate consolidation of authority in the territories taken over by the Soviet Army as a result of a victorious war. They pointed out the fact that in the last war, especially in its first stage, the U.S.S.R. lost control of almost 50 per cent of its population, about 45 per cent of its grain production, about 55 per cent of its output of coal, iron, aluminum and steel, and about 90 per cent of its key armament industries. These losses may be compared to the losses which a war using weapons of mass destruction would bring about, and yet they did not cause the U.S.S.R. to capitulate.

United States strategy is usually evaluated as unscientific and being the expression of "some monopolistic groups in the U.S.A. and their advocates in the Pentagon" who, deriving "enormous profits from filling government orders," dictate the type of strategy and weapons to be used. In the book of Major General Milsztein and Col. A. Slobodenko, *Voennyie Ideologi* (The Ideologists of War), mentioned before, it was stated that the views of American military ideologists, tying their hopes in future war only to aviation, and under-evaluating the roles of other branches of the armed forces, border on adventurism.

The U.S.S.R. military press never ceases to emphasize the aggressive character of "American imperialism," which thinks that military bases can assure victory over the U.S.S.R. The Commander in Chief of the Soviet Air Forces, Marshal of Aviation Vershinin declared in 1957 that one can only wonder at the shortsightedness of those who do not consider that if these bases are close to us, then they are also not far from us. Soviet strategy does not, therefore, consider these bases dangerous. It assumes they can be smashed very quickly and at the same time an attack by the planes of the American Strategic Air Command on Soviet territory can be effectively prevented. At the moment of the outbreak of war, the Soviet armed forces will conduct military operations on the territory of the enemy and, if necessary, advance on the territory of other states in order to destroy barbarous imperialist robbers and defend to the end the state interests of the U.S.S.R. This same view appeared for the first time, I think, in the magazine *Krasnaia Zvezda* (The Red Star) in May, 1955. From then on it has been often repeated in various magazines and textbooks.

Text books on war problems are mass-published and can be found in any large Soviet library. In the catalogue of the reference department of a medium-sized library in an industrial establishment in Moscow I found the following titles, some in two or three copies: "Marxism-Leninism, O Voine, Armii i Voennoi Nauke" (Marxism-Leninism on War, the Army, and Military Science) A collection of articles. Moscow 1955.

COL. A. N. LAGOVSKY. *Strategia i Ekonomika* (Strategy and Economics) Moscow, 1957.

COL. E. A. KHOMENKO. *O Voinakh Spravedliwykh i Nespraved liwykh* (On Just and Unjust Wars) Moscow, 1954.

COL. N. DENISOV. *Boevaia Slava Sovetskoi Aviatsii* (The Combat Glory of Soviet Aviation) Moscow, 1953.

V. I. SKOPIN. *Militarism* (Militarism) Moscow, 1956.

"O Sovetskoi Voennoi Nauke" (On Soviet Military Science) A collection of articles. Moscow, 1954.

Sovremennaia Voennaia Tekhnika (Contemporary Military Technology) Moscow, 1957.

V. P. PETROV. *Upravliaemye Snariady i Rakety* (Guided Missiles and Rockets) Moscow, 1957.

"Sredstva i Sposoby Zashchity ot Atomnogo Oruzhiia" (Ways and Means of Defense Against Atomic Weapons) A collection of articles. Moscow, 1956.

G. N. ZAPOLSKY. *Atomnoe Oruzhie i Protivoatomnaia Zashchita Naseleniia* (The Atomic Weapon and Defense of the Population) Moscow, 1956.

I asked the smiling, attractive librarian for some of these titles. She disappeared behind a big cabinet and returned after a while to inform me that she was sorry but all the books were in use. "People read them now as they used to read novels and love stories," she said, still smiling. "But you can have this one. We have a few hundred copies." I looked at the title of the thin pamphlet she handed me: *Programma Zaniatiis*

naseleniium po protivoatomnoi zashehite v kruzhkakh pervich-
nykh organizatsiakh DOSAAF (Program of Anti-Atomic Defense
Instruction of the Population through Primary Groups of the
DOSAAF organization) Moscow, 1955.

One day I visited a small school near Kharkov. The young
teacher took me proudly around the chemistry, physics, biology
and botany laboratories, the zoological pavilion, a miniature
museum of the 1917 Revolution made by the pupils, a workshop
for manual work, two Michurinov gardens and a greenhouse.
We were accompanied by a group of boys and girls. Every one
tried to add a few words to the teacher's comments. On our
way out towards the main corridor we passed another group
of students in the course of hanging up a large wall newspaper.
These posters are published at certain intervals by alternate
groups of students. This particular copy bore the title "Fighting
Against Imperialism." It was made of cardboard and represented
the five continents of the world. Against the background of
each continent were pasted cut-outs of rebellious people with
broken chains around their wrists and rifles or red flags in their
hands. These figures appeared in relief in Latin America, Africa,
the Middle and Far East, South Asia, and Europe. To the
territory of the United States was pasted a caricature of the
Statue of Liberty, cut out of the Soviet satirical magazine
Krokodil (Crocodile). The eyes of the statue were two police-
men, and their two clubs hung from the eyes in the form of
tears. Another cut-out represented a group of masked Ku Klux
Klansmen lynching a Negro. There was a group of obese capitalists watching a ragged mob of workers from luxurious limousines. Eisenhower and Dulles were handing atom and hydrogen bombs to West European armies with the inscription "A
Gift from the U.S.A." American soldiers were running their
tanks over Korean mothers with babies in their arms.

I came closer to the newspaper. It was very carefully done.
There was evidence that much work and effort had been put
into it. In the center, between the continents, there was an article:
"The Hour of Imperialism Has Struck." Here are fragments
from the articles: "The colonial and dependent nations, oppressed and exploited by the American and European imperialists, break their fetters. . . . Under the leadership of the

communist parties and inspired by the ideals of brotherhood of nations they rise against their oppressors, they rise to the struggle against imperialism. . . . The hour strikes for the bloody hangmen of the Pentagon and its masters in Wall Street. The plans of the American warmongers, the bloody murderers of Korean children in their cradles and of nursing mothers, are crumbling into pieces . . . The great Chinese nation, and the nations of Mexico, Uruguay, Venezuela, Argentina and Chile, looking to the U.S.S.R. and to the building of a new system, turn their backs on the cunning plans of the American capitalists. The tribes of East and West Africa, the nations of the Arab countries, of Indonesia, Thailand, Burma, Laos, and Cambodia rise in arms for the right of self-determination, progress, and freedom. . . . Communists of all the countries unite under the command of the heroic Communist Party of the Soviet Union. The slogan 'Proletarians of the world, unite!' becomes reality, and the coming years will make it real for the whole world under the leadership of the great U.S.S.R."

Three other teachers joined me in reading the wall newspaper and then took me with them to the school canteen for lunch. The teachers were very pleased with their students. Though some students lagged behind in their work or showed an improper attitude towards the group, they were easily handled by the youth organizations with the help of the teaching staff. We talked about the method of teaching and its results.

The biology teacher said, "The principle of our method is very simple. The point is that all the subjects must constitute one entity. This means that, for instance, the conclusions reached from learning biology, mathematics, and physics must concur with the conclusions learned from history, economics, and literature. Of course, the most important part of our outlook is the political premises on which it is founded. A moment ago in the corridor you saw the wall newspaper whose subject matter was politics. All the sciences in our system lead to these same political formulations. They all establish in the student's mind the conviction of the uniformity of the materialistic world and its objective dialectic and historical laws, and an understanding of the materialistic world outlook as applied to social, economic, and political sciences by our Party. In this way a problem like, for instance, the development of a live cell is closely knit to the problem of defeating imperialism. The political reasons for teaching biology are just as vital as the political reasons for teaching history or economics. Didactics and methodology are the great successes of Soviet pedagogy."

Said the history teacher, "Dialectic and historical materialism is the foundation of all teaching. Our task in teaching history is reduced to this fundamental conclusion: socialism is a higher type of social-political system and must win, because such is the mechanism of the development of the world, and because objectively operating historical and economic laws lead to this conclusion. The Communist Party is armed with scientific knowledge of these laws and is vitally interested in knowing more about them and using them in practice for the purposes of socialism. Basing its work on these laws, the Party cannot be mistaken as to the basic direction of the development of the U.S.S.R. and of the struggle with imperialism. Contemporary imperialism is, as we say, 'pregnant with war.' This means that for imperialism, war is a life necessity and that the imperialists, driven by the laws of capitalistic economy, of which laws they are not aware, will try to bring war about at any cost. Therefore, peace seriously weakens imperialism and may lead, with the ever-shrinking world market, to a violent internal crisis. On the other hand, war will be a debacle for imperialism because of the U.S.S.R.'s military power and scientific war strategy. In other words, the crisis of imperialism becomes a reality. The struggle of socialism with imperialism enters its last and decisive state."

There's one more conversation to put down, perhaps the longest. It took place towards the end of my sojourn in the Soviet Union, and the other party was a member of the staff of one of the Scandinavian embassies in Moscow. A career diplomat with more than ten years in the U.S.S.R., he spoke Russian perfectly, was interested in Russian and Soviet art and literature, and as a side interest did much research on the cultures of some of the Soviet Republics. He had many friends among the Moscow and Leningrad intelligentsia. I had a chance to notice that both his knowledge and culture were highly regarded.

When I learned that he intended to write a book about the

U.S.S.R. and international problems, I decided to compare the material I had collected with his opinions on a number of subjects.

Here are some of his views and observations. "You see, the so called 'Soviet problem' emerged during the last war. Up to the outbreak of the war, Western Europe and America considered the Soviets and Stalinism as a local affair only affecting the U.S.S.R. After 1946, the West European democracies and the United States were not able to grasp the historical significance of a new fact. This new fact was that the U.S.S.R. was succeeding in building the world empire which Hitler had failed to create. Once again history was playing a trick on the historians. The victor was accomplishing that for which the conquered had perished.

"Preoccupied with Hitler and the ruins of the Third Reich, the western democracies did not notice until it was too late that the Soviet Union had gained domination over Eastern Europe and the Balkans and had become master of the Chinese land mass, thus establishing itself as the first world power of the post-war world and creating ideal conditions for its continued conquests. The significance of Soviet power was intensified by the division of Germany, the disarmament of Japan, and disagreement among the Western countries in their appraisal of the new situation, especially by the shortsightedness of the politicians and governing circles of the United States.

"The West failed to understand the danger of this new power with its ability for ideological and political expansion, just as it failed to recognize the danger from a military standpoint.

"Soviet strategy, especially in the second half of the war, proved to be more successful than the strategy of the Allies, which they used from 'Normandy to the Baltic Shores.' The artillery and tanks of the Soviet Army were decidedly superior to those of the Americans, and equal to those of the Germans.

"Nor did the West pay any attention to the enormous interest the Soviets displayed in foreign scientists right after the war, nor in their feverish activity in recruiting and bringing to the U.S.S.R. and the satellite countries great numbers of scientists from all over the world to work in strategically important fields.

"Even the thousands of orders for strategically important equipment and research apparatus placed by the U.S.S.R. in the capitalistic countries of the whole world, including the United States, did not alert the West. And this indifference continued. Even today, no one bothers about the fact, generally known in the U.S.S.R., that thousands of scientists all over the world are co-operating with Soviet industry by means of various intermediary agencies located mostly in Europe. These scientists are very well paid for their reports and scientific works.

"While the West was forgetting World War II, the Soviet Union was already thinking of World War III. The voices of the few West European statesmen who tried to point this out were drow̄ned in the arguments and futile discussions by the crowd of idiots and braggarts which fill the diplomatic services of some capitalistic powers. It is a well-known fact that the financial prospects offered by the diplomatic service to young diplomats are pretty grim. Naturally only those who cannot find a place for themselves in more profitable and creative work, due to lack of intelligence or crudeness, stick to it.

"I remember vividly how the ablest of these dunces prophesied the complete destruction of the Soviet system in 1941, regardless of the result of the war. In 1944 they claimed that the contact of the Soviet troops with Allied troops, plus the destruction suffered by the U.S.S.R., would lead to the overthrow of the Soviet Regime in Russia. In 1945 the U.S.S.R. was already the second power in the world, yet the dunces and braggarts in well-pressed evening suits delivered speeches about Lend-Lease written for them by their blonde secretaries.

"The era of post-war prosperity with speculative opportunities to get rich quick caused many of the dunces to leave the diplomatic service and try their hands at the business of trading in war equipment, uniforms, and other surpluses which the war ended too soon to absorb. I was in Brussels and Paris then, and I saw how trainloads of military equipment, acres of automobiles, and useless bombers were sold 'privately.'

"In 1946 a new generation began to swell the ranks of the diplomatic service of some of the capitalistic countries. These were even no good at business speculation. In time this generation was assigned the mission of conducting the cold war.

Probably they tried, but from the very beginning the war was being won by someone else.

"The cold war was a good idea, but it was tackled in a cowboy spirit. Its main result was to reduce greetings to Soviet diplomats to cold bows and extending only rare invitations to them for banquets and receptions. Nobody knew how to consolidate the anti-Soviet forces, how to take a definite stand on Soviet organizations, or what to do about the hundreds and thousands of spies and collaborators of the U.S.S.R. who were operating everywhere.

"The most the cold war accomplished was to freeze the policy of the Western world which had not been very agile anyway. It did not freeze Soviet policy. On the contrary, it lit a fire under it.

"The policy of the Western World, especially American policy, still does not understand the full danger of current U.S.S.R. policy. The United States cannot, or does not want to, revise its ineffective moves . . . moves which are certainly not in its own interests and may be altogether suicidal. Compared with the far seeing Soviet policy, perhaps a hundred years ahead of our times, the Western World under the leadership of the White House indulges in an imitation of nineteenth-century politics with all its standard slogans about 'democracy' and 'freedom.'

"The totalitarian system of the U.S.S.R. requires a totalitarian opponent. Unfortunately, the contemporary capitalist world is not able to understand this. Probably it is afraid of the very idea of totalitarianism, allegedly contradictory to the spirit of 'democracy.' As a result, the flexible Kremlin collective which can make decisions within hours and carry them out within weeks has for an adversary a powerful, complicated, and heavy, but democratic, bureaucratic political machine in the U.S.A. The political paralysis of this system, in which America seems to delight, makes it possible for the politicians of the U.S.S.R. and its satellites to consistently perform political acrobatics in the well-founded knowledge that the White House and the Pentagon are having too much trouble with their own government to have time left for dealing with the policies of other governments. Therefore, in the U.S.A. only science fiction writers and writers of suspense stories, with an occasional gifted journalist, deal with real politics.

"No vaccine has been found for this type of paralysis so common in the U.S.A. Nor do the electric shocks occasionally applied to Washington by some new Kremlin success help. Washington does not lose credit in the American or major European banks. But among the smaller European allies this credit has been sharply reduced.

"Up to now, the U.S.A. has not worked out any realistic doctrine concerning peace or war, just as it has failed to build foundations for its attitude towards Soviet imperialism since 1945. The method of flying from one extreme to the other, which may be considered the only doctrine of the White House in the past few years, has not passed the test. But neither has it been given up.

"And another problem, is that the faith in the 'anti-government' attitude of Soviet society continues to be the prevailing view of the West. The Western statesmen stick stubbornly to the theory that secret police hold this nation of two hundred million people in their omnipotent tentacles, forcing obedience to a hated government. But this theory is fantasy. With the possible exception of Communist China, the U.S.S.R. today is the only country in the world where 99 per cent of the people will back up any policy of the government in the conviction that this policy is necessary, made so by the mechanics of a historical process or by the need for the defense of the gains of socialism from imperialistic aggression. We must not forget that the masses working in Soviet industry or agriculture are completely tied to the policy of their government and Party in life and in politics. At least 15 per cent of the population, the most privileged portion, are completely dedicated to the causes of the Party and the government, no matter where it would lead them. The rest are, at best, neutralized social strata incapable of any move unforeseen by the government.

"This tremendous society, heterogeneous historically, culturally, linguistically, and economically, was put into an extremely well-knit social, occupational, and administrative framework as far back as the twenties. There is no room in this organization for a 'lost individual.' Man is firmly bound to the group and authority and cannot free himself. Usually he does not even believe that there can be any existence outside of the group.

"The entire society, in Central Russia as well as in Central Asia, was subjected to intensive propaganda by the Party and government in every sphere of life while the entire country was at the same time cut off from any foreign influence. This system, which has been at work for forty years, is beginning to pay off. The younger generations are ready to do anything asked by the government. They are not only driven by the energy generated by the Party and government, but they also have the tremendous momentum acquired through forty years of communist policy universally applied.

"These are obvious processes, and there's no reason why everybody should not see them. Failure to recognize these facts in the post-war years, and even today, is as dangerous as awakening too late to the pro-war and imperialistic policy of the U.S.S.R.

"The consolidation of the entire nation around Kremlin policies is not only an ideological success. It is also the result of long and intensive historical, social, economic, and cultural processes. In developing these processes, the Soviet government did not begin from scratch, did not start to 'build on a vacant lot.' The Soviet authorities tied these processes to existing national and cultural forces, national traditions, national pride, and they succeeded, especially in the last decade, in creating real economic and political motivations.

"The daydreams cultivated in the West about the ever-present possibility of a rebellion by the masses against their Red oppressors and about the pro-Western feelings of the Russian people belong in a museum of political curios. There, they could be placed next to the daydreams of the French aristocrats who refused to believe the truth about the victories won by Napoleon Bonaparte. This kind of thinking, together with faith in the peaceful intentions of the U.S.S.R., is particularly dangerous because it disarms the West and misleads Western public opinion with a false image of the U.S.S.R.

"Does all this mean that the Western world, under the leadership of the U.S.A., is caught in a trap without any way out? In my opinion, part of the answer is 'yes.' The West is in a trap, but there *still* is a way out. The path is narrower than it was ten years ago, but still wide enough. It consists in the adoption of a consistent policy towards the U.S.S.R. and towards the Allies, as long as there are still some allies in existence. The initiative must be taken by the U.S.A., and this cannot be done without substantial changes in the American system of government, whether the people like it or not. The existing bureaucratic government machinery can only, at best, conduct a bureaucratic policy whose results are well-known to all of us and which are a godsend to the Kremlin.

"At the foundation of this new policy, realistic goals and principles conforming to the truth must replace the moral teachings and commandments of the ancestors of American democracy, which have stubbornly been dragged out of the dusty attic. These teachings have long since ceased to be practical in the internal policy of the U.S.A., let alone its foreign policy.

"This new policy, in relations with existing and potential allies, should avail itself less of the talent of American advisors for complicated geometrical forms on the basis of which pacts, treaties, and defensive-offensive alliances are built. As long as there's still time, let them give up geometry for the sake of an honest analysis of the concrete political, economic, and social conditions which should be made by experts, not by politicians who, unfortunately, are not even real politicians.

"The statesmen implementing this policy would have to understand in advance that the foreign policy of the most powerful capitalist power of the second half of the twentieth century cannot depend exclusively on stockpiling rockets, canned goods, and nineteenth-century moral teachings or in putting handicaps in the way of their allies in the name of these same teachings."

The diplomat stopped, then added after a minute, "These are the problems I wanted to deal with in my book about the U.S.S.R. and international policy. However, as a diplomat of a country which doesn't have an independent policy of its own, which is dependent in this area on what we jokingly call the 'Atomamerican Bombassador,' I cannot publish these views. The principle of American business, which tolerates no interference by its neighbors, has been transferred from the sphere of business to international politics. This is probably the cause of the isolation of these bombassadors in all friendly countries. But tell me, what is your opinion of it all?"

I had no opinion. I had always thought that the moves made by politicians and statesmen were just as puzzling to the man in the street as his views were to the politicians.

However, if in this book I have dwelt on the relationship of the man in the street in the U.S.S.R. to the question of war and peace it was no accident. I had always been taught that history was wise. After my return from the U.S.S.R., I believe that it can be cruel and cynical as well. In the U.S.S.R., the common man, hero of the gray daily life, has been dragged into politics for forty years. And now this "Soviet experiment," as we used to call it in the twenties, starts to bear fruit. Even before the state has begun to feel responsible for the small man and his human needs, he himself has come to feel responsible for the inhuman policy of his government—the government which surrounds him, shapes his imagination, limits his horizons, and cripples his character.

Let us look at this man once more. Stooped, dressed in a gray suit of shoddy material, his collar covered with dandruff, his complexion gray as the result of vitamin deficiencies, he sits and reads today's paper. Today, just as in the past forty years, the newspaper brings him news in the same spirit, interpreted in the same way. The small man believes that this news is true and lives up to the title of the paper, *Pravda* (Truth). He believes the paper he holds in his hands. He trusts it blindly. He lives by it, because what else can he do?

WORDS INSTEAD OF
AN EPILOGUE

AND SO THE DAY TO SAY GOOD-BY CAME. I HAD DECIDED TO LEAVE the U.S.S.R., after all. My bags were packed and already at the airport. The pockets of my jacket bulged with the wide airplane tickets and baggage checks.

In this country, parting is a real sorrow. They are real "good-bys," seldom "till we meet again." My friends looked at me searchingly, trying to read from my face what motives influenced my decision and what memories I would carry with me.

"So you are leaving, after all," someone said. On their faces disappointment and wonder were mirrored. "You are leaving Soviet Russia just like that. You don't even say that you'd like to live here, work here, marry here, have children. Why?"

"It's so seldom that anybody leaves this country," said another. "It's hard to realize that in a few hours you won't be in the U.S.S.R. any more."

"You can't escape the U.S.S.R.," someone else had said, "just as you can't escape history or fate. So long. We'll see each other again, the world is getting so small."

"Be sure *not* to send any cards or letters to us," some said. "Forget that you knew us. You understand, memory is the worst thing. Try to forget whatever you remembered."

The last formalities. An official carefully checked my papers, investigated the contents of my briefcase. His attention was caught by the sheets of densely written notes. He looked at them for a moment, then shut the briefcase, and with a wooden smile wished me a good journey.

I found my seat on the plane. There were not many passengers. The plane circled on the runway. Soon the strips of concrete and the airport buildings began to recede beyond the round window. In another moment we were leaving behind roads winding like rope between fields that were studded with small square houses beside which were white dots of clothes hanging on lines.

I began to check my notes from my trip through the U.S.S.R. and to arrange them. They made quite a collection. Behind each of them I saw a human being living his daily life with its joys, worries, and apathy.

I made the notes principally for myself, to satisfy my own passionate curiosity and as a record of my own experiences. As in every society, the life of a man in the U.S.S.R. is too complicated to be described by a few generalizations and labels. I did not go to the U.S.S.R. to find the answers to questions such as "Is this life good or bad?" To me, the important thing was that this life is led by human beings and therefore warranted careful study.

I realize that in my contacts with daily life in the U.S.S.R. I inevitably added my own subjectivity to the subjectivity of those describing their part in that life. In an effort to cut this down to a minimum, I was always glad to let other people talk and limited my role to listening and faithfully recording the conversations.

As society is what the people who live in it believe it to be, this was the only picture of the U.S.S.R. I wanted to obtain on my visit there. Therefore I did not try to collect objective data. But the picture of a man in his daily life, drawn by himself and by the people around him, will always be a subjective picture. This cannot be avoided.

There are some who will say that in an era of mass conflict endangering the existence of the whole of mankind, a small man with his individual experiences and his one-sided appraisal of them ceases to count.

My answer is that these great mass conflicts count only so far as they affect the life, the thoughts, and the fate of the small man, the hero of gray everydayness.

The plane climbed higher. The steamy, curling clouds which hugged it tightly fell away. The sky contrasted sharply with the earth below, on which darkness had already fallen.

Date Due